CLIENT/SERVER COMPUTING

[SECOND EDITION]

Dr. Munesh Chandra Trivedi
Institute of Management Studies
Ghaziabad (NCR)

KHANNA BOOK PUBLISHING CO. (P) LTD.
DELHI

CLIENT/SERVER COMPUTING
Dr. MUNESH CHANDRA TRIVEDI

Published by **KHANNA BOOK PUBLISHING CO. (P) LTD.**
1694-95 Nai Sarak, Delhi - 110 006
Ph : 011-23256658, 23283211, Fax : 011-23256658
E-mail : contact@khannaedu.com
Website : www.khannaedu.com

ISBN : 978-93-80016-60-3

First Edition : ***2008***
Second Edition : ***2010***

Reprint : 2014

Printed by :
Ziya Offset Works, Delhi

Preface To Second Edition

Client/Server Computing is a subject that is an integralcomponent of the ubiquitous soft computing paradigm. An in depth understanding and appreciations of the field requires some background knowledge of the Accounting, Computer Network and Operating System, this is a difficult task. The second edition of "Client/Server Computing" aims to achieve a balanced of these areas. Client/Server Computing is the discipline that attempts to provide methods to handle this complexity and enable us to produce reliable real time systems with maximum productivity.

This book is for students who have not had previous training is Client/Server Computing, and is suitable for a one-semester course. This book covers syllabus of all India Universities. This is also useful for a project based introducing course in Client/Server Computing in which both the students and the instructor can follow the chapters is the order given both in the lectures as well as in the project.

The emphasize of second edition throughout this book is not an abstract theory but on the practical utility of Client/Server Computing. This is our pleasure to offer second edition to the readers of various universities. Utmost care has been taken in the formation of this book as per syllabus of various universities. I would always gracefully welcome any kind of suggestions and positive criticism to improve the subsequent editions of this book. Kindly mail E-mail your suggestion and feedback to : munesh.trivedi@gmail.com

Munesh Chandra Trivedi

SYLLABUS

CLIENT/SERVER COMPUTING

Unit I : **Introduction :** Client Server Computing. DBMS concepts and architecture. Single system image, Client Server computing. Mainframe centric client serve computing downsizing and client server computing. Preserving Mainframe application investment through porting, client server development tools, Advantage of client server computing.

Unit II : **Components of Client Server Application :** The client services, Request for services, RPC, Window services, Remote boot services, Other remote services, Other remote services, Utility services, Dynamic data exchange, Object linking and embedding, Common object request broker architecture. The server Detailed server functionality. The networking operating system, Available platforms. The server operating system.

Unit III : **Components of Client Server Application :** Connectivity, Communication interface technology, Inter-process communication, Wide area network technologies network management, Client-server system development software.

Client-Server System Development : Hardware, Network Acquisition PC-level processing unit, Macintosh, Notebooks, Pen, UNIX work station. X-terminals. Server hardware. Data storage, Magnetic disk.

Unit IV : **CD rom WORM Erasable Optical, Mirroed Disk :** RAID disk array, tape, Optical disks, Network protection devices UPS. Surge protectors. Client server systems development services and support, System administration. Availability, Reliability Serviceability, Software Distribution performance Network Management, Help Desk, Remote Systems Management Security, LAN and Network Management issues.

Unit V : **Client/Server System Development :** Training, Training Advantage of GUI Application, System Administration Training, Database Administrator training, END-user training, The Future of Client Server Computing Enabling Technologies, The Transformational System.

CONTENTS

1. CLIENT/SERVER COMPUTING 1 - 18

2. COMPONENTS OF CLIENT/SERVER APPLICATION 19 - 92

3. CLIENT/SERVER SYSTEM DEVELOPMENT 93 - 119

4. CLIENT/SERVER SYSTEM DEVELOPMENT SOFTWARE 120 - 141

5. NETWORK INTERFACES 142 - 190

6. CLIENT/SERVER SYSTEMS DEVELOPMENT 191 - 195

7. CLIENT/SERVER TRAINING CONCEPTS 196 - 248

Chapter 1

Introduction

1.1 Client/Server Computing

In 1960, After the NATO Science summit some agreed upon concept of network resource sharing were developed and called as Client/Server Computing.

As Client/Server Computing with resource shares the information resources so it take into consideration some network concept, Concept of Operating System, Concept of DBMS, and some practical aspects of MIS.

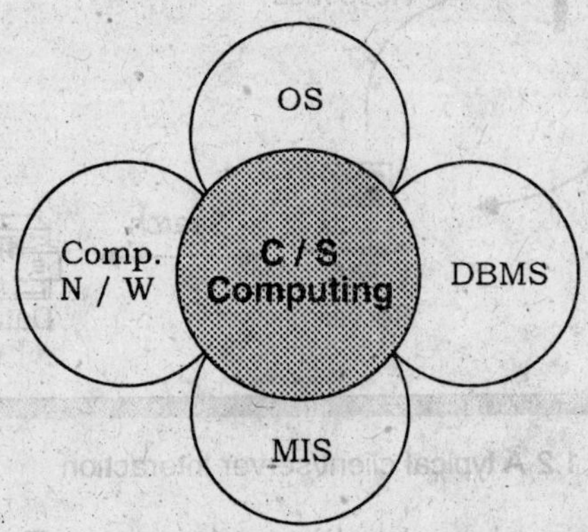

Fig 1.1 Client\Server Computing

1.2 Client/Server Model of Computing

To truly understand how much of the Internet operates, including the Web, it is important to understand the concept of client/server computing. The client/server model is a form of distributed computing where one program (the client) communicates with another program (the server) for the purpose of exchanging information.

The client's responsibility is usually to:

1. Handle the user interface.
2. Translate the user's request into the desired protocol.
3. Send the request to the server.
4. Wait for the server's response.
5. Translate the response into "human-readable" results.
6. Present the results to the user.

The serve's functions include:

1. Listen for a client's query
2. Process that query.
3. Return the results back to the client.

A typical client/server interaction goes like this:

1. The user runs client software to create a query.
2. The client connects to the server.
3. The client sends the query to the server.
4. The server analyzes the query.
5. The server computes the results of the query.
6. The server sends the results to the client.
7. The client presents the results to the user.
8. Repeat as necessary.

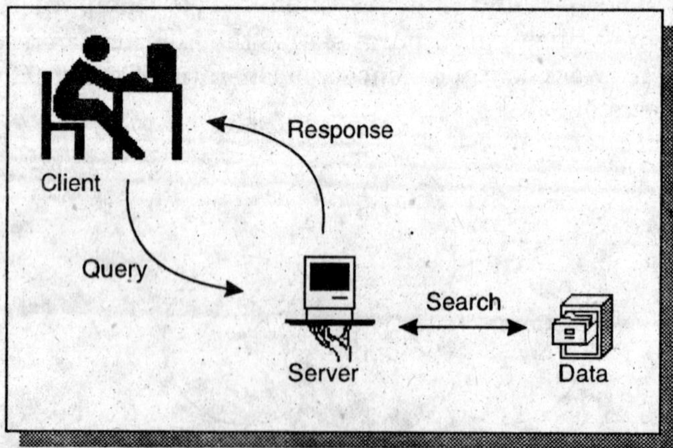

Fig 1.2 A typical client/server interaction

This client/server interaction is a lot like going to a French restaurant. At the restaurant, you (the user) are presented with a menu of choices by the waiter (the client). After making your selections, the waiter takes note of your choices, translates them into French, and presents them to the French chef (the server) in the kitchen. After the chef prepares your meal, the waiter returns with your diner (the results). Hopefully, the waiter returns with the items you selected, but not always; sometimes things get "lost in the translation."

Flexible user interface development is the most obvious advantage of client/server computing. It is possible to create an interface that is independent of the server hosting the data. Therefore, the user interface of a client/server application can be written on a Macintosh and the server can be written on a mainframe. Clients could be also written for DOS- or UNIX-based computers. This allows information to be stored in a central server and disseminated to different types of remote computers. Since the user interface is the responsibility of the client, the server has more computing resources to spend on analyzing queries and disseminating information. This is another major advantage of client/server computing; it tends to use the strengths of divergent computing platforms to create more powerful applications. Although its computing and storage capabilities are dwarfed by those of the mainframe, there is no reason why a Macintosh could not be used as a server for less demanding applications.

In short, client/server computing provides a mechanism for disparate computers to cooperate on a single computing task.

1.3 Client/Server Software Architectures

The term client/server was first used in the 1980s in reference to personal computers (PCs) on a network. The actual client/server model started gaining acceptance in the late 1980s. The client/server software architecture is a versatile, message-based and modular infrastructure that is intended to improve usability, flexibility, interoperability, and scalability as compared to centralized, mainframe, time sharing computing.

A client is defined as a requester of services and a server is defined as the provider of services. A single machine can be both a client and a server depending on the software configuration.

Mainframe architecture is not client/server architecture. With mainframe software architectures all intelligence is within the central host computer. Users interact with the host through a terminal that captures keystrokes and sends that information to the host. Mainframe software architectures are not tied to a hardware platform. User interaction can be done using PCs and UNIX workstations. A limitation of mainframe software architectures is that they do not easily support graphical user interfaces or access to multiple databases from geographically dispersed sites. In the last few years, mainframes have found a new use as a server in distributed client/server architectures.

File sharing architecture also not client/server architecture. The original PC networks were based on file sharing architectures, where the server downloads files from the shared location to the desktop environment. The requested user job is then run (including logic and data) in the desktop environment. File sharing architectures work if shared usage is low, update contention is low, and the volume of data to be transferred is low. In the 1990s, PC LAN (local area network) computing changed because the capacity of the file sharing was strained as the number of online user grew (it can only satisfy about 12 users simultaneously) and graphical user interfaces (GUIs) became popular (making mainframe and terminal displays appear out of date). PCs are now being used in client/server architectures.

Due to limitations of file sharing architectures, the client/server architecture emerged. This approach introduced a database server to replace the file server. Using a relational database management system (DBMS), user queries could be answered directly. The client/server architecture reduced network traffic by providing a query response rather than total file transfer. It improves multi-user updating through a GUI front end to a shared database. In client/server architectures, Remote Procedure Calls (RPCs) or standard query language (SQL) statements are typically used to communicate between the client and server. The client\server architecture are of following types:

1.3.1 Two Tier Architectures

With two tier client/server architectures, the user system interface is usually located in the user's desktop environment and the database management services are usually in a server that is a more powerful machine that services many clients. Processing management is split between the user system interface environment and the database management server environment. The database management server provides stored procedures and triggers. There are a number of software vendors that provide tools to simplify development of applications for the two-tier client/server architecture.

The two-tier client/server architecture is a good solution for distributed computing when work groups are defined as a dozen to 100 people interacting on a LAN simultaneously. It does have a number of limitations. When the number of users exceeds 100, performance begins to deteriorate. This limitation is a result of the server maintaining a connection via "keep-alive" messages with each client, even when no work is being done. A second limitation of the two tier architecture is that implementation of processing management services using vendor proprietary database procedures restricts flexibility and choice of DBMS for applications. Finally, current implementations of the two-tier architecture provide limited flexibility in moving (repartitioning) program functionality from one server to another without manually regenerating procedural code.

1.3.2 Three tier Architectures

The three-tier architecture (also referred to as the multi-tier architecture) emerged to overcome the limitations of the two-tier architecture. In the three-tier architecture, a middle tier was added between the user system interface client environment and the database management server environment. There are a variety of ways of implementing this middle tier, such as transaction processing monitors, message servers, or application servers. The middle tier can perform queuing, application execution, and database staging. For example, if the middle tier provides queuing, the client can deliver its request to the middle layer and disengage because the middle tier will access the data and return the answer to the client. In addition the middle layer adds scheduling and prioritization for work in progress. The three-tier client/server architecture has been shown to improve performance for groups with a large number of users (in the thousands) and improves flexibility when compared to the two-tier approach. Flexibility in partitioning can be a simple as "dragging and dropping" application code modules onto different computers in some three-tier architecture. A limitation with three tier architectures is that the development environment is reportedly more difficult to use than the visually oriented development of two tier applications. Recently, mainframes have found a new use as servers in three tier architectures.

1.3.3 Three tier Architecture with Transaction Processing Monitor Technology

The most basic type of three-tier architecture has a middle layer consisting of Transaction Processing (TP) monitor technology. The TP monitor technology is a type of message queuing, transaction scheduling, and prioritization service where the client connects to the TP monitor (middle tier) instead of the database server. The transaction is accepted by the monitor, which queues it and then takes responsibility for managing it to completion, thus freeing up the client. When third party middleware vendors provide the capability it is referred to as "TP Heavy" because it can service thousands of users. When it is embedded in the DBMS (and could be considered a two tier architecture), it is referred to as "TP Lite" because experience has shown performance degradation when over 100 clients are connected. TP monitor technology also provides

- The ability to update multiple different DBMSs in a single transaction
- Connectivity to a variety of data sources including flat files, non-relational DBMS, and the mainframe
- The ability to attach priorities to transactions
- Robust security

Using three-tier client/server architecture with TP monitor technology results in an environment that is considerably more scalable than a two-tier architecture with direct client to server connection. For systems with thousands of users, TP monitor technology (not embedded in the DBMS) has been reported as one of the most effective solutions. A limitation to TP monitor technology is that the implementation code is usually written in a lower level language (such as COBOL), and not yet widely available in the popular visual toolsets.

1.3.4 Three tier with Message Server

Messaging is another way to implement three tier architectures. Messages are prioritized and processed asynchronously. Messages consist of headers that contain priority information, and the address and identification number. The message server connects to the relational DBMS and other data sources.

The difference between TP monitor technology and message server is that the message server architecture focuses on intelligent messages, whereas the TP Monitor environment has the intelligence in the monitor, and treats transactions as dumb data packets. Messaging systems are good solutions for wireless infrastructures.

1.3.5 Three tier with an Application Server

The three-tier application server architecture allocates the main body of an application to run on a shared host rather than in the user system interface client environment. The application server does not drive the GUIs; rather it shares business logic, computations, and a data retrieval engine. Advantages are that with less software on the client there is less security to worry about, applications are more scalable, and support and installation costs are less on a single server than maintaining each on a desktop client. The application server design should be used when security, scalability, and cost are major considerations.

1.3.6 Three tier with an ORB Architecture

Currently industry is working on developing standards to improve interoperability and determine what the common Object Request Broker (ORB) will be. Developing client/server systems using technologies that support distributed objects holds great promise, as these technologies support interoperability across languages and platforms, as well as enhancing maintainability and adaptability of the system. There are currently two prominent distributed object technologies:

- Common Object Request Broker Architecture (CORBA)
- COM/DCOM (Component Object Model (COM),Distributed Component Object Model(DCOM)).

Industry is working on standards to improve interoperability between CORBA and COM/DCOM. The Object Management Group (OMG) has developed a mapping between CORBA and COM/DCOM that is supported by several products.

Distributed/Collaborative Enterprise Architecture

The distributed/collaborative enterprise architecture emerged in 1993.This software architecture is based on Object Request Broker (ORB) technology, but goes further than the Common Object Request Broker Architecture (CORBA) by using shared, reusable business models (not just objects) on an enterprise-wide scale. The benefit of this architectural approach is that standardized business object models and distributed object computing are combined to give an organization flexibility to improve effectiveness organizationally, operationally, and technologically. An enterprise is defined here, as a system comprised of multiple business systems or subsystems. Distributed/collaborative enterprise architectures are limited by a lack of commercially available object orientation analysis and design method tools that focus on applications.

Client/server architectures are being used throughout industry and the military. They provide a versatile infrastructure that supports insertion of new technology more readily than earlier software designs.

1.4 Client/Server Protocol

For a proper client-server communication, a protocol which is at least as powerful as a simple request-response (RR) protocol is required. The client request includes the parameters of the demanded thumbnail. The server response contains the thumbnail image. If an error occurs during the thumbnail processing, the client knows due to a response timeout exception. Such a RR protocol would be sufficient for the thumbnail service. However, a more sophisticated protocol which sends a positive acknowledgment with the thumbnail response and a negative acknowledgment including the server error is preferable. HTTP is an example of such an advanced protocol.

Furthermore, the protocol must be capable of sending a parameter for the URL of the source Web page in the request. The client specifies the URL of the desired Web page thumbnail. Additional parameters such as the width and height of the thumbnail, the encoding format of the image, caching options, and a request timeout are recommended to provide a flexible service. This list of parameters has been implemented in our application. Without doubt, more parameters could be defined to improve the service.

For our thumbnail service, we decided to use HTTP—the Web protocol—as the communication protocol between client and server. This decision has the following advantages: Firstly, it allows users to request thumbnails directly from the Web browser. Any Web browser can be used as a client for the thumbnail service; no changes to the Web browser and no extensions, such as plug-ins or external applications, are required. Secondly, using standard HTTP offers the opportunity to more easily integrate dynamically generated thumbnails into Web pages. Alternatively, any other self-implemented client programs, *i.e.*, Java programs, browser plug-ins, cgi-scripts, and servelets, all of which connect via TCP/IP to the server and communicate according to HTTP can be used as clients to access the thumbnail service.

In our implementation, the thumbnail server acts like a HTTP server for its clients. Incoming client requests are parsed to extract the request parameters such as URL, width, height, etc. of Web page thumbnails. If the request was successfully processed, the server replies with the thumbnail image. The payload contains the encoded image data. The MIME type header option is used to indicate the data encoding. Therefore, for our JPEG encoded thumbnails, we use "IMAGE/JPEG". In case of a server error, the error code is replied in the HTTP header in the same way as usual Web servers do. In this case, the page content is a HTML style error message whereas "HTML/TEXT" is used as MIME type. On using the Web browser as client program, the response of the thumbnail server will be displayed immediately in the Web browser. Either the Web page thumbnail will be displayed as an image or the server error message will be shown as HTML text.

1.5 Objectives of Client/Server Computing

The major Objectives of Client/Server Computing are:

i) Optimized utilization of Hardware resources.
ii) Bestly sharing of software systems.
iii) Highly utilization of informative resources, *i.e.*, database.
iv) Optimum use of man power.
v) To develop centrally Control System.
vi) High Security Aspects.
vii) Cost Effectiveness.
viii) Globalization of market.
ix) Requirements of globally shared information.
x) Online transaction processing.

The Client/Server model makes the enterprise available at the disk. It provides access to data that the previous architecture did not, standard have been defined for Client/ Server Computing.

The single system image is best implemented through Client/Server Computing.

Client A Client is a single user work station, which provides presentation services, appropriate computing connectivity, database services and interface relevant to business needs.

Server A Server is one or more multi-user processors with shared memory providing computing connectivity, database services and interface relevant to business needs.

Client/Server Computing is an environment that satisfies the business needs by appropriately allocating the application processing between the Client/Server processors.

The client requests services from the server; the server processes the requests and returns the result to the client. Client / Server is a software model of Computation not a hardware definition.

The Hardware platform and the operating system of the client and server are not usually the same. In such cases the communication mechanism may be further extended through a well defined set of standards, Application program interface called as API's and Remote procedure calls.

In Effective way the Client / Server Computing will be fundamentally platform independent. In the single system image environment a business system user is totally unaware of where data is stored, How client and server processes, what network is involved from connectivity and How transparent it is.

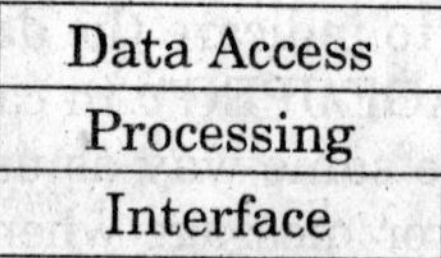

Fig 1.3 Simplified Application Model.

1.6 Advantages of Client/Server Computing

Client/server computing provides the capability to use the most cost-effective user interface, data storage, connectivity, and application services. Frequently, client/server products are deployed within the present organization but are not used effectively. The client/server model provides the technological means to use previous investments in concert with current technology options. There has been a dramatic decline in the cost of the technology components of client/server computing. Organizations see opportunities to use technology to provide business solutions. Service and quality competition in the marketplace further increase the need to take advantage of the benefits available from applications built on the client/server model.

Client/server computing in its best implementations moves the data-capture and information-processing functions directly to the knowledgeable worker that is, the worker with the ability to respond to errors in the data, and the worker with the ability to use the information made available. Systems used in the front office, directly involved in the process of doing the business, are forced to show value. If they don't, they are discarded under the cost pressures of doing business. Systems that operate in the back room after the business process is complete are frequently designed and implemented to satisfy an administrative need, without regard to their impact on business operations. Client/server applications integrate the front and back office processes because data capture and usage become an integral part of the business rather than an after-the-fact administrative process. In this mode of operation, the processes are continuously evaluated for effectiveness. Client/server computing provides the technology platform to support the vital business practice of continuous improvement.

The client/server computing model provides the means to integrate personal productivity applications for an individual employee or managers with specific business data processing needs to satisfy total information processing requirement for the entire enterprise the advantages of client / server computing are as follows:

i) Enhanced data sharing
ii) Integrated services.
iii) Sharing resources among diverse platforms
iv) Data interchangeability and interoperability
v) Masked Physical data access.
vi) Location independent of data and processing.
vii) Centralized Management.

1.6.1 Enhanced Data Sharing

Data Sharing is one of the important Aspects of Client / Server Computing, here data is collected as a part of normal business process and maintained on a server, so that it can be awaited to the authorized users.

Authorized users are the users having a grant of server, so that it can use protected and private data of the server. As DBMS is also having some priority in Client/Server Computing that is why structured query language is organized in such a manner so that the access at the data can be wait to certain user or can be restricted to certain workstation.

1.6.2 Integrated Services

In the Client/Server Computing model all information that the clients is entitled to use is available on the desktop, as such there is no need to change into terminal mode or into processes to access information.

All authorized information and processes are directly available from the desktop interfaces. Example—Internet explorer for mail and yahoo messenger for Chat system.

Desktop user can use their desktop tool in conjunction with information make available for the cooperate system to produce new & useful information.

1.6.3 Resource Sharing

Infect Client / Server Computing is oriented toward software application development in such a say, so that the inter connection of the workstation are made in such a manner as workstation can utilized best from the server software system.

Apart from this network services and protocols are also established in a way so that Hardware resources of the server could facilitate the workstation at the most.

1.6.4 Data Interchangeability and Interoperability

SQL is an industry-standard data definition and access language. This standard definition has enabled many vendors to develop production-class database engines to manage data as SQL tables. Almost all the development tools used for client/server development expect to reference a back-end database server accessed through SQL. Network services provide transparent connectivity between the client and local or remote servers. With some database products, such as Ingres Star, a user or application can define a consolidated view of data that is actually distributed between heterogeneous, multiple platforms.

Systems developers are finally reaching the point at which this heterogeneity will be a feature of all production-class database engine products. Most systems that have been implemented to date use a single target platform for data maintenance. The ability to do high-volume updates at multiple locations and maintain database integrity across all types of errors is just becoming available with production-level quality performance and recovery. Systems developed today that use SQL are inherently transparent to data storage location and the technology of the data storage platform. The SQL syntax does not specify a location or platform. This transparency enables tables to be moved to other platforms and locations without affecting the application code. This feature is especially valuable when adopting proven, new technology or if it makes business sense to move data closer to its owner.

Database services can be provided in response to an SQL request without regard to the underlying engine. This engine can be provided by vendors such as ASK/Ingres, Oracle, Sybase, or IBM running on Windows NT, OS/2, UNIX, or MVS platform. The system development environment (SDE) and tools must implement the interfaces to the vendor database and operating system products. The developer does not need to know which engine or operating system is running. If the SDE does not remove the developer fromdirect access to the database server platform, the enthusiasm to be efficient will prevent developers from avoiding the use of "features" available only from a specific vendor. The transparency of platform is essential if the application is to remain portable. Application portability is essential when taking advantage of innovation in technology and cost competitiveness, and in providing protection from the danger of vendor failure.

Database products, such as Sybase used with the Database Gateway product from Micro DecisionWare, provide direct, production-quality, and transparent connectivity between the client and servers. These products may be implemented using DB2, IMS/DB, or VSAM through CICS into DB2, and Sybase running under VMS, Windows NT, OS/2, DOS, and MacOS. Bob Epstein, executive vice president of Sybase, Inc., views Sybase's open server approach to distributed data as incorporating characteristics of the semantic heterogeneity solution.1 In this solution, the code at the remote server can be used to deal with different database management systems (DBMSs), data models, or processes. The remote procedure call (RPC) mechanism used by Sybase can be interpreted as a message that invokes the appropriate method or procedure on the open server. True, somebody has to write the code that masks the differences. However, certain partssuch as accessing a foreign DBMS (like Sybase SQL Server to IBM DB2)can be standardized.

ASK's Ingres Star product provides dynamic SQL to support a distributed database between UNIX and MVS. Thus, Ingres Windows 4GL running under DOS or UNIX as a client can request a data view that involves data on the UNIX Ingres and MVS DB2 platform. Ingres is committed to providing static SQL and IMS support in the near future. Ingres' Intelligent Database engine will optimize the query so that SQL requests to distributed databases are handled in a manner that minimizes the number of rows moved fromthe remote server. This optimization is particularly crucial when dynamic requests are made to distributed databases. With the announcement of the Distributed Relational Database Architecture (DRDA), IBM has recognized the need for open access from other products to DB2. This product provides the app-lication program interfaces (APIs) necessary for other vendors to generate static SQL requests to the DB2 engine running under MVS. Norris van den Berg, manager of Strategy for Programming Systems at IBM's

Santa Teresa Laboratory in San Jose, California, points out that IBM's Systems Application Architecture (SAA)

DBMSs are different. Even within IBM, they must deal with the issues of data interchange and interoperability in a heterogeneous environment.2 More importantly, IBM is encouraging third-party DBMS vendors to comply with its DRDA. This is a set of specifications that will enable all DBMSs to interoperate.

The client/server model provides the capability to make ad hoc requests for information. As a result, optimization of dynamic SQL and support for distributed databases are crucial for the success of the second generation of a client/server application. The first generation implements the operational aspects of the business process. The second generation is the introduction of ad hoc requests generated by the knowledgeabe user looking to gain additional insight from the information available.

1.6.5 Masked Physical Data Access

When SQL is used for data access, users can access information from databases anywhere in the network. From the local PC, local server, or wide area network (WAN) server, data access is supported with the developer and user using the same data request. The only noticeable difference may be performance degradation if the network bandwidth is inadequate. Data may be accessed from dynamic random-access memory (D-RAM), from magnetic disk, or from optical disk, with the same SQL statements. Logical tables can be accessedwithout any knowledge of the ordering of columns or awareness of extraneous columnsby selecting a subset of the columns in a table. Several tables may be joined into a view that creates a new logical table for application program manipulation, without regard to its physical storage format.

The use of new data types, such as binary large objects (BLOBs), enables other types of information such as images, video, and audio to be stored and accessed using the same SQL statements for data access. RPCs frequently include data conversion facilities to translate the stored data of one processor into an acceptable format for another.

1.6.6 Location Independence of Data and Processing

We are moving from the machine-centered computing era of the 1970s and 1980s to a new era in which PC-familiar users demand systems that are user-centered. Previously, a user logged into a mainframe, mini-, or microapplication. The syntax of access was unique in each platform. Function keys, error messages, navigation methods, security, performance, and editing were all very visible. Today's users expect a standard "look and feel." Users log into an application from the desktop with no concern for the location or technology of the processors involved.

Figure 1.4 illustrates the evolution of a user's view of the computing platform. In the 1970s, users logged into the IBM mainframe, the VAX minicomputer, or one of the early microcomputer applications. It was evident which platform was being used. Each platform required a unique login sequence, security parameters, keyboard options, and custom help, navigation, and error recovery. In the current user-centered world, the desktop provides the point of access to the workgroup and enterprise services without regard to the platform of application execution. Standard services such as login, security, navigation, help, and error recovery are provided consistently among all applications.

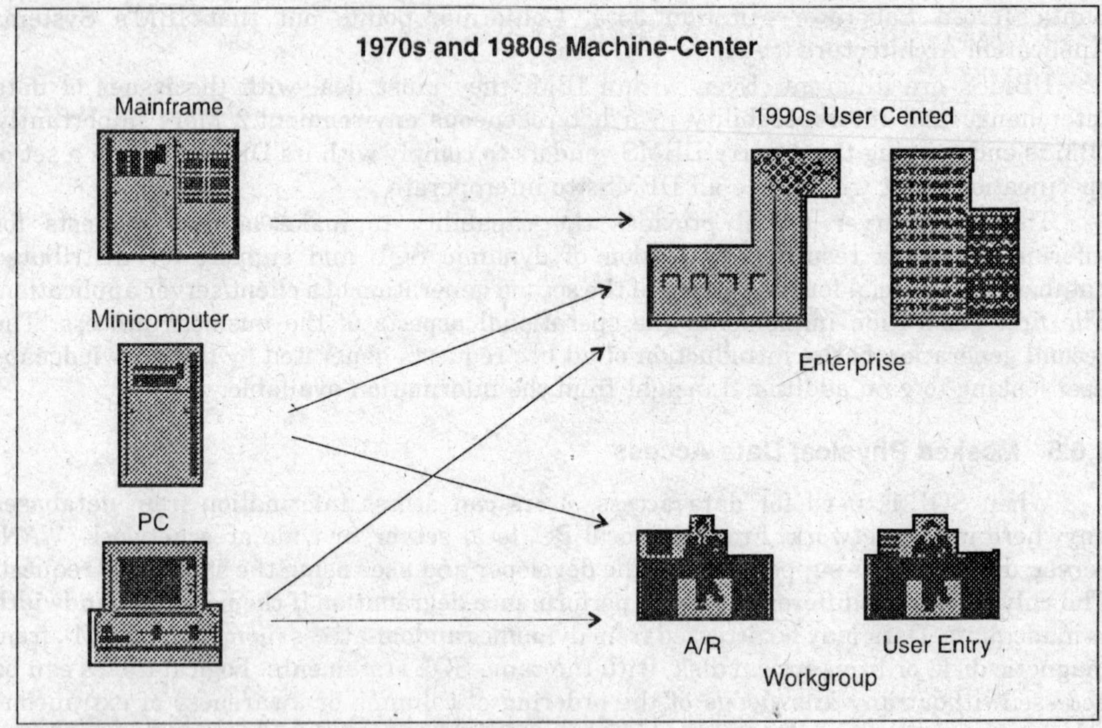

Fig 1.4. Location independence of data and processing

The application developer deals with the development language and uses a version of SDE customized for the organization to provide standard services. The specific platform characteristics are transparent and object to change without affecting the application syntax.

1.6.7 Centralized Management

As processing steers away from the central data center to the remote office and plant, workstation server, and local area network (LAN) reliability must approach that provided today by the centrally located mini- and mainframe computers. The most effective way to ensure this is through the provision of monitoring and support from these same central locations. A combination of technologies that can "see" the operation of hardware and software on the LANmonitored by experienced support personnelprovides the best opportunity to achieve the level of reliability required. The first step in effectively providing remote LAN management is to establish standards for hardware, software, networking, installation, development, and naming. These standards, used in concert with products such as IBM's Systemview, Hewlett-Packard's Openview, Elegant's ESRA, Digital's EMA, and AT&T's UNMA products, provide the remote view of the LAN. Other tools, such as PC Connect for remote connect, PCAssure from Centel for security, products for hardware and software inventory, and local monitoring tools such as Network General's Sniffer, are necessary for completing the management process.

1.7 DBMS Concepts And Architecture

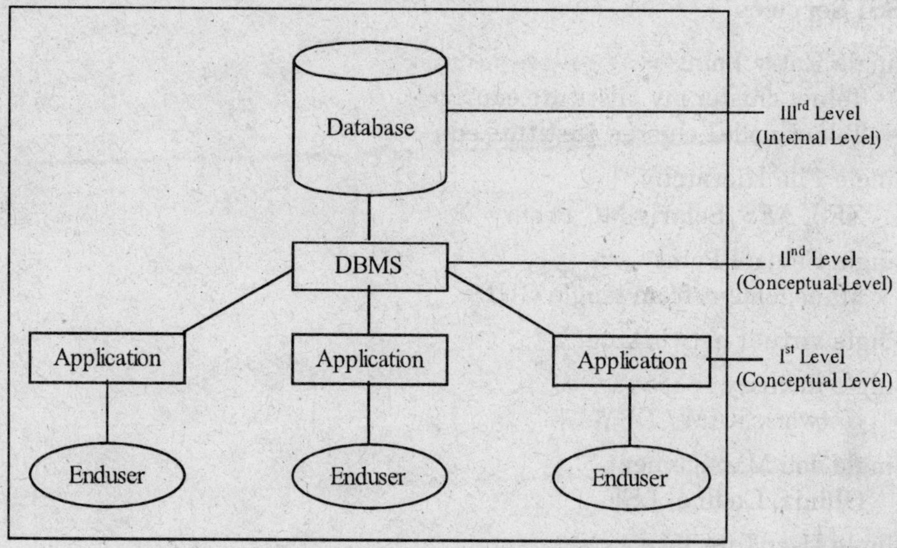

Fig 1.5 DBMS Architecture

In the DBMS concept and architecture Client / Server Computing say that Application works as client and send request to the DBMS. DBMS here acts as server and responds services to application.

Internal Level : The distribution of the database in internal level is in the form of table.

Conceptual Level : The conceptual level tells about the concepts or the way the data has been stored.

External Level : The external level tell about how data is looking to the user.

1.8 Single System Image

A single system image is the illusion, created by software or hardware, that presents a collection of resources as one, more powerful resource.

SSI makes the cluster appear like a single machine to the user, to applications, and to the network. A cluster without a SSI is not a cluster

Benefits of Single System Image

- Usage of system resources transparently
- Transparent process migration and load balancing across nodes.
- Improved reliability and higher availability
- Improved system response time and performance
- Simplified system management
- Reduction in the risk of operator errors

- User need not be aware of the underlying system architecture to use these machines effectively

Desired SSI Services

- Single Entry Point
  - Telnet cluster.my_institute.edu
  - Telnet node1.cluster. Institute.edu
- Single File Hierarchy
  - XFS, AFS, Solaris MC Proxy
- Single Control Point
  - Management from single GUI
- Single virtual networking
- Single memory space
  - Network RAM / DSM
- Single Job Management
  - Glunix, Codine, LSF
- Single User Interface
  - Like workstation/PC windowing environment (CDE in Solaris/NT), may it can use Web technology

Availability Support Functions

- Single I/O Space (SIO):
  - Any node can access any peripheral or disk devices without the knowledge of physical location.
- Single Process Space (SPS)
  - Any process on any node creates process with cluster wide process wide and they communicate through signal, pipes, etc, as if they are one a single node.
- Check pointing and Process Migration.
  - Saves the process state and intermediate results in memory to disk to support rollback recovery when node fails. PM for Load balancing...
- Reduction in the risk of operator errors
  - User need not be aware of the underlying system architecture to use these machines effectively

SSI Levels/How do we implement SSI ?

- It is a computer science notion of levels of abstractions (house is at a higher level of abstraction than walls, ceilings, and floors).the major single system image levels are as follows:

1. Application and Subsystem Level
2. Operating System Kernel Level
3. Hardware Level

SSI Characteristics

1. Every SSI has a boundary
2. Single system support can exist at different levels within a system, one able to be build on another

SSI Representative Systems

- OS level SSI
  - SCO NSC UnixWare
  - Solaris-MC
  - MOSIX, .
- Middleware level SSI
  - PVM, TreadMark (DSM), Glunix, Condor, Codine, Nimrod, .
- Application level SSI
  - PARMON, Parallel Oracle, ...

Single System Image is best implemented through C/S Model.

The concept of the single system image says that you can build systems that provide transparency of the technology platform to the user and at the largest extent possible to the developer.

Developers will need sufficient knowledge of the syntax used to solve the business problem, but will need little or no knowledge of the underlying technology infrastructure.

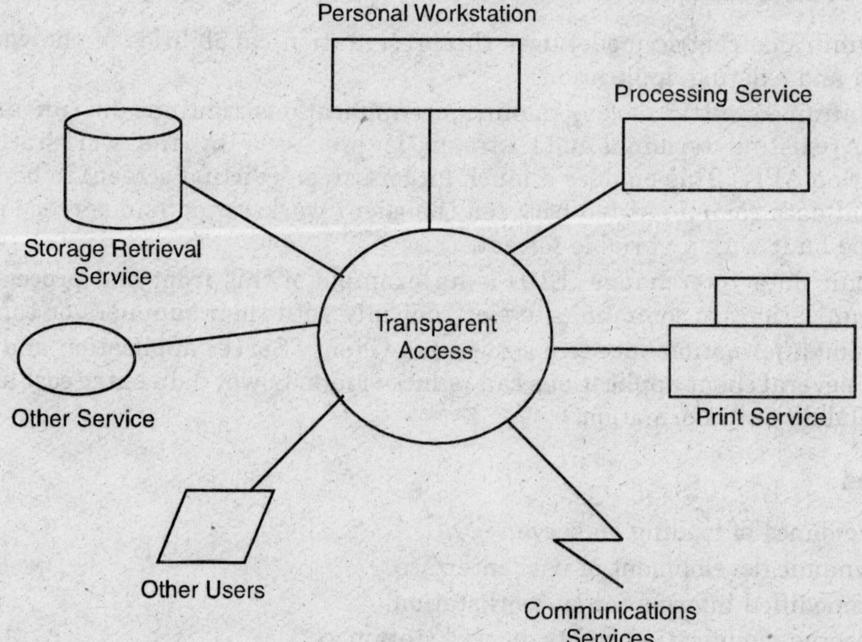

Fig 1.6. Single System Image

Systems development is not an art, it is an engineering discipline that can be learned and used. Systems can be built on the foundations established by previous projects.

Within the single-system image environment a business system user is totally unaware of where data is stored, how the client and server processors work and what networking is involved in gaining connectivity.

How is the transparency accomplished?

- Every application that the user access provides a common look and feel. Help is provided in the same way by every application.
- Errors are presented and resolved in the same way by every application.
- Access is provided through a standard security procedure for every application.
- Each user has access to all services for which he or she has a need and a right to access.
- Security layer is invisible to the Authorized and impenetrable to the unauthorized.
- Navigation from function to function and application to application is provided in the same way in every system. New Application can be added with minimum training, because the standard functions work in the same way and only the new business functions need be learned.
- Services are provided by the virtual cloud server in the sky. Figure shows the user view of these services. The work station on the desk appears to provide all services "The enterprise at the desk".

1.9 Mainframe Centric Client/Server Computing

The mainframe centric model uses the presentation capabilities of the workstation to front end and existing application.

In mainframe centric model, mainframe applications continue to run unmodified because the existing terminal data stream is processed by the workstation based communication API's. This enables a much larger screen (Virtual screen) to be used with no additional data communicated between the client workstation and server i.e. enables screens to be built with a variable format.

Electronic data Interchange (EDI) is an example of this front end processing. EDI enables organizations to communicate electronically with their suppliers or consumers.

Capturing information once to a server in a Client / Server application and receiving the data for several client applications can reduce errors. Lower data entry cost and speeds up the availability of information.

Advantages

i) Avoidance of loading on server.
ii) Dynamic development of user interface.
iii) Unmodified information at workstation.
iv) Reserve modification rights at workstation.
v) More facilities as fonts and colors at workstations.

1.10 Downsizing and Rightsizing

Rightsizing and downsizing are strategies used with the Client/Server model to take advantages of the lower cost of workstation technology.

Rightsizing and upsizing may involve the addition of more diverse or more powerful computing resources to an enterprise-computing environment.

Benefits of Right sizing

i) Reduction in cost of hardware, software and maintenance.

ii) Increased functionality performance and Flexibility in the application.

iii) Reduction of employee cost as the maintenance engineers or the hardware record tracker.

Downsizing

Downsizing is frequently implemented in concert with a flattening of the organization hierarchy, *i.e.*, the major approach of downsizing is to make more interaction among the different hierarchical levels as reduction of less facilitate hardware.

Downsizing information system is more than an attempt to use cheaper workstation technologies to replace existing mainframes and mini-computers in use and to provide the fast process execution so that the more no. of employees or clients of the organization can interact with each other without botheration.

Client/Server technology implemented on low cost standard hardware will drive downsizing client hardware updation is not come into downsizing only server hardware updation is come into downsizing.

Client/Server computing is an open computing mix and match is the rule developments tools and development environment must be created with both openness and standards in mind.

1.11 Summary

- A client is defined as a requester of services and a server is defined as the provider of services. A single machine can be both a client and a server depending on the software configuration.
- With two tier client/server architectures, the user system interface is usually located in the user's desktop environment and the database management services are usually in a server that is a more powerful machine that services many clients.
- In the three-tier architecture, a middle tier was added between the user system interface client environment and the database management server environment.
- For a proper client-server communication, a protocol which is at least as powerful as a simple request-response (RR) protocol is required. The client request includes the parameters of the demanded thumbnail. The server response contains the thumbnail image.
- A Server is one or more multi-user processors with shared memory providing

computing connectivity, database services and interface relevant to business needs.

- A single system image is the illusion, created by software or hardware, that presents a collection of resources as one, more powerful resource.
- The mainframe centric model uses the presentation capabilities of the workstation to front end and existing application.
- Rightsizing and upsizing may involve the addition of more diverse or more powerful computing resources to an enterprise-computing environment.

REVIEW QUESTIONS

1. Explain the client/server computing in details.
2. Explain the advantages of client/server computing.
3. Explain the DBMS concepts and architecture of the client\server computing.
4. Discuss the single system image in client/server computing.

Chapter 2

Client/Server Computing Application

2.1 Technology Revolution

The changes in computer technology that have taken place during the past five years are significantly greater than those of the preceding 35 years of the computer history. In technology Revolution the major focus towards the change in technology.

Technology Revolution is related to downsizing and right sizing. In downsizing if we update the hardware of the server it is called server side downsizing and if we update the Hardware of clients, it is called client side downsizing.

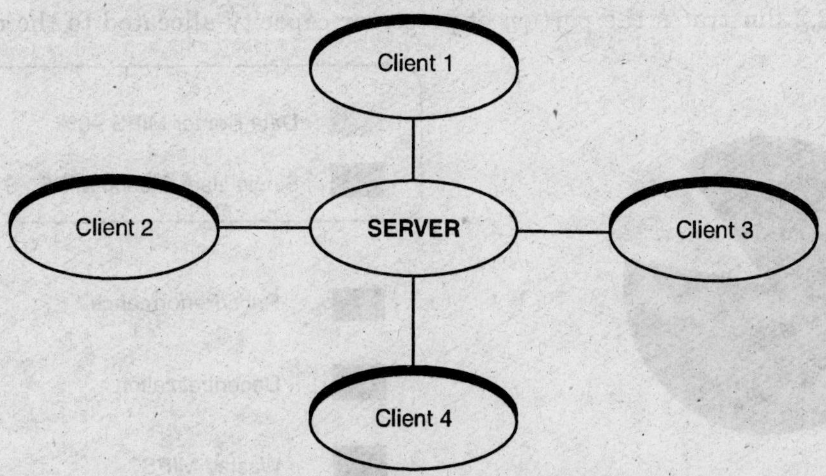

Fig 2.1. Technology Revolution

Similarly, in rightsizing if we update the software of the server, it is called server side rightsizing and if we update the software of clients, it is called client side rightsizing.

The major difference between the technology revolution and downsizing, rightsizing is that if we update server because of clients is called technology revolution and if we update clients because of server is related to downsizing and rightsizing.

2.1.1 Future Technology (Server)

Predicting the future is a risky business. Industry leaders, technicians and investors have been equally unsuccessful on occasion. It is important, however to achieve an educated view of where technology is headed during the life of a new system. The architecture on which a new system is built must be capable of supporting all users throughout its capable of supporting all users throughout its life.

The major points related to future technology of server are:

(i) What is available
  (a) Number of clients.
  (b) The current platform for operating.
  (c) Lacunas of the current platform.

(ii) What is expected
  (a) Fulfillment of lacunas.
  (b) New facilities of the new operating platform.
  (c) New restructured operating platform overcoming drawbacks.

(iii) For expectation what is required.

2.1.2 Computing Power Compared

A 1990 survey of U.S. Fortune 1000 companies, completed by a well-known computer industry research firm, found that on an MIPS (millions of instructions per second) basis, more than 90 percent of the processing power available to organizations exists at the desktop. This cheap computing power is typically underused today. It is a sunk cost available to be used as clients in the implementation of client/server applications.

Figure 2.2 illustrates the portion of processor capacity allocated to the central site

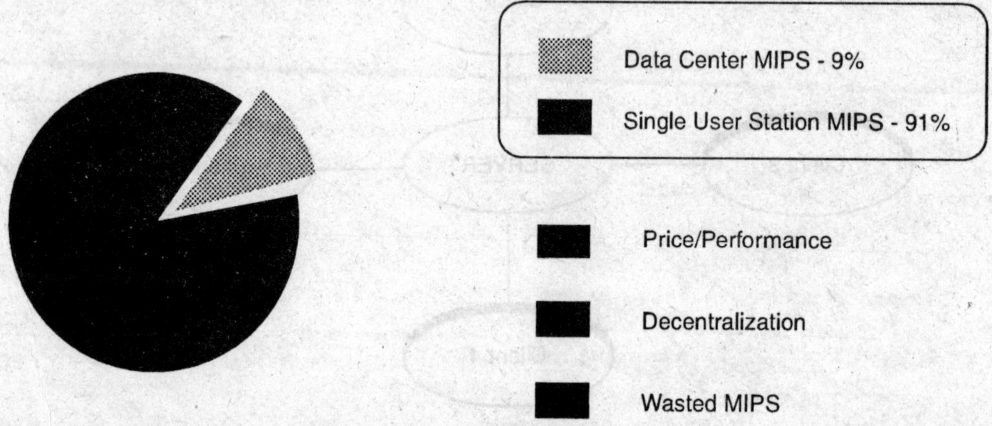

Fig 2.2. Managing the shift to distributed processing

and the desktop. In most organizations, the 9 percent of processor capacity residing in the "glass house" central computer center provides 90 percent or more of enterprise computing. The 90 percent of processor capacity on the desktop and installed throughout the organization provides less than 10 percent of the processing power to run the business. Most workstation systems are used for personal productivity applications, such as word processing, presentation graphics, and spreadsheet work. The personal productivity functions performed on these machines typically occupy the processor for a maximum of two to three hours per day.

2.1.3 Input/Output (I/O) Compared

Most applications require information that is manipulated also to be read and saved. In the next example, added to the CPU processing is the requirement to perform 1000 physical data read or write operations per second. Figure 2.3 shows the costs of performing these operations.

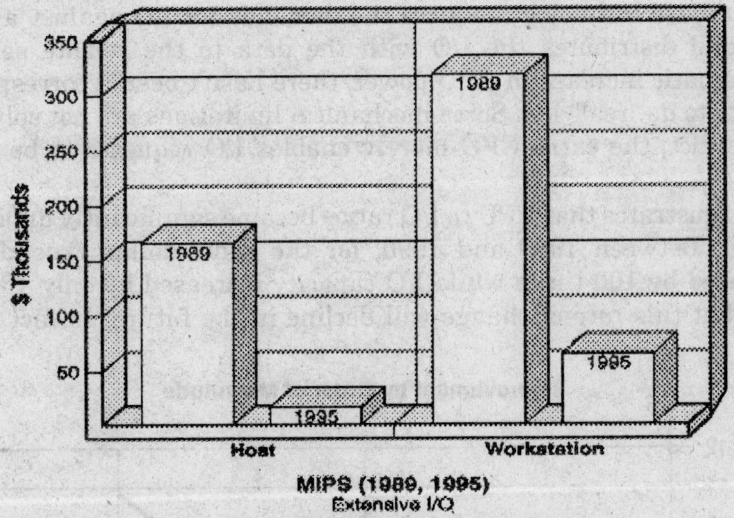

Fig 2.3. The I/O bottleneck

The same portion of the mainframe configuration required to provide one MIPS execution capability can simultaneously handle this I/O requirement. The workstation configuration required to simultaneously handle these two tasks in 1989 cost at least twice that of the mainframe configuration. In addition, the configuration involved multiple processors without shared memory access. In order to preserve data integrity, the I/O must be read only. The dramatic reduction in workstation cost projected in 1995 is predicated on the use of symmetric multiprocessors to provide CPUs with shared memory and on the use of coprocessors providing the cached controllers necessary to support parallel I/O. (Parallel I/O enables multiple I/O requests to several devices to be serviced concurrently with host CPU processing.) However,the costs are still projected to be 75 percent greater than costs on the mainframe for this high rate of I/O.

The difference in price and functionality is primarily explained by the fact that the

IBM 3090-600 is an example of a massively parallel processor optimized to do I/O. Every channel, DASD controller, tape controller, and console contains other processors. The processing capacity of these other processors is three to eight times the processing capacity of the main processor. These processors have direct memory access (DMA) to the shared memory of the configuration, with minimal impact on the processing capacity of the main processor. These processors enable I/O operations to proceed in parallel with little or no main processor involvement.

For the immediate future, forecasts show little slackening in demand for large host processors to provide enterprise database engine services for large companies, especially Fortune 500 firms. Ad hoc processing demands generated by the availability of workplace requestors will further increase the I/O demand. The RISC and Intel processors, as configured today and envisioned over the next five years, continue to use the main processor to perform much of the processing involved in I/O functions. This is an economical strategy for most client applications and many server applications where the I/O demands do not approach those found in large host mainframe configurations. Distributed database technology reduces the demands for I/O against a single database configuration and distributes the I/O with the data to the remote server processors. Despite the dramatic increase in CPU power, there hasn't been a corresponding increase in the capability to do "real" I/O. Some mechanical limitations are not solved by increased CPU power. In fact, the extra CPU merely enables I/O requests to be generated more rapidly.

Figure 2.4 illustrates that CPU to I/O ratios became significantly unbalanced between 1980 and 1990. Between 1980 and 1990, for the same dollar expenditure, processor capacity increased by 100 times while I/O capacity increased by only 18 times. There is no indication that this rate of change will decline in the future. In fact, it is likely that

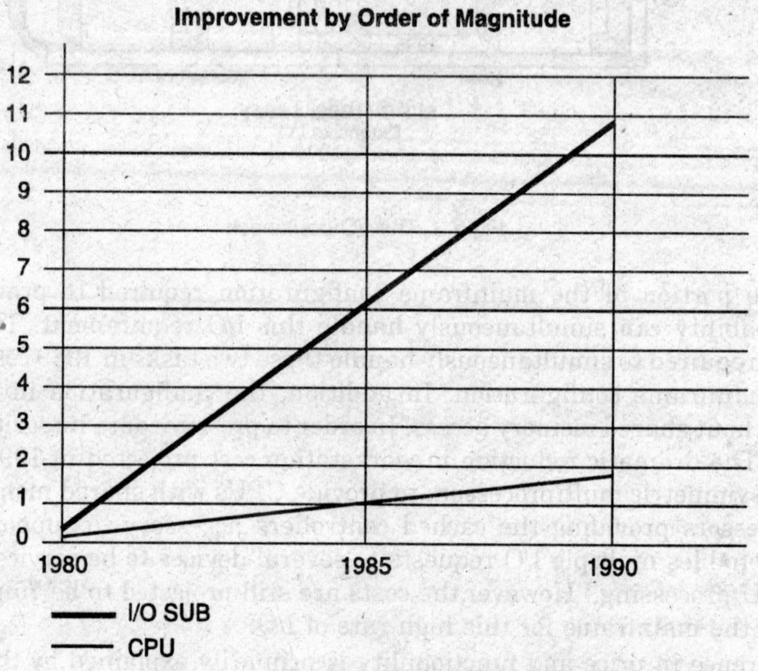

Fig 2.4 Processor power Vs I/O Capacity

with increased use of symmetric multiprocessors, CPU power availability will increase more rapidly. This in turn will generate even greater I/O demands and further widen the gap.

Only through the effective use of real storage (D-RAM) can we hope to use the available CPU power. Data can be accessed from D-RAM without the need to do physical I/O except to log the update. Database technology uses a sequential log to record changes. These sequential writes can be buffered and done very rapidly. The random updates to the database are done when the system has nothing better to do or when the shared D-RAM containing the updated data is required for other data. The log is used to recover the database after any failure that terminates the application.

Another complication in the I/O factor is the steadily decreasing cost of permanent data storage devices. As the cost of traditional data storage devicesdisk and tapedecreases, new technologies with massively greater capacity have evolved. Optical storage devices provide greater storage for less cost but with a somewhat slower rate of access than magnetic disk technologies. Most industry experience demonstrates that the amount of data an organization wants to store depends on the cost of storage, not on any finite limit to the amount of data available. If the cost of storage is halved, twice as much data will be available to store for the same budget. This additional data may come from longer histories, external sources, or totally new forms of data, such as image, audio, video, and graphics. New applications may be justified by the reduction in cost of data stores.

Workstation technologies can deal with personal data, data extracted from central systems for analysis by the end user, data from integrated external sources for comparison, and integrated new types of data such as voice annotation to documents. All these data forms provide additional uses for lower-cost, permanent data storage. Decision-support systems can use workstation technologies and massive amounts of additional data to provide useful, market-driven recommendations.

Relational database technologies also can limit the amount of real I/O required to respond to information requests. The use of descriptor indexes that contain data values extracted from columns of the database tables enables search criteria to be evaluated by accessing only the indexes. Access to the physical database itself is required only when the index search results in the identification of rows from the relational table that satisfy the search criteria. Large relational tables, which are accessed through complex searches, can demonstrate dramatically different performance and cost of access depending on the effectiveness of the database search engine. Products such as DB2 and Ingres, which do extensive query optimization, often demonstrate significantly better performance than other products in complex searches. Products that were developed to deal with a small memory model often exhibit dramatic CPU overhead when the size of resident indexes gets very large. DB2 achieves linear improvement in performance as indexes are allocated more D-RAM. Oracle, on the other hand, does not perform well in the IBM System 370 MVS implementation because of its overhead in managing very large main storage buffer pools.

2.1.4 Main Storage

Arguably, the most dramatic technological revolution affecting the computer industry today is caused by the increase in the amount of main storage (D-RAM) available to an

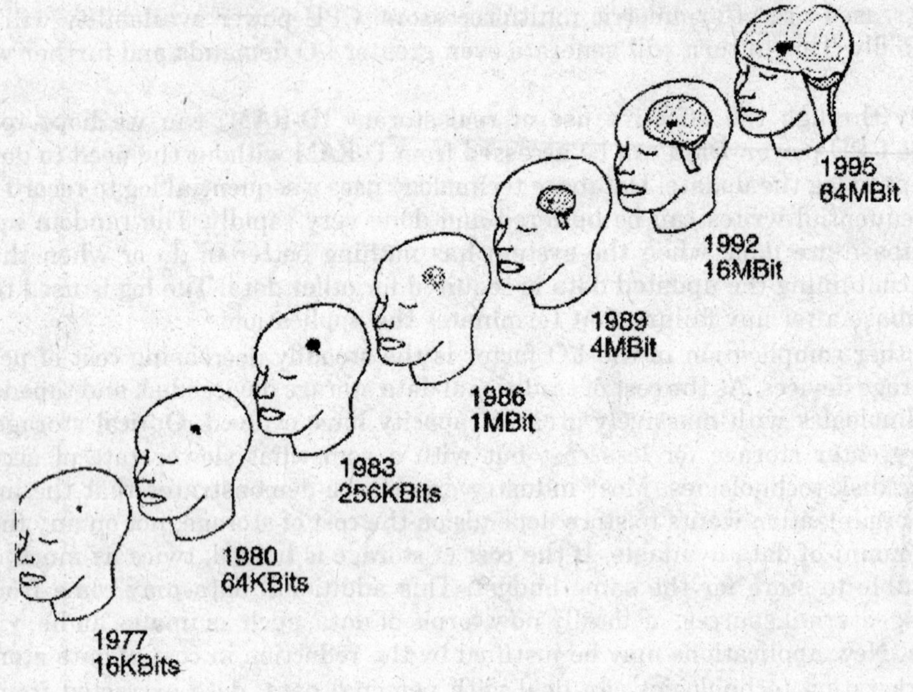

Fig 2.5. D-RAM chip evolution

application. D-RAM is used for the execution of programs and the temporary storage of permanent data.

Computer users have entered the era of very large and inexpensive D-RAM. Figure 2.10 represents the manner in which this technology has evolved and continues to evolve. Every three years, a new generation of D-RAM technology is released. Each new generation is released with four times the capacity of the previous generation for the same chip price. At the point of introduction and at any given time during its life cycle, the cost of these chips is reduced to a price equal to the price of chips from the previous generation. As the capacity of individual D-RAM chips has increased, the quantity of D-RAM available to the client (and server) has increased massively. Laboratory and manufacturing evidence reveals that this trend will continue at least through 1996.

Desktop workstations purchased in 1988 with 1 megabit (Mbit) D-RAM chips were available in 1992 with 4Mbit DRAM chips for the same or lower cost. In 1988, typical desktop workstations contained 1 to 4 megabytes (Mbytes) of D-RAM. In 1992, these same configurations contain from 4 to 16Mbytes. In 1995, these configurations will use 16Mbit chips and be available with 16 to 64Mbytes for the same price. By 1998within the life span of many applications being developed todaythese configurations will use 64Mbit chips and contain from 64 to 256Mbytes of D-RAM for the same price.

A revolutionary change is occurring in our capability to provide functionality at the desktop. Most developers cannot generate anywhere near the amount of code necessary to fill a 64Mbyte processor on the desk. Yet applications being built today will be used on desktop processors with this amount of D-RAM. It is now practical to use a multitasking client workstation with several active tasks and to switch regularly among them. Virtual storage is a reality. Workstation D-RAM costs were less than Rs. 50 per megabyte in 1992. The cost difference for an additional 4 megabytes is only Rs. 200. Only one year earlier, short-sighted application designers may have made system design decisions based on a cost of Rs. 1000 for 4Mbytes.

The same chip densities used for desktop processors are used in host servers. The typical mainframe computer in 1988 contained from 64 to 256Mbytes of D-RAM. In 1992, 256 to 1,024Mbytes were typical. By 1995, these same host servers will contain 1,024 to 4,096Mbytes of D-RAM. After 1998, host servers will contain 4,096 to 16,192Mbytes of D-RAM. These quantities are large enough to mandate that we take a completely different view of the way in which software will be built and information will be managed. During the useful life of systems being conceived today, the I/O bottleneck will be eliminated by the capability to access permanent information from D-RAM.

We are on the verge of the postscarcity era of processor power. In this era, essentially unlimited computing power will become available. With the client/server model, this processing power is available in every workplacea fundamental paradigm shift to the information-processing industry and to its customers. We expect to see a significant shakeout in the industry as hardware-only vendors respond to these changes.

What will this mean for developers and consumers?

- Only manufacturers who offer the lowest prices and who diversify into the software industry will be successful.
- Computer technology consumers are now on the verge of a related paradigm shift in the way computer technology affects their business. Only the most effective users can hope to demonstrate real value in a competitive marketplace.

2.1.5 Software Trends

To achieve the benefit of this advance in technology, organizations must choose software that can use it. Traditional development tools, operating systems, character mode user interfaces, and non-SQL-based database technology cannot take advantage of this quantity of D-RAM and the power available from workstation technology.

Graphical Screen Designs

Graphical user interfaces (GUIs) require large amounts of D-RAM to hold the screen image, pull-down lists, help text, navigation paths, and logic associated with all possible selectable events. Because a GUI enables processing to be selected randomly rather than in the traditional sequential, top-to-bottom order, all possible process logic and GUI management code associated with the image must be available in D-RAM to provide appropriate responses.

GUI functions require subsecond response time. Industry analysis has determined, and our experience confirms, that pull-down lists, button selects, and event invocation should take place within 0.1 second to provide a suitable user interface. Suitable means that the user is unaware of the GUI operations but is focused on the business function being performed. This performance is feasibly provided with today's workstations configured with reasonable amounts of Rs. 50 per megabyte D-RAM (in 1992) and properly architected applications.

CICS developers do not good GUI developers make.3 GUI application development requires a special mindset. Education, experience, and imagination are prerequisites for moving from the character mode world to the GUI world. Laying out a character mode screen requires that fields are lined up row to row and the screen is not cluttered with too many fields. GUI layout is more difficult, because there are so many options. Colors, pull-down lists, option buttons, text boxes, scrollbars, check boxes, and multiple windows are all layout capabilities. The skills that a layout artist commonly possesses are more appropriate to the task than those which a programmer usually demonstrates.

Relational Databases

Another dramatic change in software is in the area of database management. Traditional file system and database technologies rely on locality of reference for good performance in accessing data. Locality of reference implies that all data needed to satisfy a request is stored physically close together. However, t›day's business environment requires multikeyed access to rows of information derived from multiple tables. Performance is only possible in these environments when database searches are performed in main storage using extracted keys organized into searchable lists. Physical access to the database is restricted to the selection of rows that satisfy all search criteria. Relational database technology, using SQL, best meets these criteria. Despite the protestations symbolized in Figure 2.6, this commonly held view of relational technology is no longer valid. This incorrect view is frequently promulgated by those who have invested their careers in becoming experts in nonrelational technology. Experience indicates that in concert with good development standards and current technology, relational systems perform as well or better than previous technologies. In addition to providing independence of the physical storage from the logical view, SQL processors extract the row descriptors (column values) to separate indexes that are managed in main storage. The search request can be evaluated against the indexes to identify the rows that satisfy all search criteria. Only these identified rows are physically retrieved from external storage.

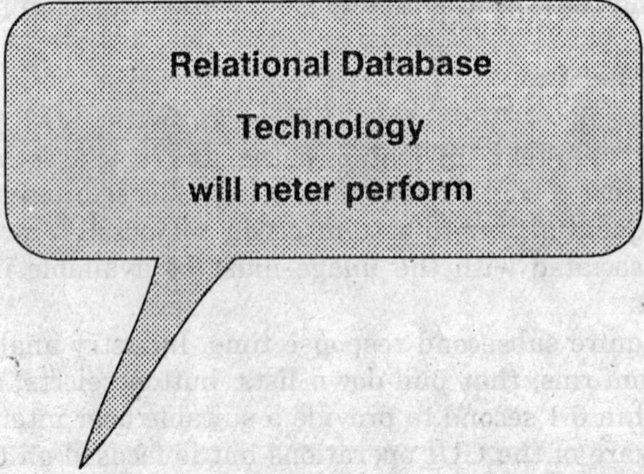

Fig 2.6. Doubting database administrators

Standards for use are an important part of a successful implementation of any tool. For example, developers can defeat the effectiveness of SQL in the client/server implementation by coding Boolean selection criteria with program logic rather than embedded SQL. Boolean selection criteria retrieves all rows that satisfy the first SELECT condition so that the program logic can be executed to filter unwanted rows. When all the application logic and database processing reside on the same processor, this is a manageable overhead. In a client/server implementation, this causes database selection to operate at the LAN or WAN communication rates rather than at the I/O subsystem rates. Frequently, developershoping to reduce the overhead of query optimizationuse the boolean technique for dynamic SQL, with the unfortunate result that performance is dramatically reduced as the additional physical data access time is incurred. It is important to select tools in the client/server world that generate fully qualified SQL SELECT statements.

Relational systems can and do perform, but poor standards of use can defeat them. An example of successful performance, this book has implemented an application, described in Appendix A, that processes more than 400 update transactions per second into a five-table relational database view. This specific example is implemented under DB2 on a midsize ES9000 processor.

2.2 Ways to Improve Performance of C/S Computing

(i) Offload work to server
(ii) Reduce total execution time.
(iii) Use multitasking clients.

2.2.1 Offload Work to Server

- Do certain things on certain clients only.
- Have distributed database systems.

To avoid load on the server or to do offloading shared databases or distributed data base systems are used as specialized communication interfaces (mediator between remote clients and the prominent centric server).

These remote clients sending the requests to the server and after analyzing certain activities on the server. These requests are diverted to the sub-server, which are handling the distributed data base as per the requests.

For example, In a yahoo website if we are using language as Indian English, the ultimately requests are dealt by yahoo based server for India Region. In a same way, in a chatting room if we are dealing with science and technology room or software development room, management roles. Chances are there that we are dealing with different database system. So that the load on the main centric server can be avoided upto certain extent.

Another Approach to avoid the load on the server, is to generate the application from the server side that the once the application is downloaded on the remote clients. The application must provide certain facilities, so that no. of queries and the validation can be settled on the client terminal only. For example, while submitting a web page with certain value, as name last name, password, confirm password, alternate Email id etc if the entered value in the field of password and the confirm password are not same then the facilities of a application downloaded on clients. These validation can be checked.

We usually use Java Script or VB Script in HTML pages to do this kind of Validation at the remote clients.

Whereas the entered user id and password to accesses the mailbox at certain .com then the validation is done on the server side.

2.2.2 Reduce Total Execution Time

- By having multiprocessors with shared memory.

By having multiprocessors with shared memory, database searches extent calculation and stored procedures execution can be performed in parallel by the server while client workstation deals directly with the current user needs.

Having multiprocessors with shared memory high speed local area networks topologies operating at 100 megabytes/sec required. It provides high speed communication to manage extra traffic in less time and saving the resources of the server for other clients.

2.2.3 Use of Multitasking Clients

- Orientation of the clients to more than one function.
- Use of CASE Tools so that Isolation can be avoided.

NOTE : * CASE—Computer added software engineering CASE Tools are basically pseudo code activity.

* SAD is global while software Eng is local concept.

↓

* Applied only for maintenance and development.

Case Environment requires the actual availability or probable availability of the requests having different seek times so that a Pseudo code can be generated by which less time required and memory required. Some processes executed initially and rest processes later on.

The way Multitasking concepts remains on the client's side as well as on the server side.

2.3 How to Reduce Network Traffic

- Minimize the Network requests
- Ease the strain on Network resources.

2.3.1 Minimize the Network Requests

In any mainframe centric server, lot more time the services from the central node are found to be chocked, because of an unexpected number of requests created either by the remote clients (Workstation) or by the next clients (*i.e.*, client or server). To remove these unexpected requests a file server model was presumed is a combination of many distributed tables having numerous fields.

In the centralized host model network traffic is reduced to the input and output of presentation speed (workstation speed). In the client server model it is possible to introduce significantly more traffic is detailed consideration (precautionary measure regarding to requests) is not given to the requestor server interface.

In the file server model as implemented by many database product such as dbase, FoxPro and MS Access. A search is processed in the client workstation record table requests are transmitted to he server and all filtering is performed on the workstation.

This filtering measurably performed by the primary key selection in the available database. In a large database the file server model breaks down when there are more authorized user at the same database, or when the database is large then a multi-key access process is required to perform on the database. For example use foreign key to take more users access.

With the introduction of the specific database server product in the client / server (oracle server) implementation the such request is packaged in and sent to the database servers for the execution. The SQL syntax is very powerful logic when the server is having database server. In this kind of database server trigger logic are there which enables all selection and rejection logic to execute on the server with this effect we can reduce a large amount f traffic on the server and on the network topologies (LAN or WAN's) from the side of clients.

2.3.2 Ease Strain on Network Resources

The use of application and database servers to produce the answer set required for client manipulation will dramatically reduce network traffic. There is no value in moving data to the client when it will be rejected.

The maximum reduction in network overhead is achieved when the only data returned to he client is that necessary to populate the presentation screen.

Client / Server applications can reduce expensive WAN overhead by using the LAN to provide local communication services between the client workstation and server. Many client/server applications use mixed LAN and WAN services.

Application design must evaluate the requirements of each application to determine the most effective location for application and database servers.

2.4 Client Services

The ideal Client / Server platform operates in an open systems environments using a requestor Server discipline that is based on well-designed standards.

The first generation client/server application using software such as Easel Enable the input and output data streams to be reformatted at the client without changes t the host applications. They use an API that defines the data stream format. Easel uses the IBM defined extended high level language application program interface (EHLL API).

Later on, GUI having good front end facilities at the client terminal were developed along with some additional functionality such as capability to select the items for input from the list, selections of the colours and fonts and also merging the other data into the existing data without changing the host application.

An example of this form of clients is an application developed for the emergency commands and control services in U.S.A. required E-911 dispatch applications. This computer application supports calls to he 911 emergency telephone no. and dispatches Fire, Police, Ambulance or Emergency vehicle to an incident.

This application provide the facility to trace down the caller no. at the dump terminal with the help of E-911 application and the information is displaced in list form which include the position of the caller, the trace from dump terminal to caller and other assisting ways to react the caller.

At the dump terminal the operator can pickup the services, which are right now available to caller with the help of list box using cursor and sending it to concern department.

In the Client / Server implementation of this kind of system, the only server part or the dump terminal deals only with the GUI and the workstation plots the address a map that enters the display of location of the Fire or Accidents. In addition the location of all Fire station and Vehicles are plotted onto map. The dispatch operator can see at a galance the entire status of Fire supports to compensate the accidents.

The GUI front end however enables the vehicles to shown in a window and selected by using a mouse pointer at the sight of remote terminal or clients. This enforces the development of highly equipped and densely functional GUI and the further development of these interfaces were develop due to the lot more error at the LAN or WAN traffic. Which again enforce to develop lot more services like

- Remote Procedure Calls (RPC).
- Fax / Print Services.
- Window Services.
- Remote Boot Services.
- Utility Services.
- Message Services.
- Database Services.
- Network Services.

2.5 Request for Service

Client workstation request services from the attached server. Whether this server is in fact the same processor or a network processor, the application format of the request is the same.

The most basic service provided by the NOS (Network Operating System) is redirection. This service intercepts client workstation operating system calls and redirects them to the server operating system. In this way, requests for disk directories, disk files, printers, printer queues, serial devices, application programs and named pipes are trapped by the redirection software and redirected (over the LAN) to the correct server locations.

How does redirection works?

1. Any requests for any drive A: or C: is passed through to the local file system by

the redirection software. Requests for other drives are passed to the server operating system.

2. The network operating system constructs the remote procedure calls, so that the certain services can avail at the remote workstation, whereas it uses certain protocol when same functionality are restricted. Example use of database services.

Novell commercialized this redirector concept for the Intel and MS-DOS platforms, and it has been adopted by all NOS and UNIX network file system vendors. The simplicity of executing standard calls to a virtual network of services is its main advantage.

2.6 Remote Procedure Calls

Remote procedure calls are the application through which the services which are available at the remote servers in form of some subroutines and procedures are called at the certain workstation through which the request is made.

For example, in yahoo website compose box while using graphical user interface, some fonts can be called at the client workstation even that fonts are not available at the workstation. Here certain RPC's are used in the coordinated network operating system. So that, these facilities can be available at the workstation.

RPC is a powerful technique for constructing distributed, client-server based applications. It is based on extending the notion of conventional, or local procedure calling, so that the called procedure need not exist in the same address space as the calling procedure. The two processes may be on the same system, or they may be on different systems with a network connecting them. By using RPC, programmers of distributed applications avoid the details of the interface with the network. The transport independence of RPC isolates the application from the physical and logical elements of the data communications mechanism and allows the application to use a variety of transports. RPC makes the client/server model of computing more powerful and easier to program. When combined with the ONC RPCGEN protocol compiler clients transparently make remote calls through a local procedure interface.

How RPC works

An RPC is analogous to a function call. Like a function call, when an RPC is made, the calling arguments are passed to the remote procedure and the caller waits for a response to be returned from the remote procedure. Figure 2.7 shows the flow of activity that takes place during an RPC call between two networked systems. The client makes a procedure call that sends a request to the server and waits. The thread is blocked from processing until either a reply is received, or it times out. When the request arrives, the server calls a dispatch routine that performs the requested service, and sends the reply to the client.

After the RPC call is completed, the client program continues. RPC specifically supports network applications.

A remote procedure is uniquely identified by the triple: (program number, version number, procedure number) the program number identifies a group of related remote procedures, each of which has a unique procedure number. A program may consist of one or more versions. Each version consists of a collection of procedures, which are available

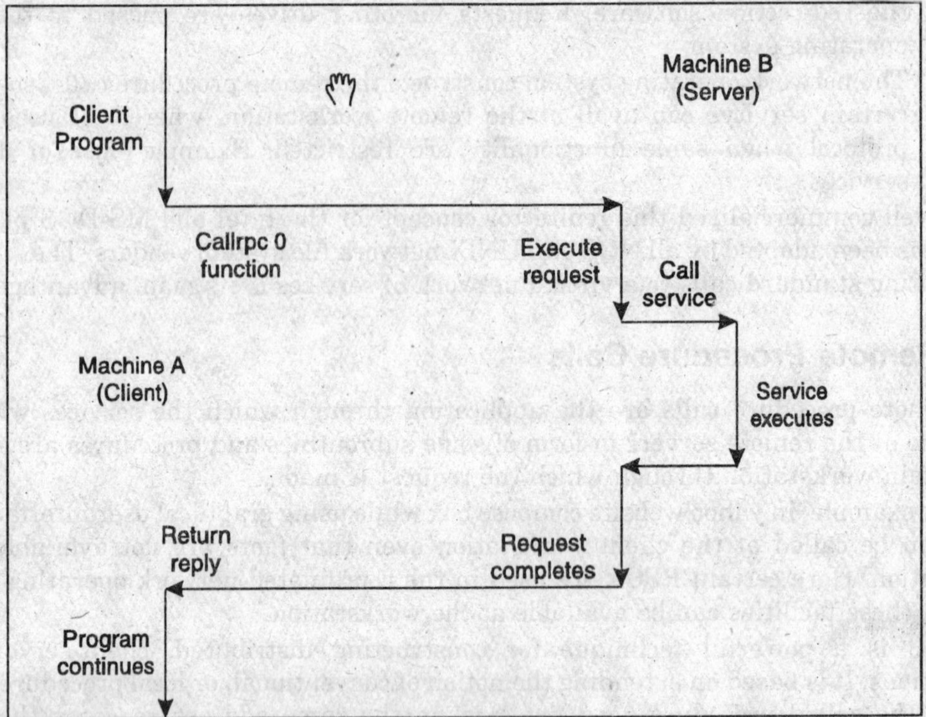

Fig. 2.7 Remote Procedure Calling Mechanism

to be called remotely. Version numbers enable multiple versions of an RPC protocol to be available simultaneously. Each version contains a number of procedures that can be called remotely. Each procedure has a procedure number.

RPC Application Development

Consider an example:

A client/server lookup in a personal database on a remote machine. Assuming that we cannot access the database from the local machine (via NFS).

We use UNIX to run a remote shell and execute the command this way. There are some problems with this method:

- The command may be slow to execute.
- You require a login account on the remote machine.

The RPC alternative is to

- Establish a server on the remote machine that can respond to queries.
- Retrieve information by calling a query, which will be quicker than previous approach.

To develop an RPC application the following steps are needed:

- Specify the protocol for client server communication.
- Develop the client program.
- Develop the server program.

The programs will be compiled separately. Generated stubs achieve the communication protocol and these stubs and rpc (and other libraries) will need to be linked in.

Defining the Protocol

The easiest way to define and generate the protocol is to use a protocol complier such as rpcgen. For the protocol you must identify the name of the service procedures, and data types of parameters and return arguments.

The protocol compiler reads a definitio and automatically generates client and server stubs. Rpcgen uses its own language (RPC language or RPCL), which looks very similar to preprocessor directives. Rpcgen exists as a standalone executable compiler that reads special files denoted by a .x prefix.

So to compile a RPCL file you simply do

rpcgen rpcprog.x

This will generate possibly four files:

- rpcprog_clnt.c—The client stub.
- rpcprog_svc.c—The server stub.
- rpcprog_xdr.c—If necessary XDR (external data representation) filters.
- rpcprog.h—The header file needed for any XDR filters.

The external data representation (XDR) is a data abstraction needed for machine independent communication. The client and server need not be machines of the same type.

Defining Client and Server Application Code

We must now write the client and application code. They must communicate via procedures and data types specified in the Protocol.

The service side will have to register the procedures that may be called by the client and receive and return any data required for processing.

The client application calls the remote procedure pass any required data and will receive the returned data.

There are several levels of application interfaces that may be used to develop RPC applications.

Compiling and running the application

Let us consider the full compilation model required to run a RPC application. Make files are useful for easing the burden of compiling RPC applications but it is necessary to understand the complete model before one can assemble a convenient make file.

Assume the client program is called rpcprog.c, the service program is rpcsvc.c and that the protocol has been defined in rpcprog.x and that rpcgen has been used to produce the stub and filter files: rpcprog_clnt.c, rpcprog_svc.c, rpcprog_xdr.c, rpcprog.h.

The client and server program must include (#include “rpcprog.h”

You must then:

- compile the client code:
  - cc -c rpcprog.c
- compile the client stub:
  - cc -c rpcprog_clnt.c
- compile the XDR filter:
  - cc -c rpcprog_xdr.c
- build the client executable:
  - cc -o rpcprog rpcprog.o rpcprog_clnt.o rpcprog_xdr.c
- compile the service procedures:
  - cc -c rpcsvc.c
- compile the server stub:
  - cc -c rpcprog_svc.c
- build the server executable:
  - cc -o rpcsvc rpcsvc.o rpcprog_svc.o rpcprog_xdr.c

Now simply run the programs rpcprog and rpcsvc on the client and server respectively. The server procedures must be registered before the client can call them.

Overview of Interface Routines

RPC has multiple levels of application interface to its services. These levels provide different degrees of control balanced with different amounts of interface code to implement. In order of increasing control and complexity. This section gives a summary of the routines available at each level. Simplified Interface Routines.

The simplified interfaces are used to make remote procedure calls to routines on other machines, and specify only the type of transport to use. The routines at this level are used for most applications. Descriptions and code samples can be found in the section, Simplified Interface @ 3-2.

Simplified Level Routine Function

- rpc_reg()—Registers a procedure as an RPC program on all transports of the specified type.
- rpc_call()—Remote calls the specified procedure on the specified remote host.
- rpc_broadcast()—Broadcasts a call message across all transports of the specified type. Standard Interface Routines The standard interfaces are divided into top level, intermediate level, expert level, and bottom level. These interfaces give a developer much greater control over communication parameters such as the transport being used, how long to wait beforeresponding to errors and retransmitting requests, and so on.

Top Level Routines

At the top level, the interface is still simple, but the program has to create a client handle before making a call or create a server handle before receiving calls. If you want the application to run on all transports, use this interface. Use of these routines and code samples can be found in Top Level Interface

- clnt_create()—Generic client creation. The program tells clnt_create() where the server is located and the type of transport to use.
- clnt_create_timed()—Similar to clnt_create() but lets the programmer specify the maximum time allowed for each type of transport tried during the creation attempt.
- svc_create()—Creates server handles for all transports of the specified type. The program tells svc_create() which dispatch function to use.
- clnt_call()—Client calls a procedure to send a request to the server.

Intermediate Level Routines

The intermediate level interface of RPC lets you control details. Programs written at these lower levels are more complicated but run more efficiently. The intermediate level enables you to specify the transport to use.

- clnt_tp_create()—Creates a client handle for the specified transport.
- clnt_tp_create_timed()—Similar to clnt_tp_create() but lets the programmer specify the maximum time allowed. svc_tp_create() Creates a server handle for the specified transport.
- clnt_call()—Client calls a procedure to send a request to the server.

Expert Level Routines

The expert level contains a larger set of routines with which to specify transport-related parameters. Use of these routines

- clnt_tli_create()—Creates a client handle for the specified transport.
- svc_tli_create()—Creates a server handle for the specified transport.
- rpcb_set()—Calls rpcbind to set a map between an RPC service and a network address.
- rpcb_unset()—Deletes a mapping set by rpcb_set().
- rpcb_getaddr()—Calls rpcbind to get the transport addresses of specified RPC services.
- svc_reg()—Associates the specified program and version number pair with the specified dispatch routine.
- svc_unreg()—Deletes an association set by svc_reg().
- clnt_call()—Client calls a procedure to send a request to the server.

Bottom Level Routines

The bottom level contains routines used for full control of transport options.

- clnt_dg_create()—Creates an RPC client handle for the specified remote program, using a connectionless transport.
- svc_dg_create()—Creates an RPC server handle, using a connectionless transport.

- clnt_vc_create()—Creates an RPC client handle for the specified remote program, using a connection-oriented transport.
- svc_vc_create()—Creates an RPC server handle, using a connection-oriented transport.
- clnt_call()—Client calls a procedure to send a request to the server.

The Programmer's Interface to RPC

This section addresses the C interface to RPC and describes how to write network applications using RPC. For a complete specification of the routines in the RPC library, see the rpc and related man pages.

Simplified Interface

The simplified interface is the easiest level to use because it does not require the use of any other RPC routines. It also limits control of the underlying communications mechanisms. Program development at this level can be rapid, and is directly supported by the rpcgen compiler. For most applications, rpcgen and its facilities are sufficient. Some RPC services are not available as C functions, but they are available as RPC programs. The simplified interface library routines provide direct access to the RPC facilities for programs that do not require fine levels of control.

Routines such as rusers are in the RPC services library librpcsvc. rusers.c, below, is a program that displays the number of users on a remote host. It calls the RPC library routine, rusers.

The program.c program listing:

```
#include <rpc/rpc.h>
#include <rpcsvc/rusers.h>
#include <stdio.h>
/*
* a program that calls the
* rusers() service
*/
main(int argc,char **argv)
{
int num;
if (argc != 2) {
fprintf(stderr, "usage: %s hostname\n",
argv[0]);
exit(1);
}

if ((num = rnusers(argv[1])) 0) {
fprintf(stderr, "error: rusers\n");
```

```
exit(1);
}

fprintf(stderr, "%d users on %s\n", num, argv[1] );
exit(0);
}
Compile the program with:
cc program.c -lrpcsvc -lnsl
```

The Client Side

There is just one function on the client side of the simplified interface rpc_call(). It has nine parameters:

```
int
rpc_call (char *host /* Name of server host */,
u_long prognum /* Server program number */,
u_long versnum /* Server version number */,
xdrproc_t inproc /* XDR filter to encode arg */,
char *in /* Pointer to argument */,
xdr_proc_t outproc /* Filter to decode result */,
char *out /* Address to store result */,
char *nettype /* For transport selection */);
```

This function calls the procedure specified by prognum, versum, and procnum on the host. The argument to be passed to the remote procedure is pointed to by the in parameter, and inproc is the XDR filter to encode this argument. The out parameter is an address where the result from the remote procedure is to be placed. outproc is an XDR filter which will decode the result and place it at this address.

The client blocks on rpc_call() until it receives a reply from the server. If the server accepts, it returns RPC_SUCCESS with the value of zero. It will return a non-zero value if the call was unsuccessful. This value can be cast to the type clnt_stat, an enumerated type defined in the RPC include files (<rpc/rpc.h>) and interpreted by the clnt_sperrno() function. This function returns a pointer to a standard RPC error message corresponding to the error code. In the example, all "visible" transports listed in /etc/netconfig are tried. Adjusting the number of retries requires use of the lower levels of the RPC library. Multiple arguments and results are handled by collecting them in structures.

The example changed to use the simplified interface, looks like

```
#include <stdio.h>
#include <utmp.h>
#include <rpc/rpc.h>
#include <r[csvc/rusers.h>

/* a program that calls the RUSERSPROG
* RPC program
```

```
*/

main(int argc, char **argv)

{
unsigned long nusers;
enum clnt_stat cs;
if (argc != 2) {
fprintf(stderr, "usage: rusers hostname\n");
exit(1);
}

if( cs = rpc_call(argv[1], RUSERSPROG,
RUSERSVERS, RUSERSPROC_NUM, xdr_void,
(char *)0, xdr_u_long, (char *)&nusers,
"visible") != RPC_SUCCESS ) {
clnt_perrno(cs);
exit(1);
}

fprintf(stderr, "%d users on %s\n", nusers, argv[1] );
exit(0);
}
```

Since data types may be represented differently on different machines, rpc_call() needs both the type of, and a pointer to, the RPC argument (similarly for the result). For RUSERSPROC_NUM, the return value is an unsigned long, so the first return parameter of rpc_call() is xdr_u_long (which is for an unsigned long) and the second is &nusers (which points to unsigned long storage). Because RUSERSPROC_NUM has no argument, the XDR encoding function of rpc_call() is xdr_void() and its argument is NULL.

The Server Side

The server program using the simplified interface is very straightforward. It simply calls rpc_reg() to register the procedure to be called, and then it calls svc_run(), the RPC library's remote procedure dispatcher, to wait for requests to come in.

```
rpc_reg() has the following prototype:
rpc_reg(u_long prognum /* Server program number */,
u_long versnum /* Server version number */,
u_long procnum /* server procedure number */,
char *procname /* Name of remote function */,
xdrproc_t inproc /* Filter to encode arg */,
xdrproc_t outproc /* Filter to decode result */,
char *nettype /* For transport selection */);
```

svc_run() invokes service procedures in response to RPC call messages. The dispatcher in rpc_reg() takes care of decoding remote procedure arguments and encoding results, using the XDR filters specified when the remote procedure was registered. Some notes about the server program:

- Most RPC applications follow the naming convention of appending a _1 to the function name. The sequence _n is added to the procedure names to indicate the version number n of the service.
- The argument and result are passed as addresses. This is true for all functions that are called remotely. If you pass NULL as a result of a function, then no reply is sent to the client. It is assumed that there is no reply to send.
- The result must exist in static data space because its value is accessed after the actual procedure has exited. The RPC library function that builds the RPC reply message accesses the result and sends the value back to the client.
- Only a single argument is allowed. If there are multiple elements of data, they should be wrapped inside a structure which can then be passed as a single entity.
- The procedure is registered for each transport of the specified type. If the type parameter is (char *)NULL, the procedure is registered for all transports specified in NETPATH.

You can sometimes implement faster or more compact code than can rpcgen. rpcgen handles the generic code-generation cases. The following program is an example of a hand-coded registration routine. It registers a single procedure and enters svc_run() to service requests.

```
#include <stdio.h>
#include <rpc/rpc.h>
#include <rpcsvc/rusers.h>

void *rusers();

main()
{
if(rpc_reg(RUSERSPROG, RUSERSVERS,
RUSERSPROC_NUM, rusers,
xdr_void, xdr_u_long,
"visible") == -1) {
fprintf(stderr, "Couldn't Register\n");
exit(1);
}
svc_run(); /* Never returns */
fprintf(stderr, "Error: svc_run returned!\n");
exit(1);
}
```

rpc_reg() can be called as many times as is needed to register different programs, versions, and procedures.

Passing Arbitrary Data Types

Data types passed to and received from remote procedures can be any of a set of predefined types, or can be programmer-defined types. RPC handles arbitrary data structures, regardless of different machines' byte orders or structure layout conventions, by always converting them to a standard transfer format called external data representation (XDR) before sending them over the transport. The conversion from a machine representation to XDR is called serializing, and the reverse process is called deserializing. The translator arguments of rpc_call() and rpc_reg() can specify an XDR primitive procedure, like xdr_u_long(), or a programmer-supplied routine that processes a complete argument structure. Argument processing routines must take only two arguments: a pointer to the result and a pointer to the XDR handle.

The following XDR Primitive Routines are available:

```
xdr_int() xdr_netobj() xdr_u_long() xdr_enum()
xdr_long() xdr_float() xdr_u_int() xdr_bool()
xdr_short() xdr_double() xdr_u_short() xdr_wrapstring()
xdr_char() xdr_quadruple() xdr_u_char() xdr_void()
```

The nonprimitive xdr_string(), which takes more than two parameters, is called from

```
xdr_wrapstring().
```

For an example of a programmer-supplied routine, the structure:

```
struct simple {
int a;
short b;
} simple;
```

Contains the calling arguments of a procedure. The XDR routine xdr_simple() translates the argument structure as shown below:

```
#include <rpc/rpc.h>
#include "simple.h"

bool_t xdr_simple(XDR *xdrsp, struct simple *simplep)

{
if (!xdr_int(xdrsp, &simplep-a))
return (FALSE);
if (!xdr_short(xdrsp, &simplep-b))
return (FALSE);
return (TRUE);
}
```

An equivalent routine can be generated automatically by rpcgen (See Chapter 33).

An XDR routine returns nonzero (a C TRUE) if it completes successfully, and zero otherwise.

For more complex data structures use the XDR prefabricated routines:

```
xdr_array() xdr_bytes() xdr_reference()
xdr_vector() xdr_union() xdr_pointer()
xdr_string() xdr_opaque()
```

For example, to send a variable-sized array of integers, it is packaged in a structure containing the array and its length:

```
struct varintarr {
int *data;
int arrlnth;
} arr;
```

Translate the array with xdr_array(), as shown below:

```
bool_t xdr_varintarr(XDR *xdrsp, struct varintarr *arrp)
{
return(xdr_array(xdrsp, (caddr_t)&arrp-data,
(u_int *)&arrp-arrlnth, MAXLEN, sizeof(int), xdr_int));
}
```

The arguments of xdr_array() are the XDR handle, a pointer to the array, a pointer to the size of the array, the maximum array size, the size of each array element, and a pointer to the XDR routine to translate each array element. If the size of the array is known in advance, use xdr_vector() instread as is more efficient:

```
int intarr[SIZE];

bool_t xdr_intarr(XDR *xdrsp, int intarr[])
{
return (xdr_vector(xdrsp, intarr, SIZE, sizeof(int),
xdr_int));
}
```

XDR converts quantities to 4-byte multiples when serializing. For arrays of characters, each character occupies 32 bits. xdr_bytes() packs characters. It has four parameters similar to the first four parameters of xdr_array().

Null-terminated strings are translated by xdr_string(). It is like xdr_bytes() with no length parameter. On serializing it gets the string length from strlen(), and on deserializing it creates a null-terminated string.

xdr_reference() calls the built-in functions xdr_string() and xdr_reference(), which translates pointers to pass a string, and struct simple from the previous examples. An example use of xdr_reference() is as follows:

```
struct finalexample {
char *string;
struct simple *simplep;
} finalexample;

bool_t xdr_finalexample(XDR *xdrsp, struct finalexample
*finalp)

{  if (!xdr_string(xdrsp, &finalp-string, MAXSTRLEN))
return (FALSE);
if (!xdr_reference( xdrsp, &finalp-simplep, sizeof(struct
simple), xdr_simple))
return (FALSE);
return (TRUE);
}
```

Note thatxdr_simple() could have been called here instead of xdr_reference() .

Developing High Level RPC Applications

Let us now introduce some further functions and see how we develop an application using high level RPC routines. We will do this by studying an example.

We will develop a remote directory reading utility.

Consider the program to consist of two files:

```
lls.c -- the main program which calls a routine in a local
module read_dir.c
/*
* ls.c: local directory listing main - before RPC
*/
#include <stdio.>h
#include <strings.h>
#include "rls.h"

main (int argc, char **argv)

{
char    dir[DIR_SIZE];
/* call the local procedure */
strcpy(dir, argv[1]);/* char dir[DIR_SIZE] is coming and
going... */
read_dir(dir);
```

```
/* spew-out the results and bail out of here! */
printf("%s\n", dir);

exit(0);
}
read_dir.c -- the file containing the local routine
read_dir().
/* note - RPC compliant procedure calls take one input and
return one output. Everything is passed by pointer.  Return
values should point to static data, as it might have to
survive some while. */
#include <stdio.h>
#include <sys/types.h>
#include <sys/dir.h>        /* use <spg2include/sys/dirent.h>
(SunOS4.1) or
<sys/dirent.h> for X/Open Portability Guide, issue 2
conformance */
#include "rls.h"

read_dir(char    *dir)
/* char dir[DIR_SIZE] */
{
DIR * dirp;
struct direct *d;
printf("beginning ");

/* open directory */
dirp = opendir(dir);
if (dirp == NULL)
return(NULL);
/* stuff filenames into dir buffer */
dir[0] = NULL;
while (d = readdir(dirp))
sprintf(dir, "%s%s\n", dir, d-d_name);

/* return the result */
printf("returning ");
closedir(dirp);
return((int)dir);   /* this is the only new line from
Example 4-3 */
}
the header file rls.h contains only the following (for now
at least)
#define DIR_SIZE 8192
```

Clearly we need to share the size between the files. Later when we develop RPC versions more information will need to be added to this file.

This local program would be compiled as follows:

```
cc lls.c read_dir.c -o lls
```

Now we want to modify this program to work over a network: Allowing us to inspect directories of a remote server accross a network.

The following steps will be required:

- We will have to convert the read_dir.c, to run on the server.
  - We will have to register the server and the routine read_dir() on the server/.
- The client lls.c will have to call the routine as a remote procedure.
- We will have to define the protocol for communication between the client and the server programs.

Defining the Protocol

We can can use simple NULL-terminated strings for passing and receivong the directory name and directory contents. Furthermore, we can embed the passing of these parameters directly in the client and server code.

We therefore need to specify the program, procedure and version numbers for client and servers. This can be done automatically using rpcgen or relying on prdefined macros in the simlified interface. Here we will specify them manually.

The server and client must agree ahead of time what logical adresses thney will use (The physical addresses do not matter they are hidden from the application developer) Program numbers are defined in a standard way:

- ?0x00000000 - 0x1FFFFFFF: Defined by Sun
- ?0x20000000 - 0x3FFFFFFF: User Defined
- ?0x40000000 - 0x5FFFFFFF: Transient
- ?0x60000000 - 0xFFFFFFFF: Reserved

We will simply choose a user deifnined value for our program number. The version and procedure numbers are set according to standard practice.

We still have the DIR_SIZE definition required from the local version as the size of the directory buffer is rewquired by bith client and server programs.

Our new rls.h file contains:

```
#define DIR_SIZE 8192
#define DIRPROG ((u_long) 0x20000001)    /* server program
(suite) number */
#define DIRVERS ((u_long) 1)     /* program version number
*/
```

```
#define READDIR ((u_long) 1)     /* procedure number for
look-up */
```

Sharing the data

We have mentioned previously that we can pass the data a simple strings. We need to define an XDR filter routine xdr_dir() that shares the data. Recall that only one encoding and decoding argument can be handled. This is easy and defined via the standard xdr_string() routine.

The XDR file, rls_xrd.c, is as follows:

```
#include <rpc/rpc.h>
#include "rls.h"
bool_t xdr_dir(XDR *xdrs, char *objp)
{ return ( xdr_string(xdrs, &objp, DIR_SIZE) ); }
```

The Server Side

We can use the original read_dir.c file. All we need to do is register the procedure and start the server.

The procedure is registered with registerrpc() function. This is prototypes by:

```
registerrpc(u_long prognum /* Server program number */,
u_long versnum /* Server version number */,
u_long procnum /* server procedure number */,
char *procname /* Name of remote function */,
xdrproc_t inproc /* Filter to encode arg */,
xdrproc_t outproc /* Filter to decode result */);
```

The parameters a similarly defined as in the rpc_reg simplified interface function. We have already discussed the setting of the parametere with the protocol rls.h header files and the rls_xrd.c XDR filter file.

The svc_run() routine has also been discussed previously.

The full rls_svc.c code is as follows:

```
#include <rpc/rpc.h>
#include "rls.h"

main()
{
extern bool_t xdr_dir();
extern char * read_dir();

registerrpc(DIRPROG, DIRVERS, READDIR,
read_dir, xdr_dir, xdr_dir);

svc_run();
}
```

The Client Side

At the client side we simply need to call the remote procedure. The function callrpc() does this. It is prototyped as follows:

```
callrpc(char *host /* Name of server host */,
u_long prognum /* Server program number */,
u_long versnum /* Server version number */,
char *in /* Pointer to argument */,
xdrproc_t inproc /* XDR filter to encode arg */,
char *out /* Address to store result */
xdr_proc_t outproc /* Filter to decode result */);
```

We call a local function read_dir() which uses callrpc() to call the remote procedure that has been registered READDIR at the server.

The full rls.c program is as follows:

```
/*
* rls.c: remote directory listing client
*/
#include <stdio.h>
#include <strings.h>
#include <rpc/rpc.h>
#include "rls.h"

main (argc, argv)
int argc; char *argv[];
{
char     dir[DIR_SIZE];
/* call the remote procedure if registered */
strcpy(dir, argv[2]);
read_dir(argv[1], dir); /* read_dir(host, directory) */

/* spew-out the results and bail out of here! */
printf("%s\n", dir);

exit(0);
}

read_dir(host, dir)
char    *dir, *host;
{
extern bool_t xdr_dir();
enum clnt_stat clnt_stat;
```

```
clnt_stat = callrpc ( host, DIRPROG, DIRVERS, READDIR,
xdr_dir, dir, xdr_dir, dir);
if (clnt_stat != 0) clnt_perrno (clnt_stat);
}
```

2.7 Fax / Print Services

Whenever a request is made from the remote workstation to print certain document at the server. Then print services comes into actions (i.e. the application made for printing requests for remote terminal comes into actions) and redirected by network operating system redirector software and managed by the server either for printing and in case busy then to the server queue manager and simultaneously server also sends some messages to the clients workstation that the request is turndown, by using print services of the server.

The client workstation can view the status of the print queue at any time, but if having the sharing of the print services as well as the server.

2.8 Window Services

A client workstation may have several windows open on screen at any time. The capability to activate, view, move, size or hide a particular window is provided by the window services of the client operating system.

These services are essential in a Client / Server implementation, because they interact with message services provided to notify the user of events that occur on a server. Because of these windows services of the clients sometimes if happen a webpage is view without scrolling at a maximize position on a certain workstation whereas the same page may be viewing with scrolling when at the maximize position at the different workstation.

2.9 Remote Boot Services

Some applications operate well on workstations without any focal disk storage. The client workstation must provide sufficient software burned into erasable programmable read only memory (E-PROM) to start the initial program load (IPL) *i.e.*, Boot process. E-PROM is included in all workstations to hold the Basic Input/output (BIOS) services.

This mini operating system is powerful enough to load the remote software that provides the remaining services and applications functions to the client workstation.

Applications can be invoked from the client to execute remotely on a server. Backup services are an example of services that might be remotely invoked from a client workstation. Business functions such as downloading data from a host or checking a list of stock prices might also be invoked locally to run remotely. Software is provided by the NOS to run on the client workstation to initiate these remote applications.

2.10 Utility Services

The operating system provides local functions such as copy, move, edit, compare and help that execute on the client workstation.

2.10.1 Message Services

Messages can be sent and received synchronously to or from the network. The message services provide the buffering, scheduling and arbitration services to support this function.

2.10.2 Network Services

The client workstation communicates with the network through a set of services and API's that create, send, receive and format network messages. These services provide support for communications protocols such as IPX, TCP/IP, APPC, Ethernet, Token Ring, FDDI, X-25 and SNA.

2.10.3 Application Services

In addition to the remote execution services that the NOS provides, customs applications will use their own API's embedded in an RPC to invoke specialized services from a remote server.

2.10.4 Database Services

Database requests are made using the SQL syntax. SQL is an industry standard language supported by many vendors. Because the language uses a standard from, the same application may be run on multiple platforms. There are syntactical differences and product extensions available form most vendors.

These are provided to improve developer productivity and system performance and should be carefully evaluated to determine whether their uses are worth the incompatibility implied by using proprietary components.

2.11 Dynamic Data Exchange

VB (Interface) ⟶ Connected Database
Data

HTML - ASP (Interface) ⟶ Connected Database
Data

The transferring of data through one package to another package is called dynamic data exchange.

Dynamic Data Exchange is one of the prominent features of some operating system from window 3.X onwards by which a data of one package enables to get transferred onto the another package with the help of some application programming interface. In standardized manner we can say "The transferring of data through one package of a vendor to another package of the same vendor or the different vendor is called the dynamic data Exchange. i.e. if we considered visual basic generated form as an integrated interface for the user through which a data is posted to any database, *i.e.*, Oracle or MS-Access by some connectivity then above is formed as dynamic data exchange.

In a same manner if we are using HTML-ASP interface for the user and connected to data entered by user with the help of ODBC to any database *i.e.*, SQL server, MS-Access, Oracle is also formed as dynamic data Exchange.

If a word file data is saved as the another word file data the process is called Static data Exchange, As both the packages are same and vendors are same, whereas if we are saving the data of the some word file as a file of some another package by giving a relevant extension then it is formed as dynamic data exchange as the packages are different.

Because of the above concept of website receiving or retrieving the data to or from the database are formed as the dynamic cum informative website, whereas the website intimating different WebPages through the hyperlink but not receiving and retrieving any database are formed as static cum informative website.

It sends data between applications using Windows messages according to a documented protocol. Saying that DDE is old-fashioned and is being replaced by COM is something you see repeated parrot fashion over and over again. DDE and COM do not work in the same way and they solve different problems. Here are some points of difference:

- COM is synchronous, one party makes subroutine calls into the other and must wait until the call returns. If the called component is busy the caller is blocked until it becomes free. DDE is asynchronous, a well-programmed client sends a Windows message to the server and carries on processing. Windows holds the message and sends it to the server when the server is ready to process it.
- COM is complex to program but powerful. The client can manipulate objects within the server as if they belonged to the client. DDE is straightforward to implement but all it can do is transmit data. It can only control another application because the recipient can treat data as a command.
- COM works well when the client creates an instance of a server object or application for its own use. Programming a continuously running server, to which clients can attach when they wish, is possible but tricky. DDE of itself is incapable of creating objects (although OLE1 used it as a transport mechanism). The essence of DDE is that clients attach to an already running server.
- Applications using COM almost always need support DLLs such as the VB runtimes or MFC. Programs using DDE can be mean and lean and do not need extra support DLLs.
- COM interfaces are tightly specified and contained within the software component. Some documentation is normally built into the interface. The user of a COM component knows exactly which methods are available and how to call them. DDE interfaces are specified only in external documentation.
- Because of the tight interface specification, upgrading COM components can be a nightmare. With DDE the server or client can be changed independently.
- COM is frequently used to communicate with a DLL in the same process space (called an in-process server). Such as server is often termed an ActiveX control and has the extension OCX. Our DDClient and DDServer Visual Basic components are in-process servers. Using DDE to communicate between components of the same application is possible but has no benefits.
- COM communication with a remote machine is called DCOM (Distributed COM). If you make a DCOM call to a remote machine which does not respond, your

program (or at least the thread making the call) is stuck. DCOM has a fixed built-in timeout which you cannot change. DDE with a remote machine is called NETDDE, it is used by the Hearts game and Chat which come with Windows. Timeout is controlled by the program.

- Under Windows 3.1 and 9x it is possible to crash the system by badly programmed DDE, because the message queue can be filled. NT does not crash in this way, COM does not suffer from the problem at all.
- DDE is totally "Bit blind", neither the client nor server can tell whether the other application is 16-bit or 32-bit. Indeed, the server cannot know whether the client is on the same computer or not. Connecting 16 to 32 bit COM components is not usually possible.

It is easy to see from the above points why a DDE server is the most widely used way of providing data obtained from any form of hardware interface. In particular:

- The server can run continuously.
- It will probably serve a wide range of clients but can be updated without requiring them all to be recompiled.
- It is immune from the problems associated with different versions of the system DLLs on different machines.
- It can be small and self-contained.
- Clients cannot interfere with the running of the server by being slow or busy.

When is DDE more suitable? or When using COM is impossible?

- **Connecting to a running instance of a program, which does not register in the Running Object Table (ROT).**
  For example, ActiveX server applications written in Visual Basic do not register themselves in the ROT. (It is possible by a piece of 'Black Belt' programming)
- **Connecting to a particular instance of an application**
  Some applications such as Excel do register themselves in the ROT and support multiple instances. However, there is no way to connect to a particular instance of Excel with COM. For example, the Get Object () method in Visual Basic returns a random instance, even when a file name is specified.

With DDE you can manipulate any worksheet without regard to the instance hosting it, because Excel offers a separate topic name for each worksheet. For more information on controlling Excel go to Controlling Excel with DDE.

With some care it is possible to connect to particular instances with DDE, even when the topics supported by each instance are the same. The client must start when at most one of the instances of the server is running. The client must capture the instance handle of each instance as it registers with DDEML, and connect using it. Connections made using a string for the service name, *e.g.*, IExplore, will connect to a random instance.

Writing compact programs, or when the compiler does not make COM easy

The amount of code required to operate a DDE interface is trivial compared to that required for COM. In the DDE Software download area there are sample programs (with full source), which manipulate Microsoft Excel using DDE. The compiled C program is only 17kb, and it does not rely on any external DLLs (apart from the Common Controls which is for the status bar, not DDE). The Visual Basic example uses the Evaluation version of DDClient, so you can modify the project. VB does make COM easy, but if you need to hook up to a running instance of Excel, DDE is the only way you can be certain of connecting to the required worksheet.

When the server is a self-standing program, which must execute whether or not is has clients

In other words, when the server is the primary application or must have priority on processor time. Hardware monitoring is an example of this situation. The overhead of queuing a message is fixed and the process cannot hang. Quite apart from the complexity of programming COM events, the server must wait for each client to process the data, and its performance therefore depends upon the performance of the clients. If just one of the clients hangs in the COM (or DCOM) event routine the server, or at least one thread, is brought down with it.

A DDE server is the most widely used way of providing data obtained from any form of hardware interface because:

- The server can run continuously.
- It will probably serve a wide range of clients but can be updated without requiring them all to be recompiled.
- It is immune from the problems associated with different versions of the system DLLs on different machines.
- It can be small and self-contained.
- Clients cannot interfere with the running of the server by being slow or busy.

Networked DDE is suitable when a server is supplying data to a number of clients on different machines. Messages are queued within the client machines and do not affect server performance. NetDDE depends on Net BIOS, which can use TCP/IP, so NetDDE works over the Internet.

When the complexity and tight specification of COM, and the requirement to use GUIDs would be a hindrance rather than help.

An example is the way the Windows shell launches programs, using DDE to pass a filename or command. COM would be gross overkill for this simple task.

For program monitoring

DDE is ideal for allowing one program to monitor another, because neither program ever executes in the context of the other so they cannot interfere with each other. Internet Explorer and Netscape Navigator provide a DDE interface for monitoring the URLs they load. It is a good example of an application for which DDE is much more suitable than COM (ActiveX). Web Spy can run without a browser running. Web Spy or the browser(s) can be started first, Web Spy does not interfere with browsing in any way, and either program can be terminated at any time without affecting the other.

COM and DDE data transfer speeds compared

The transfer rates in the first group are estimated ballpark figures for 300MHz machines driven as fast as possible. We accept no responsibility for their accuracy; your mileage may vary widely. They are based on a small number of tests; the tests were not checked to ensure comparing like with like, there were only a small number of measurements. Remember that Windows can queue DDE messages, but COM is synchronous and the caller must wait for the other application to finish processing the call.

- Sending data to a client on an advice loop using DDEML - 1000 transactions/sec.
- Sending data to a client on an advice loop using our Data Send control - 2000 transactions/sec.
- Sending data to a client on an advice loop using raw DDE - 2000 transactions/sec.
- Sending data by NetDDE with DDEML - 1300 transactions/sec. (The server and client can process in parallel.)
- DDE transactions in Visual Basic using the built-in mechanism 100 - transactions/sec.
- Out-of-process COM calls - 2000-3000 transactions/sec.
- DCOM calls are slower than out-of-process, similar to NetDDE.

The following numbers are taken from the COM tutorial at DevelopMentor for 100 (lower figure) and 4 (higher figure) bytes of parameters. They are slower than our figures. DevelopMentor say the numbers are fairly old, this probably means that they were measured on a slower machine.

- In-process COM calls — 119,240-129,041 transactions/sec.
- Out-of-process COM calls — 968-1765 transactions/sec.
- DCOM calls (LAN) — 342-495 transactions/sec.
- DCOM calls (WAN) — 16-19 transactions/sec.

Do not be mislead by figures quoted for in-process COM calls, an in-process server is called in a similar way to a normal DLL. ActiveX which does not involve interprocess communication is much faster, as can be seen from the DevelopMentor table.

Network DDE (NetDDE)

DDE across a network is simple to set up. It uses Net BIOS and since this can be run over TCP/IP, NetDDE can use the Internet. Given a fast connection, network DDE is if anything faster than between two programs on one machine, because the server and client can process in parallel. In order to operate DDE over a network the following steps are necessary.

1. On both machines, a DDE agent called NETDDE.EXE must be running, its job is to transmit the data across the network. Under Windows for Workgroups and Windows 9x NETDDE.EXE can be put in the Startup Group or be started manually. Under Windows NT it is a service, which is started when required.
2. On the server side only, DDE shares must be created. These bind a service/topic name pair to a share name. For example, the pair WinChat/Chat has the share name Chat$. All the share information is stored in the registry, which has a different format under 3x/9x and NT. You may read that altering the registry by hand is required on Windows 9x, but this is not true.

   The Windows API NDde makes the registry entries; it has calls such as

NDdeShareAdd (). Application programs can use the API to share their DDE services automatically. The user creates shares manually with the program DDESHARE.EXE, which makes the necessary API calls.

In Windows for Workgroups 3.11 and Windows 9x only a 16-bit API is provided, so DDESHARE for those systems is a 16-bit program. If you do not have this program you can get it from the DDE download area. The display of the program is not bug free. If it gets confused, which it may after deleting a share, exit and re-run. Under Windows NT only a 32-bit NDde API is available, so the NT version of DDESHARE is a 32-bit program. The DDE server has no knowledge of the share and does not know if its clients are local or remote.

3. The client program must be changed to use the special service/topic pair \\computer-name\NDDE$/Share-name, for example service "\\RHAMINISYS\NDDE$" and topic "Chat$".

The client and server both hold a DDE conversation with NETDDE.EXE on the local machine. To make a connection, the client NETDDE sends the requested share name to the remote computer. The remote NETDDE agent looks in the registry for the share name. If it exists the permissions are checked. At the server end NETDDE then attempts to connect to the real service and topic names specified in the registry. The server may be started automatically. Once the conversation has been established all DDE transactions are the same as between two programs on the same machine. When connecting to NT the user may be prompted for the password and the number of sessions is limited.

2.12 Object Linking and Embedding (OLE)

Object Linking and Embedding (OLE) is a distributed object system and protocol developed by Microsoft.OLE allows an editor to "farm out" part of a document to another editor and then reimport it. For example, a desktop publishing system might send some text to a word processor or a picture to a bitmap editor using OLE. The main benefit of using OLE, next to reduced file size, is the ability to create a master file. References to data in this file can be made and the master file can then have changed data which will then take effect in the referenced document.

Its primary use is for managing compound documents, but it is also used for transferring data between different applications using drag and drop and clipboard operations. The concept of "embedding" is also central to much use of multimedia in Web pages, which tend to embed video, animation (including Flash animations), and audio files within the hypertext markup language (such as HTML or XHTML) or other structural markup language used (such as XML or SGML). However, OLE uses a fat client architecture, which means that the file type or the application which is being embedded must be present on the machine which is being operated upon. For instance, if a Microsoft Excel spreadsheet is to be manipulated or even viewed, then there must be a copy of Excel or an Excel viewer installed on the user's machine.

Technology

OLE 1.0, released in 1990, was the evolution of the original dynamic data exchange, or DDE, concepts that Microsoft developed for earlier versions of Windows. While DDE was limited to transferring limited amounts of data between two running applications,

OLE was capable of maintaining active links between two documents or even embedding one type of document within another.

OLE servers and clients communicate with system libraries using virtual function tables, or VTBLs. The VTBL consists of a structure of function pointers that the system library can use to communicate with the server or client. The server and client libraries, OLESVR.DLL and OLECLI.DLL, were originally designed to communicate between themselves using the WM_DDE_EXECUTE Windows message.

OLE 1.0 later evolved to become an architecture for software components known as the component object model (COM), and later DCOM.When an OLE object is placed on the clipboard, it is stored in native Windows formats (such as a bitmap or metafile), as well as being stored in its own, native format. This native format allows an OLE-aware application to embed a portion of another document cut or copied to the clipboard by the user by storing it in the current document.

OLE 2.0 was the next evolution of OLE 1.0, sharing many of the same goals, but was re-implemented over top of the Component Object Model instead of using VTBLs. New features were automation, drag-and-drop, in-place activation and Structured storage.

ActiveX

In 1996, Microsoft renamed the OLE 2.0 technology to ActiveX. ActiveX introduced ActiveX Controls, Active Documents and Active Scripting (built on top of OLE Automation). This version of OLE is commonly used by Web designers to embed multimedia files in Web pages.

In the wake of losing a patent lawsuit with Eolas, Microsoft announced on December 2, 2005, that "native" support for ActiveX has been dropped: "After a forthcoming update, Microsoft Internet Explorer users will not be able to directly interact with Microsoft ActiveX controls loaded by the APPLET, EMBED, or OBJECT elements." Functionally, this means that Internet Explorer users would still be able to use ActiveX but would have to explicitly "activate" objects such as Flash navigation bars and QuickTime movies before they could interact with them. The objects still display, but the user can no longer do anything with them (for example, pause a playing movie) until they activate them. When users move their cursors over such an object a pop-up window directs them to "Click to activate and use this control." If they then click on the object, they may subsequently use it in the old fashion.

The further extended feature of the dynamic data exchange is formed as OLE. By discussing OLE a term aware is focused. Aware means a reference to the object or one of its components that automatically launches the appropriate software to manipulate the data.

For example, an ODBC is one of the components of the MS-Access through which the database connectivity of ASP interface is provided is formed as object linking. If, we have generated an image in Microsoft word document and we are saving it as Photoshop file it is called dynamic data exchange but at the same time, if we are cropping this image and a gif image, then this crop is similar components in forms of application interface as ODBC.

By discussing OLE, two important forms are viewer and launcher. The viewers are the application component, which make us aware how the things or data will be view when it is transferred to another package. The viewers and launchers are the custom build application.

With the viewer, users can see data from one software package while they are running another package, launchers, invoke the software package that created the data and thus provide the full functionality of the launched software. OLE enabled application can use any software that supports these data interchange API's. An e-mail application will be able to attach any no. of components into mail object with the need to provide custom viewers or launchers.

2.13 Common Object Request Broker Architecture (CORBA)

Object oriented concepts have been used to design and implement operating system Kernels, bringing benefits of flexibility, manageability and portability. The application of object oriented techniques to the design and implementation of distributed software is referred to as Distributed Object Computing (DOC).

There are three main computing technologies in the DOC market:

- The object management group (OMG) architecture called CORBA (Common Object Request Broker Architecture).
- The Java Remote Method Innovation (RMI) system.
- Microsoft is distributed component object model (DCOM).

The CORBA is the most advanced and well established of the three. A number of industry leaders, including IBM, SUN, Netscape and Oracle support CORBA and Microsoft has announced that it will link its windows only, Dcom with CORBA.

What is CORBA?

In short, the CORBA is specification from the object management group (ONG), a UNIX vendor consortium. OLE focuses on data sharing between applications on a single desktop and CORBA addresses cross platform data transfer and the process of moving objects over networks. A CORBA support enables windows and UNIX clients to share objects. A word processor graphics generated from a UNIX workstation.

Common Object Request Broker Architecture (CORBA) is a competing distributed systems technology that offers greater portability than remote method invocation. Unlike RMI, CORBA isn't tied to one language, and as such, can integrate with legacy systems of the past written in older languages, as well as future languages that include support for CORBA. CORBA isn't tied to a single platform (a property shared by RMI), and shows great potential for use in the future. That said, for Java developers, CORBA offers less flexibility, because it doesn't allow executable code to be sent to remote systems.

CORBA services are described by an interface, written in the Interface Definition Language (IDL). IDL mappings to most popular languages are available, and mappings can be written for languages written in the future that require CORBA support. CORBA allows objects to make requests of remote objects (invoking methods), and allows data to be passed between two remote systems. Remote method invocation, on the other hand, allows Java objects to be passed and returned as parameters. This allows new classes to be passed across virtual machines for execution (mobile code). CORBA only allows primitive data types, and structures to be passed - not actual code.

Under communication between CORBA clients and CORBA services, method calls are passed to Object Request Brokers (ORBs). These ORBs communicate via the Internet Inter-ORB Protocol (IIOP). IIOP transactions can take place over TCP streams, or via other protocols (such as HTTP), in the event that a client or server is behind a firewall. The following diagram shows a client and a servant communicating.

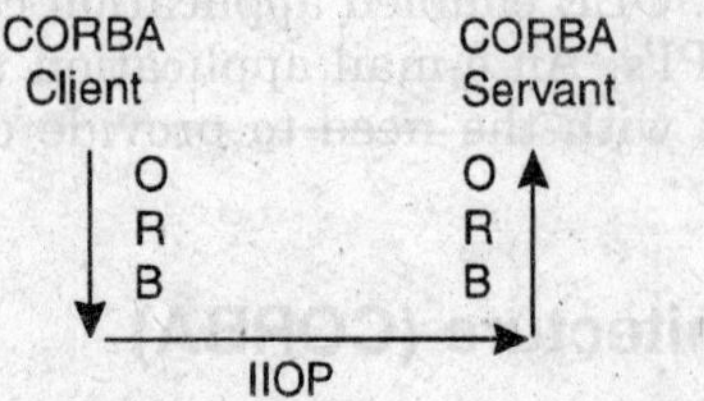

CORBA client sends a request through its local ORB to a remote ORB's servant

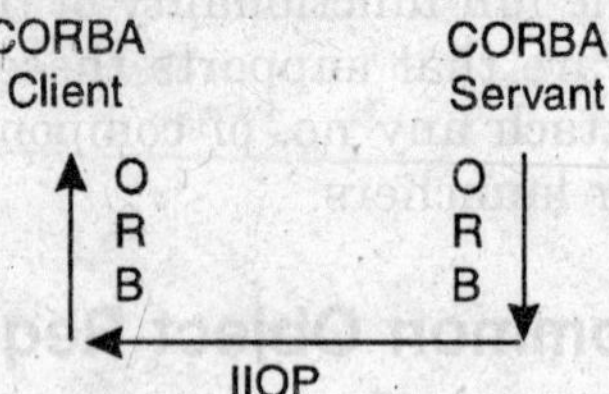

CORBA servant sends back a response to a remote ORB

RMI vs CORBA

Comparing RMI and CORBA doesn't reveal an optimum solution - one is not "better" than the other. The properties of these two technologies lend themselves to different situations. A comparison of RMI and CORBA helps to highlight individual strengths and weaknesses, but the applicability of one technology over the other depends largely on the purposes for which it is to be used, the experience of the developers who will design, implement and maintain the distributed system, and whether non-Java systems are intended to access the system now or in the future.

RMI Pros and Cons

Remote method invocation has significant features that CORBA doesn't possess - most notably the ability to send new objects (code and data) across a network, and for foreign virtual machines to seamlessly handle the new objects .Remote method invocation has been available since JDK 1.02, and so many developers are familiar with the way this technology works, and organizations may already have systems using RMI. Its chief limitation, however, is that it is limited to Java Virtual Machines, and cannot interface with other languages.

Remote Method Invocation

Pros	Cons
(i) Portable across many platforms	Tied only to platforms with Java support
(ii) Can introduce new code to foreign JVMs	Security threats with remote code execution, and limitations on functionality enforced by security restrictions
(iii) Java developers may already have experience with RMI (available since JDK1.02)	Learning curve for developers that have no RMI experience is comparable with CORBA
(iv) Existing systems may already use RMI - the cost and time to convert to a new technology may be prohibitive	Can only operate with Java systems - no support for legacy systems written in C++, Ada, Fortran, Cobol, and others (including future languages).

CORBA Pros and Cons

CORBA is gaining strong support from developers, because of its ease of use, functionality, and portability across language and platform CORBA is particularly important in large organizations, where many systems must interact with each other, and legacy systems can't yet be retired. CORBA provides the connection between one language and platform and another - its only limitation is that a language must have a CORBA implementation written for it. CORBA also appears to have a performance increase over RMI, which makes it an attractive option for systems that are accessed by users who require real-time interaction.

Common Object Request Broker Architecture

Pros	Cons
(i) Services can be written in many different languages, executed on many different platforms, and accessed by any language with an interface definition language (IDL) mapping.	(i) Describing services require the use of an interface definition language (IDL) which must be learned. Implementing or using services require an IDL mapping to your required language - writing one for a language that isn't supported would take a large amount of work.
(ii) With IDL, the interface is clearly separated from implementation, and developers can create different implementations based on the same interface.	(ii) IDL to language mapping tools create code stubs based on the interface - some tools may not integrate new changes with existing code.
(iii) CORBA supports primitive data types, and a wide range of data structures, as parameters	(iii) CORBA does not support the transfer of objects, or code.
(iv) CORBA is ideally suited to use with legacy systems, and to ensure that applications written now will be accessible in the future.	(iv) The future is uncertain - if CORBA fails to achieve sufficient adoption by industry, then CORBA implementations become the legacy systems.
(v) CORBA is an easy way to link objects and systems together	(v) Some training is still required, and CORBA specifications are still in a state of flux.
(vi) CORBA systems may offer greater performance	(vi) Not all classes of applications need real-time performance, and speed may be traded off against ease of use for pure Java systems.

Java and CORBA

CORBA, for those who haven't heard of it before, stands for Common Object Request

Broker Architecture. This architecture allows clients to invoke methods of objects running on remote servers. The idea is nothing new - many developers will have come across similar systems such as RPC (remote procedure call), or Java's own RMI (remote method invocation). The difference between these and CORBA is that CORBA is much more interoperable with other platforms - a C++ object running on a Wintel system can communicate with a Java object on a Unix box. Developers don't need to know what language a CORBA service is written in, or even where it is physically located. This makes CORBA systems very versatile - one can change the location of a CORBA object, and then re-register with a nameserver. Clients that look up the service can then find its new location, and then continue to make requests. Java makes it easy to integrate support for CORBA into applications and applets.

Interface Definition Language (IDL)

Developers use the Interface Definition Language (IDL) to describe the interface to a CORBA object. An IDL schema can then be used to generate Java code for the client and server that will use the object. The same IDL schema could be used to generate either a client or server in C++, Ada, or any other language that supports CORBA. You don't write your implementation of a CORBA service in IDL - so you can continue to write in pure Java code if you so wish.

Let's start by taking a look at a sample IDL schema, to give you an idea what I'm talking about. The following schema shows a very simple CORBA service, which allows clients to get and store the name associated with an email address. For the purposes of this example, we won't worry about modifying or deleting an existing user.

```
// Address book system module
module address_book_system
{
    // Specify interface to our address book
    interface address_book
    {
  // Unknown user exception
  exception unknown_user {};

  // User already exists exception
  exception user_exists {};

  // Lookup name from email address
  string name_from_email(in string email)
                raises (unknown_user);

  // Lookup email from full name
  string email_from_name(in string name)
                raises (unknown_user);

  // Record a new name and email
```

```
    void record_user(in string name, in string email)
            raises user_exists;
    };
};
```

Listing 1-0 AddressBook.idl

We start by declaring a module for our address book system (modules can be mapped to Java packages). Inside the module, we declare our interfaces and the exceptions they can raise. Since its such as simple system, the methods of the interface will only return a string, but we can create more complex return values if needed. As well as returning values, we accept as input two strings for our record_user method. As you can see, IDL really isn't to hard to pick up.

Once you've written your interface using IDL, you can then begin to write client and servers in the language of the choice. We'll choose Java for now, but there's no reason why the client or the server couldn't be written in another language. Provided you have an interface in IDL format, you could write code that interacts with the object it describes.

From IDL to Java

Converting an IDL schema into Java source code is quite straightforward. Sun provides a free tool, idltojava, that creates the source code for you. This tool is currently distributed separately to JDK 1.2, but is freely available for members of the Java Developer Connection.

```
idltojava -fno-cpp AddressBook.idl
```

Based on the name of your IDL schema's module, a package will be generated that contains skeleton source code for your CORBA client and server, as well a second package to cover our two exceptions. The following is a list of the files it creates for us

```
\address_book_system\
  _address_bookStub.java
  address_book.java
  address_bookHolder.java
  address_bookHelper.java
  address_bookPackage
  _address_bookImplBase.java

  address_bookPackage\
    unknown_user.java
    unknown_userHelper.java
    unknown_userHolder.java
    user_exists.java
    user_existsHelper.java
    user_existsHolder.java
```

As you can see, there are a lot of files! Fortunately, we only need three to implement a complete CORBA client and server. The first file is a servant, which serves the requests made by clients. The second is a server, which will accept requests, and the third is a standalone application which will issue requests.

Implementing a CORBA Servant

Under CORBA, a servant is responsible for handling service requests. When we ran the idltojava tool, an abstract class was created that handles most of the hard work for us. All we need to do is create an AddressBookServant class, that implements the _address_bookImplBase. It will contain the code for our three methods described in the IDL schema.

```
package address_book_system;
import  address_book_system.address_bookPackage.*;

import  java.util.Hashtable;
import  java.util.Enumeration;
//
//
// AddressBookServant
//
// This servant class is responsible for implementing
// three methods
//
//    * String name_from_email ( String email );
//    * String email_from_name ( String name   );
//    * void    record_user ( String name, String email );
//
//
class AddressBookServant extends _address_bookImplBase

{
    private Hashtable name2email;

    public AddressBookServant()

    {
  // Create a new hashtable to store name & email
  name2email = new Hashtable();
    }

    // Get the name of this email user
    public String name_from_email ( String email )
            throws unknown_user
```

```
    {
if (name2email.contains(email))
{
    // Begin search for that name
    for (Enumeration e = name2email.keys();
                e.hasMoreElements();)
    {
  String name = (String) e.nextElement();
  String e_mail = (String) name2email.get(name);

  // Match on email ?
  if (email.compareTo(e_mail) == 0)

  {
    return name;
  }
   }
}

// User not found - throw unknown user exception
throw new unknown_user();
  }

  // Get the email of this person
  public String email_from_name ( String name  )
          throws unknown_user
  {
// If user exists
if (name2email.containsKey(name))
{
  // Return email address
  return (String) name2email.get(name);
}

// User doesn't exist
throw new unknown_user();
  }

  // Add a new user to the system
  public void record_user ( String name, String email )
          throws user_exists
  {
// Is the user already listed
if (name2email.containsKey( name ) ||
```

```
        name2email.contains( email ) )
    {
      // If so, throw exception
      throw new user_exists();
    }

    // Add to our hash table
    name2email.put (name, email);
      }
  }
```

The servant class maintains a list of people's email addresses, and stores this information inside a Hashtable. When the CORBA server receives a request, it will call upon the name_from_email, email_from_name, and record_user methods of the servant to fulfill the request.

Writing a CORBA Server

Writing a CORBA server is pretty straightforward. We need to create an ORB (object-request-broker), and register our servant with it. We'll also notify a nameserver of our ORB, so that CORBA clients can access our address book. Once we've registered, CORBA clients will be able to look for our interface, and send requests through our ORB to the servant object.

```
package address_book_system;
import org.omg.CORBA.*;
import org.omg.CosNaming.*;
import org.omg.CosNaming.NamingContextPackage.*;

//
//
// AddressBookServer
//
// This server is responsible for creating an object
// request broker (ORB), and registering an
AddressBookServant
// with a naming service
//
//
public class AddressBookServer
{
      public static void main(String args[])
      {
    try
    {
      // Create a new object request broker
```

```
        ORB orb = ORB.init(args, null);

        // Create a new address book ...
        AddressBookServant servant = new AddressBookServant();

        // ... and connect it to our orb
        orb.connect(servant);

        // Object Request Broker Initialised
        System.out.println ("Address book ORB initialised");

        // Obtain reference for our nameservice
        org.omg.CORBA.Object object =
        orb.resolve_initial_references("NameService");

            // Since we have only an object reference, we must
            // cast it to a NamingContext. We use a helper
            // class for this purpose
            NamingContext namingContext =
            NamingContextHelper.narrow(object);

            // Add a new naming component for our interface
            NameComponent list[] =
            { new NameComponent("address_book", "") };

            // Now notify naming service of our new interface
            namingContext.rebind(list, servant);

            // Wait for clients
            for (;;){}
        }
        catch (Exception e)
        {
            System.err.println ("ORB Error - " + e);
            e.printStackTrace(System.out);
            System.exit(0);
        }
    }
}
```

Writing a CORBA Client

Now that we have a finished server, we need to write a client to show that the server works. Our client is very simple. It looks up our AddressBook service through a naming service, and then sends requests in response to commands made by the user. The client also traps exceptions thrown by the AddressBook service, in the event that a user's details doesn't exist or that a duplicate is being inserted into the system.

```
package address_book_system;
import address_book_system.address_bookPackage.*;

import org.omg.CORBA.*;
import org.omg.CosNaming.*;
import java.io.*;

//
//
// AddressBookClient
//
// This client demonstrates the AddressBook server and
servant.
// A menu is presented to the user, allow he or she to add
// users, and look up their names & email addresses
//
//
public class AddressBookClient

{
    public static void main(String args[]) throws
IOException
    {
        try
  {
      // Create an object request broker
      ORB orb = ORB.init(args, null);

      // Obtain object reference for name service ...
            org.omg.CORBA.Object object =
            orb.resolve_initial_references("NameService");

            // ... and narrow it to a NameContext
            NamingContext namingContext =
            NamingContextHelper.narrow(object);

            // Create a name component array
            NameComponent nc_array[] =
            { new NameComponent("address_book","") };

            // Get an address book object reference ...
```

```
        org.omg.CORBA.Object objectReference =
        namingContext.resolve(nc_array);

        // ... and narrow it to get an address book
        address_book AddressBook =
        address_bookHelper.narrow(objectReference);

        // DataInputStream for system.in
        DataInputStream din = new DataInputStream
        (System.in);

        for (;;)
        {
             try
             {

  // Print menu
               System.out.println ("1- Add user");
               System.out.println ("2- Look up email");
               System.out.println ("3- Look up name");
               System.out.println ("4- Exit");

    System.out.print ("Command :");

    // Read a line from user
    String command = din.readLine();

    // Convert to number
    Integer num = new Integer (command);
    int choice = num.intValue();

    // Variables we'll need for service calls
    String name;
    String email;

    switch (choice)
    {
    case 1:
    System.out.print ("Name:");
    name  = din.readLine();
    System.out.print ("Email:");
    email = din.readLine();
```

```
// Call AddressBook service
AddressBook.record_user(name,email);
break;

case 2:
System.out.println ("Name:");
name   = din.readLine();

// Call AddressBook service
email = AddressBook.email_from_name(name);
System.out.println ("Email of" + name + "is" + email);
break;

case 3:
System.out.println ("Email:");
email  = din.readLine();

  // Call AddressBook service
name = AddressBook.name_from_email(email);
System.out.println ("Name of" + email + "is" + name);
break;

case 4:
System.exit(0);
                    }
               }

catch (user_exists  already_there)
{
System.out.println ("User already exists - cannot be
added to address book");
}
catch (unknown_user bad_user)
{
System.out.println ("User doesn't exist");
}
                 }
          }
catch (Exception e)
{
              System.err.println ("CORBA error - " + e);
}
     }
}
```

Putting it all together

Now that we have a CORBA server and a CORBA client, the next step is to have the client connect to the server. If you've already compiled the source code, then you're ready to begin. Otherwise, download the source code (available as a .ZIP file), and extract it to its own directory.

Next, you need to do the following :

1. Start the nameservice that comes with JDK1.2
2. Start the server
3. Start the client

Start the nameservice that comes with JDK1.2

If your Java installation directory is in the path, you can type the following from your prompt

```
tnameserv -ORBInitialPort 2000
```

The port parameter is necessary for Unix users who aren't logged it as root. Windows users can omit the parameter. If you do specify a port parameter, make sure you do so for the client and server as well.

Start the Server

All of the examples are part of the address_book_system package. Some users have reported problems running the examples. Make sure that the current directory is in the classpath, and then go to the directory where you've compiled the examples, or where you've unzipped them. Next, start the server

java address_book_system.AddressBookServer

- ORBInitialPort 2000
- ORBInitialHost myhost

The port parameter is optional (but needed if you've specified a port for your nameservice). You'll also need to specify the hostname if you run the server on a different machine to the nameservice (omit it if running everything locally).

Start the Client

You'll need to go to the directory where the examples are stored. Make sure that the nameservice and server are already running, and then start the client

java address_book_system.AddressBookClient -ORBInitialPort 2000

- ORBInitialHost myhost

The port parameter is optional (but needed if you've specified a port for your nameservice). You'll also need to specify the hostname if you run the client on a different machine to the nameservice (omit it if running everything locally).

Running the Client

The client is capable of invoking all the methods defined in our IDL. It can record new users, look up an email address, and look up a name. While the demonstration is relatively simple, it does show how easy it is to write clients that interact with services on remote systems. This demo is a standalone application, but you could just as easily write an applet that implemented the same functionality.

```
1- Add user
2- Look up email
3- Look up name
4- Exit

Command :1
Name: David Reilly
Email: dodo@fan.net.au

1- Add user
2- Look up email
3- Look up name
4- Exit

Command :2
Name:
David Reilly
Email of David Reilly is dodo@fan.net.au
```

Summary

CORBA technology offers developers many benefits over other techniques for distributed computing, but its most compelling is the ease with which developers can create distributed services that are platform independent. Once a service is described by an IDL schema, the developer can choose to implement either client or server (or both) in Java. Being able to use Java is an attractive option, because Java brings platform portability - but its nice to know that one can also connect a C++ module to Java. CORBA allows developers to connect objects together, and developers can still choose the versatility and familiarity of Java.

A further advantage is that CORBA services can be moved throughout the network or intranet. Java 1.2 includes a nameservice, which allows ORBs to register (or bind) their services. This means that services can be moved from system to system as needed, and that clients don't need to be aware of the physical location of the service. CORBA is a powerful technology for distributed computing, and the introduction of support for CORBA in JDK1.2 offers developers greater freedom when they create distributed systems.

2.14 The Role of the Server

As we have discussed in client role, the services which are activated by the clients whenever request is made from the user at the client. Client using certain services (i.e. Client services) sends these requests to the server. Now server deals with these kinds of request with the according server services.

For example, if a request is made by a client to print certain document. As the request reaches to server, the response made by the server (whether it is printing the document, asking the queue manager to place the request in a queue or deny the request) by using the print services of the server.

Likewise the other services of the server are:

- Fax Services,
- Image Services,
- Communication Services,
- Database Services,
- Security Services,
- Network management Services.

The major Client/Server architecture role emphasizes on mainly security, database and the network management services. While discussing the role of server, it is important to understand the architecture concept of the server. A concept of the server is not the physical implementation but a conceptual view of sharing the data and services of the server at the different level.

The client and server functions can be provided by the some physical device which is used for LAN or WAN network. By excepting any request from the remote client the RPC are get activated, so that the server are classified accordingly and facility from the server to the client is in the form of given some sub-programs and sub-routines.

Apart from this the server roles also come whenever the memory allocation, disk allocation of the remote clients are given at the server. For example — The memory (disk) space for the remote clients at the application yahoo.com mail is 6MB. For public user whenever a public user is exceeding with the used disk space on the server more than 6 MB. The server protocol directs the server to stop the facility using disk space to the clients. Fax server provides supports similar to that provided by the print services that are why the fax / print services of the server are integrated.

2.15 Server Services

In this we describe the functions provided by the server in a NOS environment. The requests are issued by a client to the NOS services software resident on the client machine. These services format the request into an appropriate RPC and issue the requests to the application layer of the client protocol stock. This request is received by the application layer of the protocol stock on the server. The major server services are:

- Shorting physical records services,
- Hierarchical database services,
- Relational database service,

- Communication Services,
- Security Services,
- File Services,
- Fax / Print / Image Services,
- Database Services.

2.15.1 Sorting Physical Records Service (Flat Files)

Many organizations today still use the flat file approach to data management for reporting and batch update input. Data is extracted and sorted for efficient input to a batch report. Data TS captured for update and sorted for more efficient input to a batch update program.

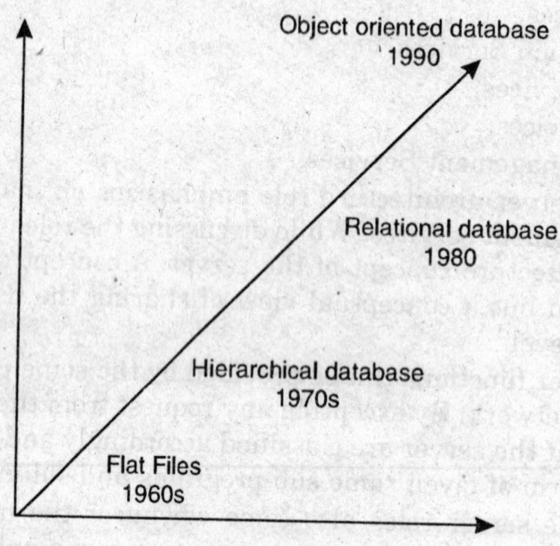

Fig 2.8 Database Trends

2.15.2 Hierarchical Database : Adjacent storage of Related Records Types

The hierarchical database, could store related record types physically or logically next to each other. In the Hierarchical model implementation, when a user accesses a physical record type, other application related data is usually stored physically close and will be moved from skid to DRAM all together.

Internally stored pointers are used to navigate from one record to the next if there is insufficient space close by at data creation time to insert the related data.

The major disadvantage with the hierarchical technique is that only applications that access data according to its physical storage sequence benefits from locality of reference.Application sensitivity to physical implementation is the main problem with the hierarchical database systems

2.15.3 Relational Databases Services

Relational database technology provides the current data management solution to many of the problems inherent in the flat file and hierarchical technologies.

The first relational products were introduced by ADR with dotcoms DB and Computer Corporation of America with model 204.

In the client/server implementation, you should off load database processing to the server. Therefore the database engine should accept SQL requests from the client and execute them totally on the server, returning only the answer set to the client requestor.

The C/S model implies that there will be multiple concurrent user access. The database engine must be able to manage this access without requiring every developer to write well behaved applications. The following feature must be part of the database engine

- Locking mechanisms to guarantee data integrity,
- Deadlock detection and prevention,
- Multithreaded application processing,
- User access to multiple databases on multiple servers.

2.15.4 Communication Services

The application which are required to make the transfer of information from one node to another node (client to server) **interims of byte transferred**, are required to coordinated by certain services from the server. The request integrated with network operating system can be made are called communication services.

2.15.5 Security Services

The security services prominently deals with information available at the database of the server. For example if a user with certain user-id and password want to access certain information or data these services get activated, whether the entered password with corresponding user-id is correct.

2.15.6 File Services

File services handle access to the virtual directories and files located on the client workstation and to the server's permanent storage. These services are provided through the redirection software implemented as part of client workstation operating environment.

The minimize the effort and effect of installation and maintenance of software, for execution on the client. New versions can be updated on the server and made immediately available to all users.

In addition, installation in a central location reduces the effort required for each workstation user to handle the installation process. Because each client workstation user uses the same installation of the software, optional parameters are consistent and remote help disk operators are aware of them.

2.15.7 FAX / PRINT / IMAGE Service

High quality printers, workstation generated Faxes, and plotters are natural candidates for support from a shared server. The server can accept input from many clients, queue if according to the priority of the request and handle it when the device is available.

In the client/server model, work queues are maintained at the server by a supervisor in concert with default algorithms that determine how to distribute the queued work. Centralized capture and distribution enables images to be centrally indexed. This index can be maintained by the database services for all authorized users to query.

In this way, Images are captured once and are available for distribution immediately to all authorized users. There are dramatic opportunities for Cost Savings and improvements in efficiency if this technology is properly implemented and used.

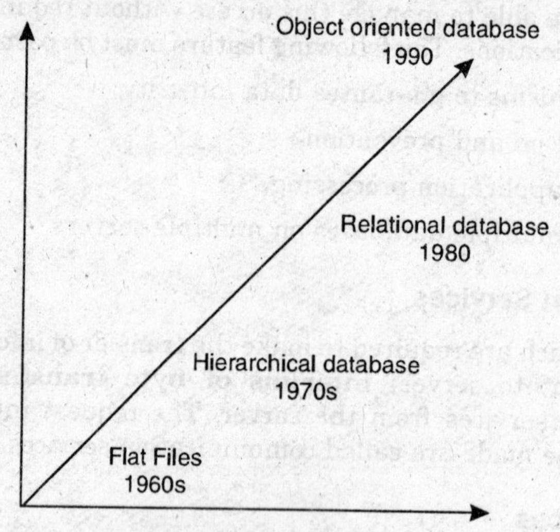

Fig 2.9 Database Trends

2.15.8 DATABASE Services

Barley database servers were actually file servers with a different interface. Products such as dBase, clipper, FoxPro execute the database engine primarily on the client machine and use the file services provided by the file server for record access and free space management. There are no facilities to execute procedural code at the server.

Client / Server database engines such as Sybase, IBM's database manager, Oracle provide support at the server to execute SQL requests issued from the client workstation. The file services are still used for space allocation and basic directory services, but all other services are provided directly by the database server. Relational database management systems are the current technology for data management.

2.16 Network Operating Systems

An operating system that includes special functions for connecting computers and devices into a local-area network (LAN). Some operating systems, such as UNIX and the Mac OS, have networking functions built in. The term network operating system, however, is generally reserved for software that enhances a basic operating system by adding networking features. Novell Netware, Artisoft's LANtastic, Microsoft Windows Server, and Windows NT are examples of NOS.

Network operating systems (NOS) typically are used to run computers that act as servers. They provide the capabilities required for network operation. Network operating systems are also designed for client computers and provide functions so the distinction between network operating systems and stand-alone operating systems is not always obvious. Network operating systems provide the following functions:

- File and print sharing.
- Account administration for users.
- Security.

Installed Components

- Client functionality
- Server functionality

Functions provided:

- Account Administration for users
- Security
- File and print sharing

Network services

- File Sharing
- Print sharing
- User administration
- Backing up data

Network Protocol Levels

You should be aware of the fact, that when talking about networking you will hear the word "protocol" all the time. This is because protocols are sets of standards that define all operations within a network. They define how various operations are to be performed. They may even define how devices outside the network can interact with the network. Protocols define everything from basic networking data structures, to higher level application programs. They define various services and utility programs. Protocols operate at many layers of the network models described below. There are protocols considered to be transport protocols such as TCP and UDP. Other protocols work at the network layer of the OSI network model shown below, and some protocols work at several of the network layers.

RFCs

Protocols are outlined in Request for Comments (RFCs). At the end of this document is a list of protocols and associated RFC numbers. Protocols. Although RFCs define protocols not all RFCs define protocols but may define other requirements for the internet such as RFC 1543 which provides information about the preparation of RFCs. The following RFCs are very central to the TCP/IP protocol:

- RFC 1122—Defines host requirements of the TCP/IP suite of protocols covering the link, network (IP), and transport (TCP, UDP) layers.
- RFC 1123—The companion RFC to 1122 covering requirements for internet hosts at the application layer.
- RFC 1812—Defines requirements for internet gateways which are IPv4 routers.

Network Models

There are several network models, which you may hear about, but the one you will hear about most is the ISO network model described below. You should realize, however that there are others such as:

- The internet layered protocol
- The TCP/IP layered protocol
- The Microsoft networking protocol

The OSI Network Model Standard

The International Standards Organization (ISO) has defined a standard called the Open Systems Interconnection (OSI) reference model. This is a seven-layer architecture listed below. Each layer is considered to be responsible for a different part of the communications. This concept was developed to accommodate changes in technology. The layers are arranged here from the lower levels starting with the physical (hardware) to the higher levels.

1. **Physical Layer**—The actual hardware.
2. **Data Link Layer**—Data transfer method (802x Ethernet). Puts data in frames and ensures error free transmission. Also controls the timing of the network transmission. Adds frame type, address, and error control information. IEEE divided this layer into the two following sub layers.
   (a) **Logical Link control (LLC)**—Maintains the Link between two computers by establishing Service Access Points (SAPs), which are a series of interface points. IEEE 802.2.
   (b) **Media Access Control (MAC)**—Used to coordinate the sending of data between computers. The 802.3, 4, 5, and 12 standards apply to this layer. If you hear someone talking about the MAC address of a network card, they are referring to the hardware address of the card.
3. **Network Layer**—IP network protocol. Routes messages using the best path available.
4. **Transport Layer**—TCP, UDP. Ensures properly sequenced and error free transmission.
5. **Session Layer**—The user's interface to the network. Determines when the session is begun or opened, how long it is used, and when it is closed. Controls the transmission of data during the session. Supports security and name lookup enabling computers to locate each other.
6. **Presentation Layer**—ASCII or EBCDEC data syntax. Makes the type of data transparent to the layers around it. Used to translate date to computer specific format such as byte ordering. It may include compression. It prepares the data, either for the network or the application depending on the direction it is going.
7. **Application Layer**—Provides services software applications need. Provides the ability for user applications to interact with the network.

Many protocol stacks overlap the borders of the seven-layer model by operating at multiple layers of the model. File Transport Protocol (FTP) and telnet both work at the application, presentation, and the session layers.

The Internet, TCP/IP, DOD Model

This model is sometimes called the DOD model since it was designed for the department of defense It is also called the TCP/IP four layer protocol, or the internet protocol. It has the following layers:

1. **Link**—Device driver and interface card, which maps to the data link and physical layer of the OSI model.
2. **Network**—Corresponds to the network layer of the OSI model and includes the IP, ICMP, and IGMP protocols.
3. **Transport**—Corresponds to the transport layer and includes the TCP and UDP protocols.
4. **Application**—Corresponds to the OSI Session, Presentation and Application layers and includes FTP, Telnet, ping, Rlogin, rsh, TFTP, SMTP, SNMP, DNS, your program, etc.

Each layer has a set of data that it generates.

1. The Data Link layer corresponds to the hardware, including the device driver and interface card. The data link layer has data packets associated with it depending on the type of network being used such as ARCnet, Token ring or Ethernet.
2. The network layer manages the movement of packets around the network and includes IP, ICMP, and IGMP. It is responsible for making sure that packages reach their destinations, and if they don't, reporting errors.
3. The transport layer is the mechanism used for two computers to exchange data with regards to software. The two types of protocols that are the transport mechanisms are TCP and UDP. There are also other types of protocols for systems other than TCP/IP but we will talk about TCP and UDP.
4. The application layer refers to networking protocols that are used to support various services such as FTP, Telnet, BOOTP, etc. Note here to avoid confusion, that the application layer is generally referring to protocols such as FTP, telnet, ping, and other programs designed for specific purposes which are governed by a specific set of protocols defined with RFC's (request for comments). However a program that you may write can define its own data structure to send between your client and server program so long as the program you run on both the client and server machine understand your protocol. For example when your program opens a socket to another machine, it is using TCP protocol, but the data you send depends on how you structure it.

Data Encapsulation, a Critical Concept to be Understood

When starting with protocols that work at the upper layers of the network models, each set of data is wrapped inside the next lower layer protocol, similar to wrapping letters inside an envelope. The application creates the data, then the transport layer wraps that data inside its format, then the network layer wraps the data, and finally the link (Ethernet) layer encapsulates the data and transmits it.

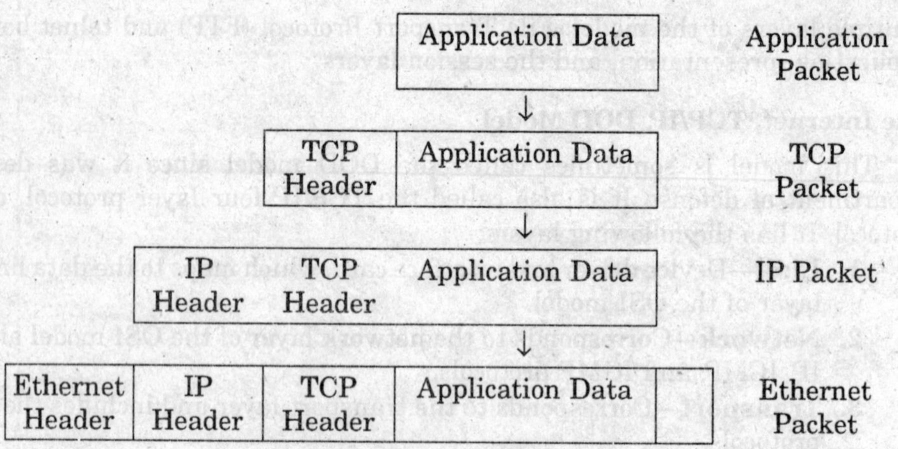

Fig 2.10. Data Encapsulation

To continue, you should understand the definition of a client and server with regards to networking. If you are a server, you will provide services to a client, in much the same way as a private investigator would provide services to their clients. A client will contact the server, and ask for service, which the server will then provide. The service may be as simple as sending a single block of data back to the client. Since there are many clients, a server must be constantly ready to receive client requests, even though it may already be working with other clients. Usually the client program will operate on one computer, while the server program will operate on another computer, although programs can be written to be both a client and a server.

Lets say you write a client chat program and a server chat program to be used by two people to send messages between their machines. You run the server program on machine B, and the client program on machine A. Tom is on machine A and George is on machine B. George's machine is always ready to be contacted, but cannot initiate a contact. Therefore if George wants to talk to Tom, he cannot, until Tom contacts him. Tom, of course can initiate contact at any time. Now you decide to solve the problem and merge the functionality of the two programs into one, so both parties may contact the other. This program is now a client/server program which operates both as a client and a server. You write your code so when one side initiates contact, he will get a dialog box, and a dialog box will pop up on the other side. At the time contact is initiated, a socket is opened between the two machines and a virtual connection is established. The program will let the user (Tom) type text into the dialog window, and hit send. When the user hits send, roughly the following will happen.

1. Your program will pass Tom's typed text in a buffer, to the socket. This happens on machine A.
2. The underlying software (Code in a library called by a function your program used to send the data) supporting the socket puts the data inside a TCP data packet. This means that a TCP header will be added to the data. This header contains a source and destination port number along with some other information and a checksum. Daemon programs (Daemon definition at the bottom of this page) may also work at this level to sort packages based on port number (hence the TCP wrapper program in UNIX and Linux).

3. The TCP packet will be placed inside an IP data packet with a source and destination IP address along with some other data for network management. This may be done by a combination of your library function, the operating system and supporting programs.
4. The IP data packet is placed inside an ethernet data packet. This data packet includes the destination and source address of the network interface cards (NIC) on the two computers. The address here is the hardware address of the respective cards and is called the MAC address.
5. The ethernet packet is transmitted over the network line.
6. Assuming there is a direct connection between the two computers, the network interface card on machine B, will recognize its MAC address and grab the data.
7. The IP data packet will be extracted from the ethernet data packet. A combination of deamons and the operating system will perform this operation.
8. The TCP data packet will be extracted from the IP data packet. A combination of deamons, the operating system, and libraries called by your program will perform this function.
9. The data will be extracted from the TCP packet. Your program will then display the retrieved data (text) in the text display window for George to read.

Be aware that for the sake of simplicity, we are excluding details such as error management, routing, and identifying the hardware address of the NIC on the computer intended to receive the data. Also we are not mentioning the possible rejection of service based on a packet's port number or sender's IP address.

A deamon program is a program that runs in the background on a computer operating system. It is used to perform various tasks including server functions. It is usually started when the operating system is booted, but a user or administrator may be able to start or stop a daemon at any time.

Network Categories

TDP/IP includes a wide range of protocols, which are used for a variety of purposes on the network. The set of protocols that are a part of TCP/IP is called the TCP/IP protocol stack or the TCP/IP suite of protocols.

Considering the many protocols, message types, levels, and services that TCP/IP networking supports, I believe it would be very helpful to categorize the various protocols that support TCP/IP networking and define their respective contribution to the operation of networking.

There are four TCP/IP layers. They are link, network, transport, and application. The link layer is the hardware layer that provides ability to send messages between multiple locations. In the case of this document, Ethernet provides this capability. Below I define several categories some of which fit into the 4 layer protocol levels described earlier. I also define a relative fundamental importance to the ability of the network to function at all. Importance includes essential, critical, important, advanced, and useful.

1. Essential—Without this all other categories are irrelevant.
2. Critical—The network, as designed, is useless without this ability.

3. Important—The network could function, but would be difficult to use and manage.
4. Advanced—Includes enhancements that make the network easier to use and manage.
5. Useful—Functionality that you would like to be able to use as a network user. Applications or some functionality is supported here. Without this, why build a network?

The categories are:

Name(layer)	Importance	Names of protocols	What it does
Hardware(link)	Essential	Ethernet, SLIP, PPP, Token Ring, ARCnet	Allows messages to be packaged and sent between physical locations.
Package management (network)	Essential	IP, ICMP	Manages movement of messages and reports errors. It uses message protocols and
Inter layer communication	Essential	ARP	Communicates between layers to allow one layer to get information to support another layer. This includes broadcasting
Service control (transport)	Critical	TCP, UDP	Controls the management of service between computers. Based on values in TCP and UDP messages a server knows what service is being requested.
Application and user support	Important	DNS, RPC	DNS provides address to name translation for locations and network cards. RPC allows remote computer to perform functions on other computers.
Network Management	Advanced	RARP, BOOTP, DHCP, IGMP, SNMP,RIP, OSPF, BGP, CIDR	Enhances network management and increases functionality
Utility (Application)	Useful	FTP, TFTP, SMTP, Telnet, NFS, ping, Rlogin	Provides direct services to the user.

The list below gives a brief description of each protocol

- Ethernet—Provides for transport of information between physical locations on Ethernet cable. Data is passed in Ethernet packets
- SLIP—Serial line IP (SLIP), a form of data encapsulation for serial lines.
- PPP—Point to point protocol (PPP). A form of serial line data encapsulation that is an improvement over SLIP.
- IP—Internet Protocol (IP). Except for ARP and RARP all protocols' data packets will be packaged into an IP data packet. Provides the mechanism to use software to address and manage data packets being sent to computers.
- ICMP—Internet control message protocol (ICMP) provides management and error reporting to help manage the process of sending data between computers.
- ARP—Address resolution protocol (ARP) enables the packaging of IP data into Ethernet packages. It is the system and messaging protocol that is used to find the Ethernet (hardware) address from a specific IP number. Without this protocol, the Ethernet package could not be generated from the IP package, because the Ethernet address could not be determined.
- TCP—A reliable connection oriented protocol used to control the management of application level services between computers.
- UDP—An unreliable connection less protocol used to control the management of application level services between computers.
- DNS—Domain Name Service, allows the network to determine IP addresses from names and vice-versa.
- RARP—Reverse address resolution protocol (RARP) is used to allow a computer without a local permanent data storage media to determine its IP address from its Ethernet address.
- BOOTP—Bootstrap protocol is used to assign an IP address to diskless computers and tell it what server and file to load, which will provide it with an operating system.
- DHCP—Dynamic host configuration protocol (DHCP) is a method of assigning and controlling the IP addresses of computers on a given network. It is a server-based service that automatically assigns IP numbers when a computer boots. This way the IP address of a computer does not need to be assigned manually. This makes changing networks easier to manage. DHCP can perform all the functions of BOOTP.
- IGMP—Internet Group Management Protocol used to support multicasting.
- SNMP—Simple Network Management Protocol (SNMP). Used to manage all types of network elements based on various data sent and received.
- RIP—Routing Information Protocol (RIP), used to dynamically update router tables on WANs or the Internet.
- OSPF—Open Shortest Path First (OSPF) dynamic routing protocol.

- BGP—Border Gateway Protocol (BGP). A dynamic router protocol to communicate between routers on different systems.
- CIDR—Classless Interdomain Routing (CIDR).
- FTP—File Transfer Protocol (FTP). Allows file transfer between two computers with login required.
- TFTP—Trivial File Transfer Protocol (TFTP). Allows file transfer between two computers with no login required. It is limited, and is intended for diskless stations.
- SMTP—Simple Mail Transfer Protocol (SMTP).
- NFS—Network File System (NFS). A protocol that allows UNIX and Linux systems remotely mounts each other's file systems.
- Telnet—A method of opening a user session on a remote host.
- Ping—A program that uses ICMP to send diagnostic messages to other computers to tell if they are reachable over the network.
- Rlogin—Remote login between UNIX hosts. This is outdated and is replaced by Telnet.

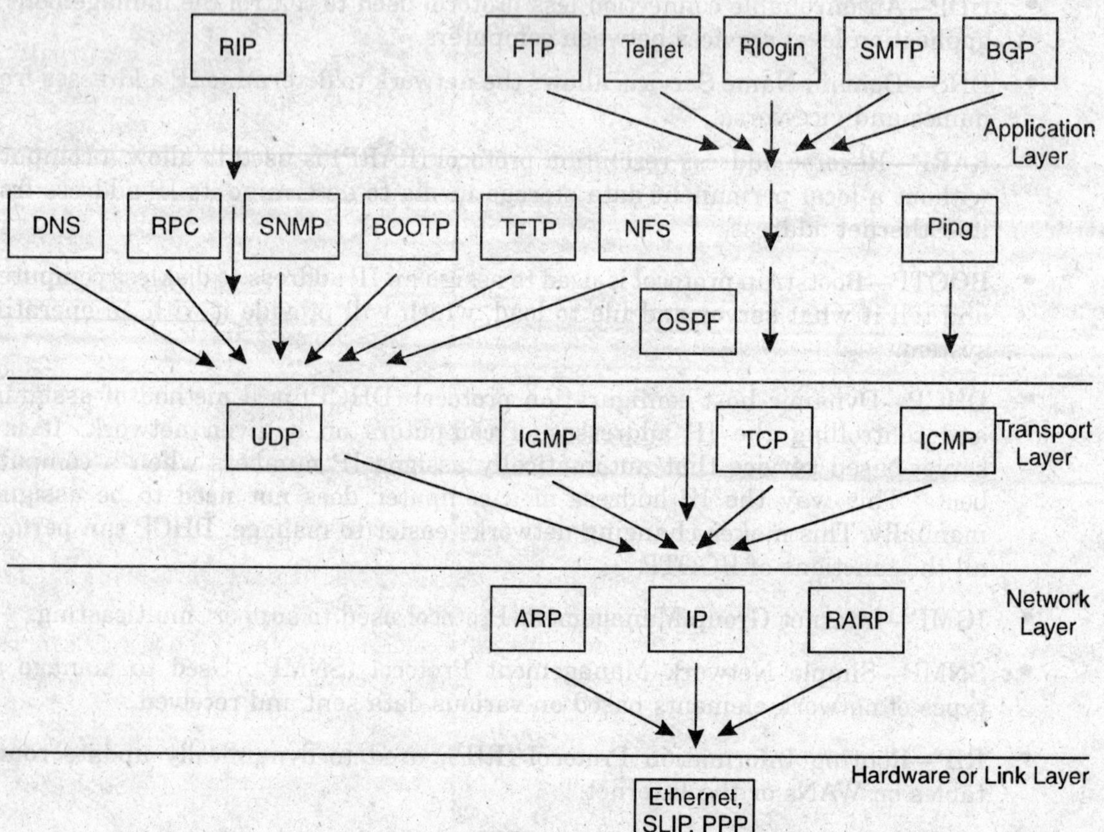

Fig 2.11 Protocol wrapper dependencies and network layers

Each protocol ultimately has its data packets wrapped in an Ethernet, SLIP, or PPP packet (at the link level) in order to be sent over the Ethernet cable. Some protocol data packets are wrapped sequentially multiple times before being sent. For example FTP data is wrapped in a TCP packet, which is wrapped in a IP packet which is wrapped in a link packet (normally Ethernet). The diagram below shows the relationship between the protocols' sequential wrapping of data packets.

2.17 Various Network Operating Systems

The network operating system provides the services not available from the client operating system.

2.17.1 Apple

Apple Computers developed the Macintosh Operating System (Mac OS). The latest version of this operating system (Mac OS X) now incorporates UNIX source code.

2.17.2 Novell Netware

The most popular network operating system in the PC world is the Novell Netware. It was designed to be used by companies down-sizing from a mainframe to a network of PC's. In such systems, each user has a desktop PC functioning as a client. In addition, some number of powerful PC's operates as servers, providing file services, database services and other services to a collection of clients.

In other words, Novell Netware is based on the client / Server model. Since Novell Netware predates OSI and is not based on it. If anything, it looks more like TCP/IP than OSI.

Application	SAP	File Server	
Transport	NCP	SPX	
Network	IPX		
Data link	Ethernet	Token Ring	ARC Net
Physical	Ethernet	Token Ring	ARC Net

Fig 2.12 Novell netware reference model

The physical and data link layers can be chosen from among various industry standards, including Ethernet, IBM token ring and ARC Net The network layer runs on unreliable connectionless internet work protocol called IPX.

It passes packets transparently from source to destination, even if the source and the destination are on different networks IPX is functionally similar to IP except that it uses 10 byte address instead of 4 byte address.

In the transport layer, NCP also provides various services (Network Core Protocol), like user data transport and really the heart of Netware. A second protocol SPX is also available but provided only transport TCP is another option.

The session and presentation layer do not exists in Novell Netware various application protocols are presents in the application layer. Each server broadcasts a packet giving it address and telling what services it offers. The broadcasts use the SAPC service advertising protocols. The packets are seen and collected by special agent processes running on the router machines.

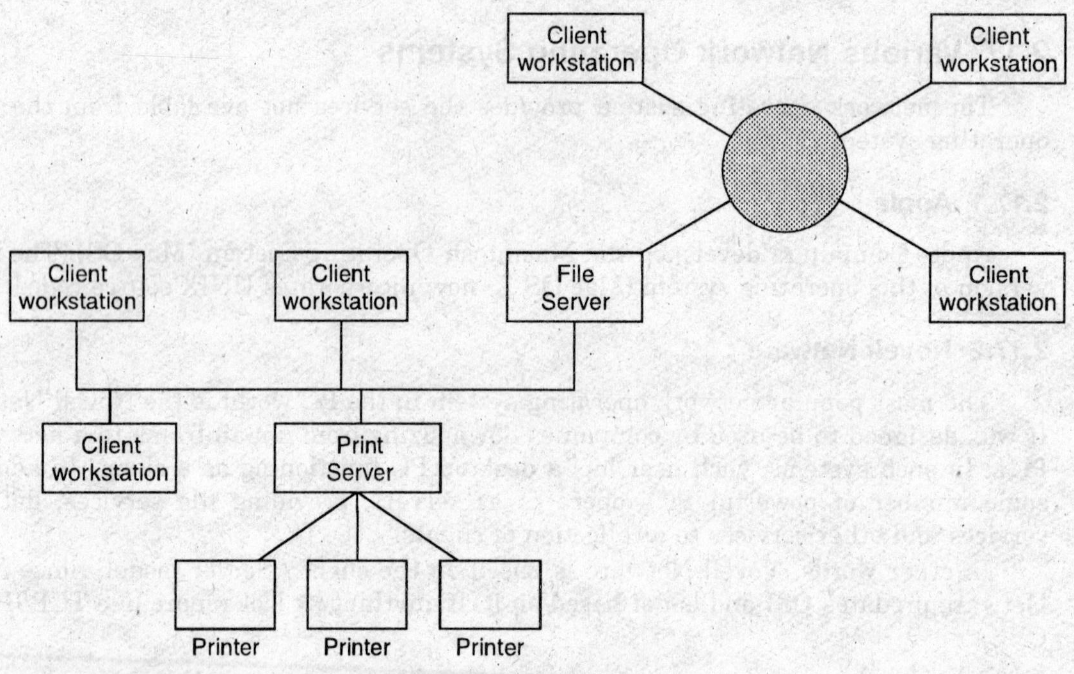

Fig 2.13. Novell Netware

When a client machine is booted it broadcasts a request asking where the nearest server is the agent on the local router machine sees this request looks in its database of servers and matches up the request with best server. The choice of server to use is then sent back to the client. The client can now establish an NCP connection with server, using this connection; the client and server negotiate the maximum packet size.

The client can access the file system services and other services using this connection. It can also query the server's database to look for other services.

2.17.3 LAN Manager

LAN manager and its IBM derivative, LAN server, are the standard products for use in client/server implementations using OS/2 as the server operating systems.

LAN manager/X is the standard Product for client/server implementations using UNIX system V as the server operating system. AT&T has taken over responsibility for the LAN manager/X version. Vendors such as Hewlett Packard (HP) have relicensed the product from AT&T. AT&T and Microsoft has an agreement to maintain compatiable API's for all base functionality.

LAN manager and advanced server provide client support for DOS, Windows, Windows NT, OS/2 and Mac system 7. Server support extends to Netware, AppleTalk,

UNIX, Window NT and OS/2. Client workstation can access data from both Netware and LAN manager servers at the same time. Redirection services are provided to map files and printers from remote workstations for client use. Advanced servers also support TCP/IP communication. Advanced server provides integrated and client / server to peer processing and client / server applications. Existing supports for Windows NT, OS/2, UNIX and Mac system 7 clients lets application, database and communication server run on the same machine as, the file and print server. This feature is attractive in small LANs.

The native operating system support for preemptive multitasking and storage protection ensures that these server applications do not reduce the reliability of other services. Even as Windows NT is rolled out to provide the database, application and communications services to client/server applications, the use of Novell as the LAN NOS of choice will continue for peripheral resource sharing applications.

Microsoft has attempted to preempt the small LAN market with its windows for work group's product. This attacks the same market as Netware life with a low cost product that is tightly integrated with windows. It is an attractive option for small organization without a requirement for larger LAN's.

NOTE : In a LAN manager environment, a workstation might acts as a client for one user while simultaneously acting as a print server for many users.

2.17.4 IBM LAN Server

IBM has entered into an agreement to resell and integrate the Novell Netware product into environments where both IBM LAN server and Novell Netware are required.

Netware are provides more functional, cashier to use and higher performance file and print services. In environments where these are the only LAN functions, Netware is preferable to LAN functions; Netware is preferable to LAN manager derivatives.

The capability to interconnect to the SNA world makes the IBM product LAN server attractive to organizations that prefer to run both products. Most large organizations have department workgroups that require only the services that Novell Netware provides well but may use LAN server for client / server applications using SNA services such as APPN.

Advantage

1. LAN server is a low cost option for small LAN's.
2. LAN server supports DOS, Windows and OS/2 clients.
3. To share data files and communication services.
4. IBM has priced LAN server very attractively so that if OS/2 clients are being used, a low cost option for small LANs.

Disadvantage

No support for MAC system 7.

2.17.5 Banyan VINES

Banyan VINES provides basic file and print services similar to those of Novell and LAN manager. VINES incorporate a facility called Street Talk that enables every resource in a Banyan enterprise LAN to be addressed by name. VINES also provide intelligent WAN routing within the communications server component.

Street Talk enables resources to be uniquely identified on the network, making them easier to access and manage. All resources including file services, users and printers are defined as objects. Each object has a street talk name associated with it.

Street Talk names follow a three-level hierarchical format: Item @ group @ organization. For example a user Munesh can be identified as

munesh@chandra@WIPRO

All Network objects are stored in a distributed database that can be accessed globally.

Novell's NDS is similar to Street Talk in functionality. However, there are key differences

(i) NDS can partition and replicate the database, which will generally improve performance and reliability and enables multiple levels of hierarchy. Street Talk supports a fixed three level hierarchy.

(ii) The NDS architecture offers more flexibility but with corresponding complexity and street talk is less flexible but fewer complexes to manage.

(iii) Street Talk objects can have unlimited attributes available for selection.

PC Network File Services (NFS)

NFS is the standard file system supports for UNIX. PC NFS is available from sun select and FTP to provide file services Support from a UNIX server to windows, OS/2, Mac and UNIX clients.

- NFS lets a client mount an NFS host is filling system as an extension of its own resources.
- NFS's resource sharing mechanisms encompass interhost printing.
- The transactions among NFS systems traditionally ride across TCP/IP and Ethernet but NFS works with any network that supports 802.3 frames.

With the increasing use of UNIX servers for application and database services, there is an increasing realization that PC NFS may be all that is required for NOS supports for many workgroups.

Advantage

A low cost and low-maintenance option because the UNIX server is easily visible from a remote location.

2.18 Server Operating System

Servers provide the platform for application database and communication services. The server operating system is based on the client / server model. In such systems, each user has a desktop PC functioning as a client. In addition, some number of powerful PCs operates as a server, providing file services, database services and communication services.

Server Operating System is designed from the ground up to provide platforms for multi-user, frequently business-critical, networked applications. As such, the focus of such operating systems tends to be security, stability and collaboration, rather than user interface.

Server OS provide a platform for multi-user applications, and most come bundled with a batch of common server applications, such as Web servers, e-mail agents and terminal services.

Common Applications for Server Operating System

File and printer sharing

File sharing involves setting up a common storage point for a company's documents—a network drive, as it were. Print sharing allows multiple computers to use a single printer. Windows 95, 98 and ME do have file and print sharing, but are not recommended for use as server OSes.

Application services (including databases)

A server OS's ability to run the applications you need is obviously crucial. Servers function as crucial database stores and shared environments for collaborative applications (such as networked MYOB or Quicken).

Web site services

A hypertext transfer protocol (HTTP) server is included with many server OSes, either via an integrated application, or other HTTP applications such as the Apache open source server. Some OSes also come with more advanced features, such as database integration (so you can dynamically build Web pages based on information in a database), personalisation and scripting. The world's most popular HTTP server application, Apache, comes with just about every version of Unix and also runs on Windows. Microsoft provides Internet Information Server (IIS) for Windows platforms.

E-mail, groupware and messaging

A central e-mail server allows you to forward and receive e-mails to and from your business, as well as control individual e-mail accounts based on a domain. Groupware applications, such as Lotus Notes, Microsoft Exchange or Novell GroupWise, provide email as well as much more sophisticated collaboration. These applications can include shared calendars, document version management, group forums, database/messaging integration, instant messaging and whiteboard sharing. Open source mail systems such as SendMail and Exim are also popular.

Terminal services

Allow a client to run a productivity application on a server, while seeing the visual results of the application on their screen. For instance, a client ('terminal') could be running Microsoft Word on the server from their desktop. The server does all the processing work, and just transmits the graphical changes to the terminal, while taking the user's input (mouse movements and key strokes) and sending them to the server. This model allows a company to use clients that don't have a lot of processing power (and enforces the storage of documents on the server, rather than on local hard drives). A server with a lot of memory and a fast processor is needed if it's going to be running productivity applications for the whole office. Nearly every current server OS can do this via Windows Terminal Server, Citrix MetaFrame or the X Window System (which is used by Novell and just about every Unix variant).

Caching

Speeding up network access (usually Internet access) by storing previously downloaded files in a cache—kind of like the way an Internet browser keeps a cache of the Web pages you have visited so it doesn't have to download the files all over again. Examples of caching server applications include Novell BorderManager, Microsoft Internet Security and Acceleration Server, Inktomi Traffic Server and Squid.

Running a server Operating System

Contractors are available for all major server OSes, including free platforms such as Linux and FreeBSD. They can give you advice on a suitable server for your needs.

A support contract is important in this circumstance. Look for uptime guarantees, support response times and availability. Make sure they document the installation properly (in case they suddenly disappear). Get several opinions from suppliers using different platforms and make sure that the product is suitably customised for your business. The server will need maintenance and patching, and proper security takes time to configure, no matter which platform is used.

Managing a support contract well can save you time and lot of headaches. It will also allow you to switch support providers at any time. Manage it badly, and you'll quickly find that your total cost of ownership starts to skyrocket.

Operating System	Company	Hardware Platform	No. of processors	Appropriate for
Windows 2000 Server/Advanced Server/Datacentre	Microsoft	Intel/AMD	4 (Server) 8 (Advanced) 32 (Datacentre)	Small, medium and large servers
Windows Server 2003 R2 Standard/ Enterprise/Data centre/Web Server/ Small Business	Microsoft	Intel/AMD & IA-64, Opteron for 64-bit versions of Windows Server 2003	4 (Standard) Up to 8 (Enterprise) Minimum 8, Maximum 64 (Datacentre)	Small, medium and large servers
Linux (Red Hat, Mandrake, Debian, SuSE, etc.)	Open Source	Many (esp. Intel/AMD)	32 (Linux is readily used on more than 4 CPUs)	Small to large servers
FreeBSD 7.0	Open Source	x86, Alpha, IA-64, PC-98 and UltraSPARC	4	Small to large servers

Mac OSX Server v10.4	Apple	PowerPC with a G3, G4, or G5 processor (Apple)	2 (4 available later)	Small to medium servers
NetWare 6.5	Novell	Intel/AMD	32	Medium to large servers
Solaris 10	Sun Microsyste ms	Sparc, Intel x64 or x86	128	Medium to enterprise servers
HP-UX 11i v1.6 & HP-UX 11i v2	Hewlett-Pa ckard	PA-RISC, Intel Itanium	64	Enterprise servers
IRIX 6.5	SGI	MIPS	64	Enterprise servers
AIX 5L 5.2	IBM	PowerPC (RS/6000)	32	Enterprise servers

Fig. 2.14 Server Operating Systems

The major six server operating systems are

(i) Netware
(ii) OS/2
(iii) Windows NT
(iv) MVS
(v) VMS
(vi) UNIX

2.18.1 Netware

NetWare is used by many organizations, large and small, for the provision of file, printer, and network services. NetWare is a self-contained operating system. It does not require a separate OS (as do Windows NT, OS/2, and UNIX) to run. Novell is taking steps to allow NetWare to run on servers with UNIX. Novell purchased USL and will develop shrink-wrapped products to run under NetWare and UNIX System V, Release 4.2. The products will enable UNIX to simultaneously access information from both a NetWare and a UNIX server.

2.18.2 OS/2

OS/2 is the server platform for Intel products provided by IBM in the System Application Architecture (SAA) model. OS/2 provides the storage protection and preemptive multitasking services needed for the server platform.

Several database and many application products have been ported to OS/2. The only network operating systems directly supported with OS/2 are LAN manager and LAN server.

Novell supports the use of OS/2 servers running on separate processors from the Netware server. The combination of Novell with an OS/2 database and application servers can provide the necessary environment for a production-quality client/server implementation.

2.18.3 Windows NT

With the release of Windows NT (New Technology) in September of 1993, Microsoft staked its unique position with a server operating system. Microsoft is previous development of OS/2 with IBM did not create the single standard UNIX alternative that was hoped for.

NT provides the preemptive multitasking services required for a functional server. It provides excellent supports for windows clients and incorporates the necessary storage protection services required for a reliable server operating system.

Its implementation of C2 level security goes well beyond that provided by OS/2 and most UNIX. Implementation. With Microsoft is prestige and marketing muscle, NT will be installed by many organizations as their server of choice?

2.18.4 MVS

IBM provides MVS as a platform for large applications. Many of the existing application services that organizations have purchased operate on system 370 compatible hardware running MVS.

The standard networking environment for many large organizations SNA is a component of MVS. IBM prefers to label proprietary systems today under the umbrella of SAA (i.e. System Application Architecture). The objective of SAA is to provide all services on all IBM platforms in a compatible way the IBM version of the single system Image.

There is a commitment by IBM to provide support for the LAN server running natively under MVS. This is an attractive option for organizations with large existing investments in MVS applications. The very large data storage capabilities provided by system 370 compatible platform with MVS make the use of MVS for LAN services attractive t large organizations.

MVS provides a powerful database server using DB2 and LU6.2 with broad industry support for LU6.2, requests that include DB2 databases as part of their view can be issued from a client/server application. Products such as Sybase provide high performance static SQL support, making this implementation viable for high performance production application.

2.18.5 OPEN VMS

Digital Equipment Corporation (DEC) provides OPEN VMS as its server platform of choice. VMS has a long history in a distributed computing arena and includes many of the features necessary to acts as a server in the client / server model.

Digital Equipment Corporation (DEC) was slow to realize the importance of this technology. Netware supports the use of OPEN VMS servers for file services. DEC provides its own server interface using a LAN manager derivative product called path works.

Path works runs native on the VAX. This is a particularly attractive configuration because it provides access on the same processor to the application, database and file services provided by a combination of OPENVMS, Netware and LAN manager.

Digital Equipment Corporation and Microsoft have announced joint agreement to work together to provide a smooth integration of windows, Windows NT, path works and OPENVMS. VAX OPENVMS supports for database products such as RDB, Sybase and Oracle enables this platform to execute effectively as a database for client/server applications.

Many organizations have large investment in VAX hardware and DEC net networking. DEC net provides ideal support for the single system image model. LAN technology is fundamental to the architecture of DEC net. Many large organizations moving into the client/server world of computing have standardized on DEC net for WAN processing. For example, Kodak selected Digital as its networking company even after selecting IBM as its mainframe outsourcing company.

2.18.6 UNIX

UNIX is a primary player as a server system in the client/server model. Dennis Ritchie and Ken Thompson created UNIX at Bell Labs in 1971. It was later rewritten in C in 1977 by them. The Two major versions of UNIX called the AT&T UNIX and Berkeley UNIX have come into existence.

UNIX consists of a Kernel and a number of Utility programs. The Kernel always resides in the memory the small SBC of the Kernel makes it easy to understand, debug and enhance it.

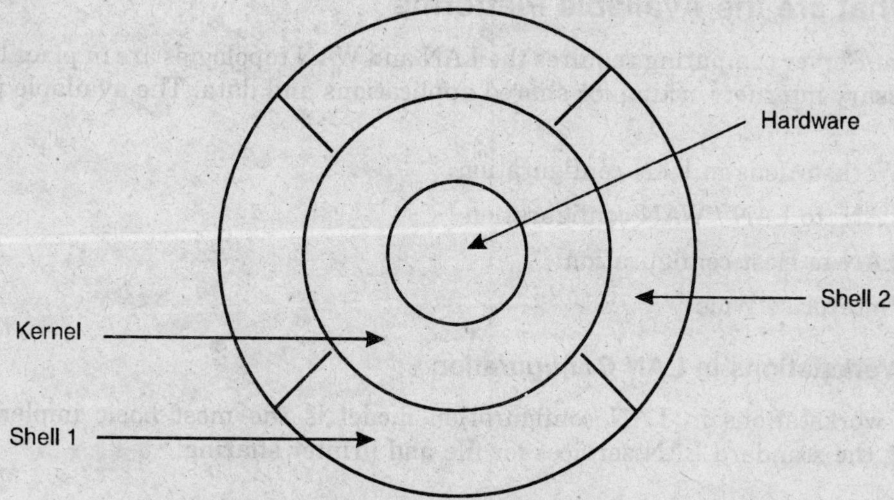

Fig. 2.15 Unit Operating System Structure.

The Kernel provides the file system. System programs use the Kernel supported system calls to provide useful functions, such as compilation and manipulation. The UNIX Kernel is divided into two parts.

- Information Management.
- Process Management.

Memory Management is very intimately linked to process management and almost driven by if. Hence memory management is assumed to be a part of the process management. It is the Kernel that manages Hardware. Application program talks to Kernel through utility.

Features

(1) UNIX is designed to be a time-sharing system.

(2) The standard user interface (Shell) is simple and can be replaced by another.

(3) UNIX supports multiple processes. A process can create another process.

UNIX is particularly desirable as a server platform for client/server computing because of the large range of platform sizes available and the huge base of application and development software available.

Applications running on operating systems that comply with these interfaces will communicate with each other and interoperate, even if the underlying operating systems are different. This is the key objective of the client / server model. Which is beastly managed in UNIX. So UNIX is most widely used as server operating system.

Disadvantage

(i) UNIX never has been widely accepted in the general corporate world that favours DOS / Windows and Novell's Netware.

(ii) A key drawback of UNIX in the corporate arena has been the lack of a single UNIX standard.

2.19 What are the Available Platforms

Client/Server computing requires the LAN and WAN topologies are in place to provide the necessary internetworking for shared applications and data. The available platforms are—

- Workstations in LAN configuration
- LAN to LAN / WAN configuration
- LAN to Host configuration
- Enterprise Wide

2.19.1 Workstations in LAN Configuration

The workstations in LAN configuration model is the most basic implementation providing the standard LAN services for file and printer sharing.

2.19.2 LAN—LAN/WAN Configuration

In the LAN—LAN or LAN-WAN configuration model, routers and communications servers will be used to provide communication services between LAN's and into the WAN. In the client / server model, these connections will be provided transparently by the SDE tools. There are significant performance implications if the traffic volumes are large.

Integrated support for TCP/IP and IPX provides a solid platform for client/server LAN to WAN implementation within DEC net.

2.19.3 LAN to Host Configuration

The lack of real estate on the desktop encouraged most organizations to move to a single device—using terminal emulation from the workstation to access existing mainframe applications. It will take considerable time and effort before all existing host based applications in organizations are replaced by client/server Applications. In the long term, the host will continue to be the location of choice for enterprise database storage and for the provision of security and network management services.

Mainframes are expensive to buy and maintain, hard to use, inflexible and large but they provide the stability and capacity required by many organizations to run their businesses.

Only organizations who create an enterprise architecture strategy and transformational plans will accomplish the migration of client/server in less than a few years. Without a well architected strategy, gradual evolution will produce failure.

2.19.4 Enterprise—Wide

Information that is of value or interest to the entire business must be managed by a central data administration function and appear to be stored on each user's desk. These applications are traditionally implemented as Online Transaction Processing (OLTP) to the mainframe or minicomputer.

With the client/server model, it is feasible to use database technology to replicate or migrate data to distributed servers. Whenever data resides or is used the location must be transparent to the user and the developer. Data should be stored where it best meets the business needs.

OLTP applications are found in such industries as insurance, finance, government and sales all of which process large number of transactions.

2.20 Summary

- Technology Revolution is related to downsizing and right sizing. In downsizing if we update the hardware of the server it is called server side downsizing and if we update the Hardware of clients, it is called client side downsizing.
- The major difference between the technology revolution and downsizing, rightsizing is that if we update server because of clients is called technology revolution and if we update clients because of server is related to downsizing and rightsizing.
- To avoid load on the server or to do offloading shared databases or distributed data base systems are used as specialized communication interfaces (mediator between remote clients and the prominent centric server).
- By having multiprocessors with shared memory, database searches extent calculation and stored procedures execution can be performed in parallel by the server while client workstation deals directly with the current user needs.
- In the file server model as implemented by many database product such as dbase, FoxPro and MS Access. A search is processed in the client workstation record table

requests are transmitted to he server and all filtering is performed on the workstation.

- Remote procedure calls are the application through which the services which are available at the remote servers in form of some subroutines and procedures are called at the certain workstation through which the request is made.
- Messages can be sent and received synchronously to or from the network. The message services provide the buffering, scheduling and arbitration services to support this function.
- The transferring of data through one package to another package is called dynamic data exchange.
- Dynamic Data Exchange is one of the prominent features of some operating system from window 3.X onwards by which a data of one package enables to get transferred onto the another package with the help of some application programming interface.
- Object Linking and Embedding (OLE) is a distributed object system and protocol developed by Microsoft.OLE allows an editor to "farm out" part of a document to another editor and then reimport it. For example, a desktop publishing system might send some text to a word processor or a picture to a bitmap editor using OLE.
- Network operating systems (NOS) typically are used to run computers that act as servers. They provide the capabilities required for network operation.
- Server Operating System is designed from the ground up to provide platforms for multi-user, frequently business-critical, networked applications. As such, the focus of such operating systems tends to be security, stability and collaboration, rather than user interface.

REVIEW QUESTIONS

1. Explain the Technology Revolution in details.
2. Explain the ways to improve performance of client\server computing.
3. Explain how to reduce the network traffic in client\server computing.
4. Discuss the request for client services in client\server computing.
5. Discuss the remote procedures calls in client\server computing.
6. Differentiate the network operating system with the server operating systems.
7. What are the available platform explain in details?

Chapter 3

Client/Server System Development

3.1 Connectivity

Connectivity is the unbiased transport of packets between two end points. This is also the essential definition of "IP" (Internet Protocol).

The era of desktop workstations began in 1981 with the introduction of the IBM personal computer (PC). The PC provided early users with the capability to do spreadsheets, word processing, and basic database services for personal data. Within three years, it became clear that high-quality printers, backup tapes, high-capacity disk devices, and software products were too expensive to put on everyone's desktop. LAN technology evolved to solve this problem. Novell is and has been the most successful vendor in the LAN market.

Step 1—Workstations Emulate Corporate Systems

Figure 3.1 shows the trend in the introduction of PCs into organizations during the period from 1980 until 1995. In most large organizations, desktop workstations provide personal productivity and some workgroup functions, but host services still provide most other business functions. The lack of desktop real estate encourages the addition of terminal emulation services to the workstation. This emulation capability connects the workstation directly to the corporate systems. The connection was and generally still is provided by a direct connection from the workstation to the host server or its controller. It is possible to use a sub-$5,000 workstation as a $500 dumb terminal.

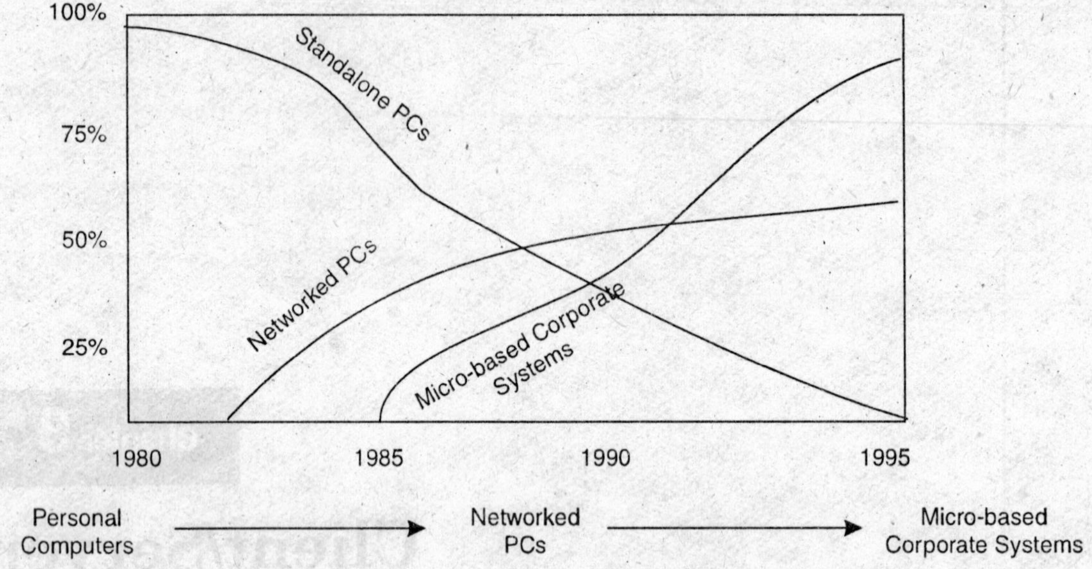

Fig 3.1 Trends in PC-micro expenditures.

Connectivity provides the opportunity to move beyond terminal emulation to use the full potential of the workstation. Often the first client/server applications in a large organization use existing mainframe applications. These are usually presentation services-only applications.

Step 2—Adding Servers for Database and Communications

The next step in connectivity is the implementation of specialized servers to provide database and communications services. These servers provide LAN users with a common database for shared applications and with a shared node to connect into the corporate network. The communications servers eliminate the need for extra cabling and workstation hardware to enable terminal emulation. The LAN cabling provides the necessary physical connection, and the communications server provides the necessary controller services.

Step 3—Full-Fledged Client/Server Applications

With its implementation of communications and database servers in place, an organization is ready for the next step up from presentation services-only client/server applications to full-fledged client/server applications. These new applications are built on the architecture defined as part of the system development environment (SDE).

User Productivity

Personal computer users are accustomed to being in control of their environment. Recently, users have been acclimated to the GUI provided by products such as Windows 3.x, OPEN LOOK, MacOS, and NeXtStep.

Productivity is enhanced by the standard look and feel that most applications running ...e environments provide. A user is trained both to get into applications and to move from function to function in a standard way. Users are accustomed to the availability of context-sensitive help, "friendly" error handling, rapid performance, and flexibility.

Compare the productivity achieved by a financial or budget analyst using a spreadsheet program such as Lotus 1-2-3 or Excel to that achieved when similar functionality is programmed in COBOL on a mainframe. Adding a new variable to an analysis or budget is a trivial task compared to the effort of making functions perform a similar change in the mainframe-based COBOL package. In the first instance, the change is made directly by the user who is familiar with the requirement into a visible model of the problem. In the instance of the mainframe, the change must be made by a programmer, who discusses the requirement with the analyst, attempts to understand the issues, and then tries to make the change using an abstraction of the problem.

The personal computer user makes the change and sees the result. The mainframe programmer must make the change, compile the program, invoke the program, and run the test. If the user understands the request, the implications, and the syntactical requirements, he or she may get it right the first time. Usually, it takes several iterations to actually get it right, often in concert with a frustrated user who tries to explain the real requirement.

We aren't suggesting that all applications can be developed by nonprogrammers using desktop-only tools. However, now that it has become rather easy to build these types of applications on the desktop, it is important for professional IS people to understand the expectations raised in the minds of the end-user community.

3.2 Communication Interface Technology

The primary function of the CIU is to collect and consolidate data from a variety of sources for use by the CANSARP application in generating search patterns. The CIU software was designed to use the EMPRESS commercial RDBMS. The CIU software uses a publicly available environmental database browser called NEONS. The software runs in a Linux (UNIX) environment using Xwindows for the Graphical User Interface.

System Description

Figure 3.2 depicts the CIU as a data concentrator, providing a unified interface between external sources of information and all of the RCC applications. The design can be implemented as a stand alone CIU prototype as or as a process running within the CANSARP workstation.

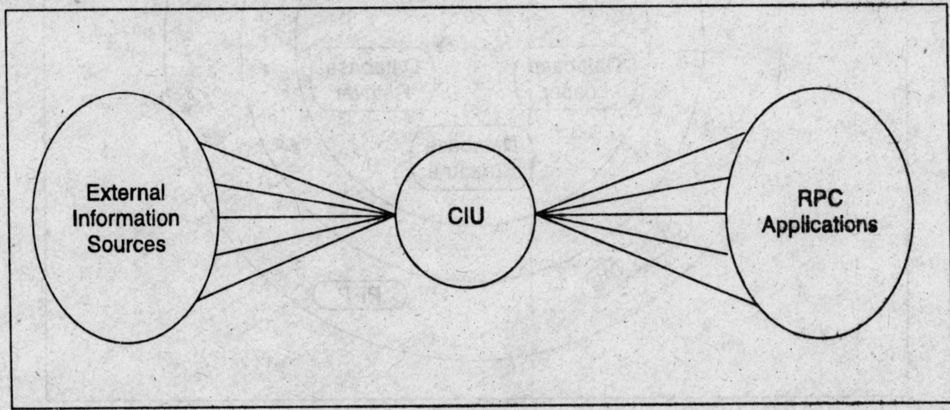

Fig. 3.2. CIU Conceptual Diagram

Figure 3.3 elaborates on this concept, and shows the internal structure of the CIU, consisting of a process controller, communication controller, data base loaders and data base retrievers which access the local data tables. The external interfaces include a modem interface to access the PSTN network and an Ethernet interface to access the RCC LAN and TC-Internet.

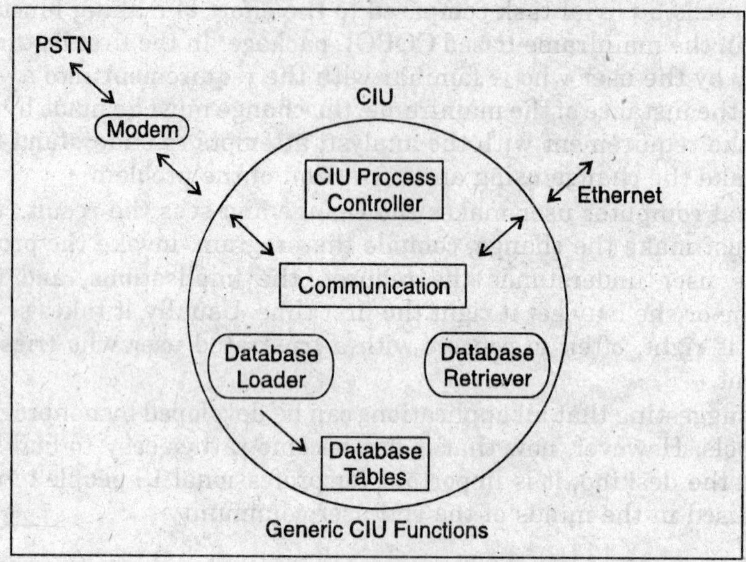

Fig. 3.3. CIU Functional Blocks

The CIU Software Architecture is shown in Figure 3.4 The data loaders and retrievers

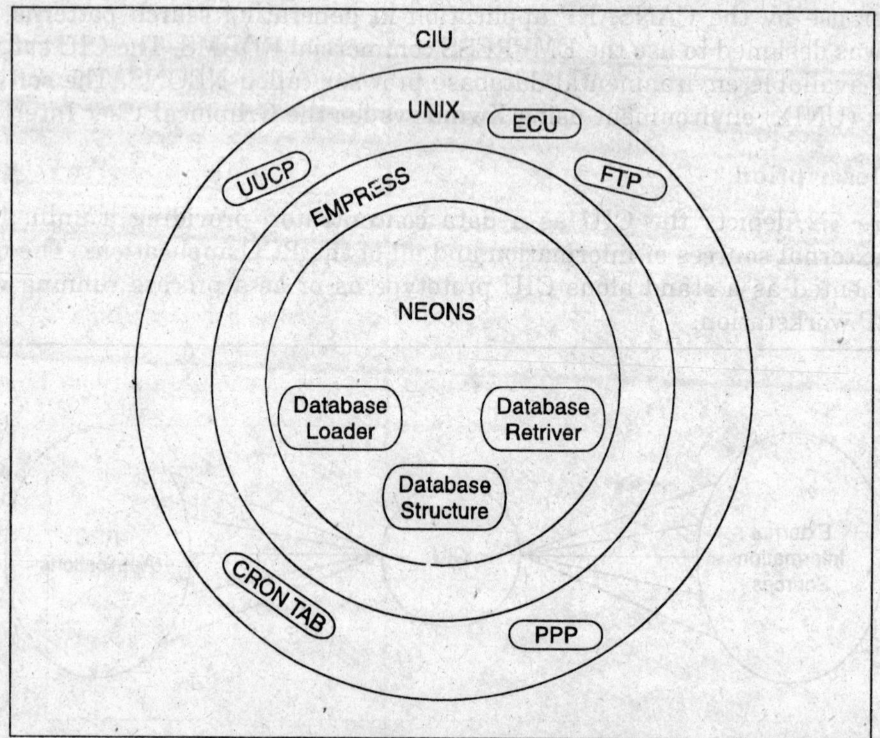

Fig. 3.4. CIU Software

and data tables are defined within the NEONs domain, which runs on top of the EMPRESS RDBMS. EMPRESS runs on top of the Linux O/S. The CRON TAB process schedules the CIU activities and uses the ECU, FTP, PPP and UUCP UNIX utilities to establish communication links with external information providers and make this data available for the data loaders.

Data Acquired

For each type of data used by the CIU, a section is created explaining the nature of the data and how that data is set up and loaded.

Wind Data Acquisition

Wind data can be provided to the CIU from the CMC AES services in Downsview and Dorval. Wind data is provided using anonymous ftp in LLT format. The data is decoded, and uncompressed before loading into the NEONS database. Two types of AES wind data are provided. Worded wind data files contain wind measurements made by human observers and manually entered into the database while AES automatic wind data is recorded by automated weather stations with no human intervention.

Surface Current Data Acquisition

Surface current data is provided by IOS, and in future, IML and BIO. Sea current data is provided via modem link from the IOS prototype BBS in LLT data format. The data is loaded into the NEONS database as LLT data. The Institute Maurice Lamontagne (IML) will soon be able to provide surface current data for the St. Lawrence river and gulf via internet ftp.

Ship Position Information

Ship position information will be provided by the CCG's Flag/Data Hail system. Ship position data can be provided via modem link from the FLAG MNET controllers. This data is decoded before loading into the NEONS database as LLT data. In future, this and more Ship data will be provided by the INNAV system and by the SATlantic Optical Feature Workstation (OFW).

CIU Interfaces

The CIU interfaces with the various environmental service agencies and the RCC monitoring centre via internet and modem link. The CIU software utilizes standard UNIX device drivers, protocols, and network interfaces for data acquisition. The conceptual

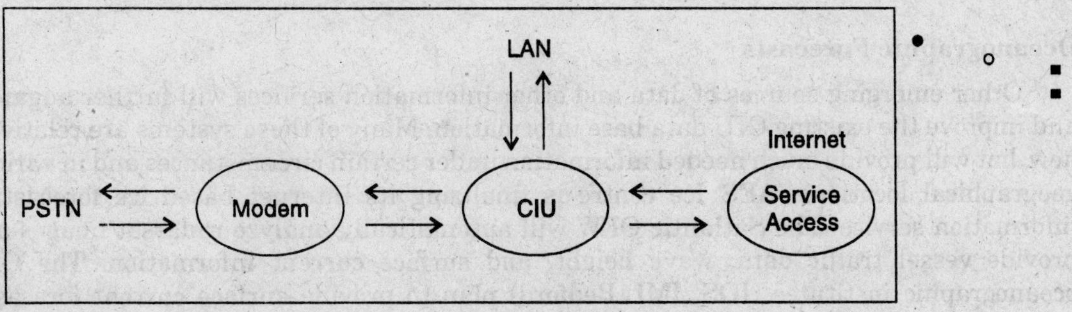

Fig. 3.5. CIU Interfaces

diagram in figure 3.5 illustrates the various external input data sources to the CIU data concentrator.

FLAG/DATA Hail

The FLAG/DATA Hail information will be accessed by the CIU. SRU position and on site reports can be monitored and analyzed and electronic messages can be sent to the ships. Flag/Data Hail is currently set up for uucp file transfer. In future, this data can be made available by the INNAV system or accessed directly on a LAN/WAN connected to the updated CCG MNET controllers.

Ocean Data and Information Network (ODIN)

The ODIN system, used by the Canadian Hydrographic service to monitor water levels in eastern Canada, may be upgraded to support a SQL database engine and to provide other coastal parameters such as temperature, salinity, weather, etc. The CIU can access ODIN data via a modem link, and in future, via dedicated LAN/WAN, or via the INNAV interface.

RCC Console

Presently, distress position estimates are provided by ELTs, PLBs and EPIRBs using the SARSAT locating system and, in future, GPS position information may also be provided by the beacon at the distress site. This position information will be part of the information that the CIU software will extract from the RCC Console and from the CMCC. This information will provide periodic updates to the actual position of the emergency site. This dynamic positioning information will allow the CANSARP software to produce very precise search plans.

ADDAM

An Internet ftp link will be provided to interface with the Argos satellite services to relay data to the CIU from ADDAM drifter buoys.

INNAV Project

The INNAV project is sponsored by the CCG VTS branch and will include both static and dynamic data on all vessels in Canadian waters. Data made available by this system will be useful to the CANSARP system and INNAV interface requirements are accommodated for in the CIU design. Distributed database calls supporting SQL and ODBC file formats will be used. ODIN, FLAG and Data Hail information will be available on the INNAV system.

Oceanographic Forecasts

Other emerging sources of data and other information services will further augment and improve the existing CIU data base information. Many of these systems are relatively new, but will provide much needed information under certain circumstances and in various geographical locations. AES Ice centre is finalizing its internet based ice forecasting information service. The Satlantic OFW will automatically analyze radarsat images and provide vessel traffic data, wave height, and surface current information. The CHS oceanographic institutes (IOS, IML Bedford) plan to provide surface current forecasts, nowcasts, and hindcasts, and these will be used by the CIU. The interfaces will be via dedicated modem link and via internet ftp.

Software Interfaces

The CIU software interfaces to the following:

(a) NEONS data management system;
(b) EMPRESS Relational Database Management System (RDBMS);
(c) Open Windows; and,
(d) CANSARP Computerized Search planning Tool.

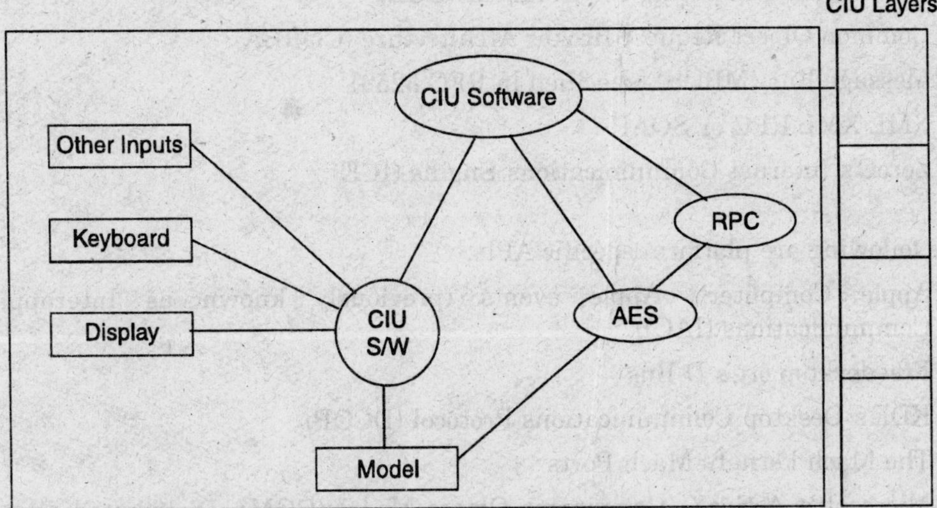

Fig. 3.6. shows the context diagram for the CIU software

3.3 Inter-process Communication

A capability supported by some operating systems that allows one process to communicate with another process. The processes can be running on the same computer or on different computers connected through a network.

IPC enables one application to control another application, and for several applications to share the same data without interfering with one another. IPC is required in all multiprocessing systems, but it is not generally supported by single-process operating systems such as DOS. OS/2 and MS-Windows support an IPC mechanism called DDE.

Inter-Process Communication (IPC) is a set of techniques for the exchange of data between two or more threads in one or more processes. Processes may be running on one computer or on two or more computers connected by a network. IPC techniques are divided into methods for message passing, synchronization, shared memory, and remote procedure calls (RPC). The method of IPC used may vary based on the bandwidth and latency of communication between the threads, and the type of data being communicated.

It is widely accepted that IPC can be implemented significantly faster in a microkernel environment than in classical monolithic kernel systems. IPC may also be referred to as inter-thread communication and inter-application communication.

Implementations

There are a number of APIs which may be used for IPC. A number of platform independent APIs include the following:

- Anonymous pipes and named pipes
- Sockets
- Distributed Computing Environment (DCE)
- Common Object Request Broker Architecture (CORBA)
- Message Bus (MBUS) (specified in RFC 3259)
- XML XML-RPC or SOAP
- ZeroC's Internet Communications Engine (ICE)

The following are platform specific APIs:

- Apple Computer's Apple events (previously known as Interapplication Communications (IAC)).
- Freedesktop.org's D-Bus
- KDE's Desktop Communications Protocol (DCOP)
- The Mach kernel's Mach Ports
- Microsoft's ActiveX, Component Object Model (COM), Distributed Component Object Model (DCOM), Dynamic Data Exchange (DDE), Object Linking and Embedding (OLE), anonymous pipes, named pipes, Local Procedure Call
- Novell's SPX
- POSIX mmap, message queues, semaphores, and shared memory
- RISC OS's messages
- Solaris's Doors
- Sun Microsystems' RPC
- System V's message queues, semaphores, and shared memory

Table of IPC Methods

Method	Provided by (Operating systems or other environments)
File	All operating systems.
Signal	Most operating systems; some systems, such as Windows, only implement signals in the C run-time library and do not actually provide support for their use as an IPC technique.
Socket	Most operating systems.
Pipe	All POSIX systems.
Named pipe	All POSIX systems.
Semaphore	All POSIX systems.
Shared memory	All POSIX systems.
Message passing (shared nothing)	Used in MPI paradigm, Java RMI, CORBA and others.
Memory map	All POSIX systems; may carry race condition risk if a temporary file is used. Windows also supports this technique but the APIs used are platform specific.
Message queue	Most operating systems.
Mailbox	Some operating systems.

3.4 Wide Area Network Technologies

A wide area network or WAN, spans a large geographical area, often a country or continent. It contains a collection of machines intended for running user (i.e., application) programs. In most WANs, the subnet consists of two distinct components

- Transmission Lines
- Switching Element.

Transmission lines (also called circuits, or channel) move bits between machines. The switching elements are specialized computers used to connect two or more transmission lines. When data arrive on an incoming line, the switching element must choose an outgoing line to forward them on.

In most WANs, the network contains numerous cables or telephone lines, each one connecting a pair of routers. If two routers that do not share a cable nevertheless wish to communicate, they must do this in directory, via other routers, when a packet is sent from one router to another via one or more intermediate routers, the packet is received at each inter mediate router in its entirely, stored until the required output line is free, and then forwarded. A subnet using this principle is called a point-to-point, store and forward or packet—switched subnet.

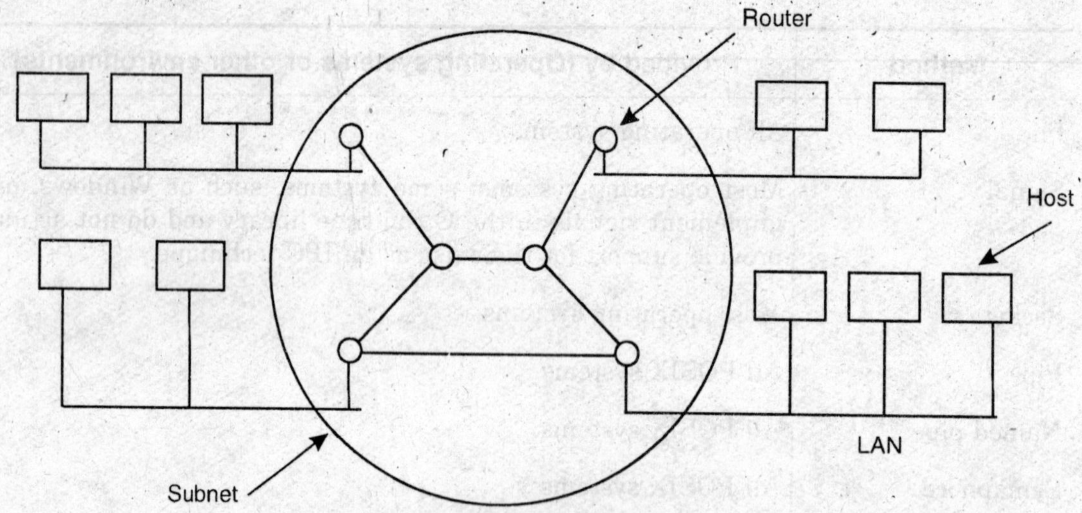

Fig. 3.7. Relation between hosts and subnet

Wide Area Networks typically have irregular topologies. WAN Bandwidth for data communications is a critical issue. In terminal to host network, traffic generated by applications could be modeled and the network would then be sized accordingly, enabling effective use of the Bandwidth. With LAN inter connections and application that enable users to transfer large files (such as through e-mail attachment) and images; this modeling is much harder to perform.

In the short term, the chances are even more dramatic as the migration from a host centric environment to a distributed client/server environment prevents the use of any past experience in guessing the actual network requirements.

Network managers must cope with these changes by seeking those technologies that will let them acquire bandwidth cost effectively while allowing flexibility to serve these new applications. WAN services have recently emerged that address this issue by providing the appropriate flexibility inherently required for these applications.

Wide Area Network

A wide area network or **WAN** is a computer network covering a broad geographical area. Contrast with personal area networks (PANs), local area networks (LANs) or metropolitan area networks (MANs) that are usually limited to a room, building or campus. The largest and most well-known example of a WAN is the Internet.

WANs are used to connect local area networks (LANs) together, so that users and computers in one location can communicate with users and computers in other locations. Many WANs are built for one particular organization and are private. Others, built by Internet service providers, provide connections from an organization's LAN to the Internet. WANs are most often built using leased lines. At each end of the leased line, a router connects to the LAN on one side and a hub within the WAN on the other. Leased lines can be very expensive. Instead of using leased lines, WANs can also be built using less costly circuit switching or packet switching methods. Network protocols including TCP/IP deliver transport and addressing functions. Protocols including Packet over

SONET/SDH, MPLS, ATM and Frame relay are often used by service providers to deliver the links that are used in WANs. X.25 was an important early WAN protocol, and is often considered to be the "grandfather" of Frame Relay as many of the underlying protocols and functions of X.25 are still in use today (with upgrades) by Frame Relay.

Academic research into wide area networks can be broken down into three areas: Mathematical models, network emulation and network simulation.

Such a network generally requires the crossing of public right-of-ways, and rely at least in part on circuits provided by a common carrier, Typically, a WAN consists of a number of interconnected switching nodes. A transmission from any one device is routed through these internal nodes to the specified destination device. These nodes (including the boundary nodes) are not concerned with the contents of data; rather their purpose is to provide a switching facility that will move the data from node to node until they reach their destination. Performance improvements are sometimes delivered via WAFS or WAN Optimization.

WAN Connectivity Options

Several options are available for WAN connectivity:

Option	Description	Advantages	Disadvantages	Bandwidth range	Sample Protocols used
Leased line	Point-to-Point connection between two computers	Most secure	Expensive		PPP, HDLC, SDLC
Circuit switching	A dedicated circuit path is created between end points. Best example is dialup connections		Call Setup		PPP, ISDN
Packet switching	Devices transport packets via a shared single point-to-point or point-to-multipoint link across a carrier internetwork. Variable length packets are transmitted over Permanent Virtual Circuits (PVC) or Switched Virtual Circuits (SVC)				X.25 Frame-Relay
Cell relay	Similar to packet switching, but uses fixed length cells instead.of variable length packets, data is divided into fixed-length cells and then transported across virtual circuits	Best for symulta neous use of Voice and data	Overhead can be consider able		ATM

Transmission rate usually range from 1200 bits/second to 6 Mbit/s. Typical communication links used in WANs are telephone lines, microwave links & satellite channels.

Wide Area Network Technologies Overview

A Wide Area Network (WAN) is a computer network covering multiple distance areas, which may spread across the entire world. WANs often connect multiple smaller networks, such as local area networks (LANs) or metro area networks (MANs). The world's most popular WAN is the Internet. Some segments of the Internet are also WANs in themselves. The key difference between WAN and LAN technologies is scalability WAN must be able to grow as needed to cover multiple cities, even countries and continents.

A set of switches and routers are interconnected to form a Wide Area Network. The switches can be connected in different topologies such as full mesh and half mesh. A wide area network may be privately owned or rented from a service provider, but the term usually connotes the inclusion of public (shared user) networks.

Both packet switching and circuit switching technologies are used in the WAN. Packet switching allows users to share common carrier resources so that the carrier can make more efficient use of its infrastructure. In a packet switching setup, networks have connections into the carrier's network, and many customers share the carrier's network. The carrier can then create virtual circuits between customers' sites by which packets of data are delivered from one to the other through the network.

circuit Switching allows data connections to be established when needed and then terminated when communication is complete. This works like a normal telephone line works for voice communication. Integrated Services Digital Network (ISDN) is a good example of circuit switching. When a router has data for a remote site, the switched circuit is initiated with the circuit number of the remote network.

Virtual private network (VPN) is a tecnology widely used in a public switched network (PSTN) to provide private and secured WAN for an organization. VPN uses encryption and other techniques to make it appear that the organisation has a dedicated network, while making use of the shared infrastructure of the WAN.

WAN technologies generally function at the lower three layers of the OSI reference model: the physical layer, the data link layer, and the network layer. Key technologies often found in WANs include SONET, Frame Relay, X.25, ATM and PPP.

- ATM: A dedicated-connection switching technology that organizes digital data into 53-byte cell units. Individually, a cell is processed asynchronously relative to other related cells and is queued before being multiplexed over the transmission path. Speeds on ATM networks can reach 10 Gbps.
- Frame Relay: (FR). A high-speed packet-switched data communications service, similar to X.25. Frame relay is widely used for LAN-to-LAN interconnect services, and is well suited to the bursty demands of LAN environments.
- SONET/SDH: Synchronous Optical Network is an international standard for high speed communication over fiber-optic networks. The SONET establishes Optical Carrier (OC) levels from 51.8 Mbps to 10 Gbps (OC-192) or even higher. Synchronous Digital Hierarchy (SDH) is a European equivalent of SONET.
- X.25: The X.25 protocol allows computers on different public networks to communicate through an intermediary computer at the network layer level.
- PPP: A point-to-point link provides a single, pre-established WAN communications path from the customer premises through a carrier network, such

as a telephone company, to a remote network. Point-to-point lines are usually leased from a carrier and thus are often called leased lines. For a point-to-point line, the carrier allocates pairs of wire and facility hardware to your line only.

IP can also be considered as a WAN technology in the packet switching environment.

Wide Area Networks (WAN)

The size of a network is limited due to size and distance constraints. However networks may be connected over a high speed communications link (called a WAN link) to link them together and thus become a WAN. WAN links are usually:

- Dial up connection
- Dedicated connection—It is a permanent full time connection. When a dedicated connection is used, the cable is leased rather than a part of the cable bandwidth and the user has exclusive use.

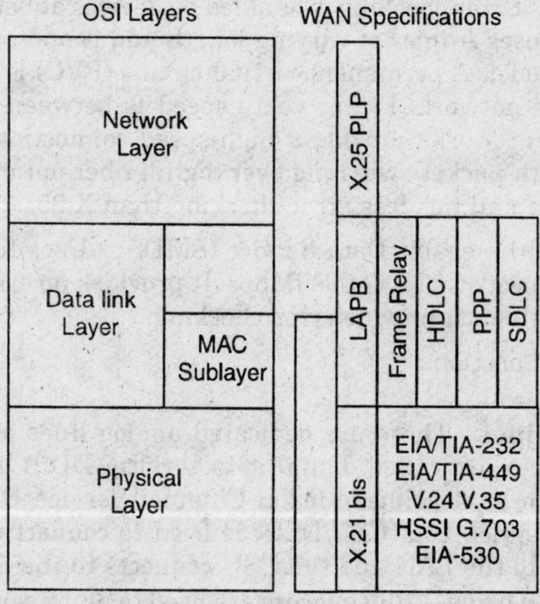

Fig 3.7 Wide Area Network Technologies Overview

- Switched Network—Several users share the same line or the bandwidth of the line. There are two types of switched networks:
    1. Circuit switching—This is a temporary connection between two points such as dial-up or ISDN.
    2. Packet switching—This is a connection between multiple points. It breaks data down into small packets to be sent across the network. A virtual circuit can improve performance by establishing a set path for data transmission. This will shave some overhead of a packet switching network. A variant of packet switching is called cell-switching where the data is broken into small cells with a fixed length.

WAN Connection Technologies

- X.25 - This is a set of protocols developed by the CCITT/ITU which specifies how to connect computer devices over an internetwork. These protocols use a great deal of error checking for use over unreliable telephone lines. They establish a virtual communication circuit. It uses a store and forward method which can cause about a half second delay in data reception when two way communications are used. Their speed is about 64Kbps. Normally X.25 is used on packed switching PDNs (Public Data Networks). A line must be leased from the LAN to a PDN to connect to an X.25 network. A PAD (packet assembler/disassembler) or an X.25 interface is used on a computer to connect to the X.25 network. CCITT is an abbreviation for International Telegraph and Telephone Consultative Committee. The ITU is the International Telecommunication Union.
- Frame Relay - Error checking is handled by devices at both sides of the connection. Frame relay uses frames of varying length and it operates at the data link layer of the OSI model. A permanent virtual circuit (PVC) is established between two points on the network. Frame relay speed is between 56Kbps and 1.544Mbps. Frame relay networks provide a high-speed connection up to 1.544Mbps using variable-length packet-switching over digital fiber-optic media. Frame relay does not store data and has less error checking than X.25.
- Switched Multi-megabit Data Service (SMDS) - Uses fixed length cell switching and runs at speeds of 1.533 to 45Mbps. It provides no error checking and assumes devices at both ends provide error checking.
- Telephone connections
  - Dial up
  - **Leased lines**—These are dedicated analog lines or digital lines. Dedicated digital lines are called digital data service (DDS) lines. A modem is used to connect to analog lines, and a Channel Service Unit/Data Service Unit or Digital Service Unit(CSU/DSU) is used to connect to digital lines. The DSU connects to the LAN and the CSU connects to the line.
  - **T Carrier lines**—Multiplexors are used to allow several channels on one line. The T1 line is basic T Carrier service. The available channels may be used separately for data or voice transmissions or they may be combined for more transmission bandwidth. The 64Kbps data transmission rate is referred to as DS-0 (Digital Signal level 0) and a full T1 line is referred to as DS-1.

Singnal	System	Total Kbps	Channels	Number of equivalent TI lines
DS-1	T1	1544	24	1
DS-2	T2	6312	96	4
Ds-3	T3	44736	672	28
DS-4	T4	274760	4032	3668

- ✦ T1 and T3 lines are the most common lines in use today. T1 and T2 lines can use standard copper wire. T3 and T4 lines require fiber-optic cable or other high-speed media. These lines may be leased partially called fractional T1 or fractional T3 which means a customer can lease a certain number of channels on the line. A CSU/DSU and a bridge or router is required to connect to a T1 line.
- ✦ Integrated Services Digital Network (ISDN)—Comes in two types and converts analog signals to digital for transmission. It is a dial up service.
  - ☐ Basic Rate ISDN (BRI)—Two 64Kbps B-channels with one 16Kbps D channel. The D-channel is used tor call control and setup.
  - ☐ Primary Rate ISDN (PRI)—23 B-channels and one D channel.
- ✦ A device resembling a modem (called an ISDN modem) is used to connect to ISDN. The computer and telephone line are plugged into it.
- ✦ Switched-56—A switched line similar to a leased line where customers pay for the time they use the line. Speed is 56Kbps. It is not dedicated and will not work to connect a WAN.
- ✦ Asynchronous Transfer Mode (ATM) - May be used over a variety of media with both baseband and broadband systems. It is used for audio, video, and data. It uses fixed length data packets of 53 8 bit bytes called cell switching. 5 bytes contain header information.

- The cell contains path information that the packet is to use. It uses hardware devices to perform the switching of the data. Speeds from 155Mbps to 622 Mbps are achieved. Error checking is done at the receiving device, not by ATM. A permanent virtual connection or circuit (PVC) is established. It may also use a switched virtual circuit (SVC). Service classes:
- Constant bit rate for data.
  - ✦ Variable bit rate for audio or video.
  - ✦ Connection less for data.
  - ✦ Connection oriented for data.

ATM can be embedded in other protocols such as ATM-25, T1, T3, OC-1, OC-3, OC-12, and OC-48. Some ATM technologies include:

- ✦ ATM-25 - 25Mbps speed.
- ✦ STS-3 - 155Mbps on fiber or category 5 cable.
- ✦ STS-12 - 620 Mbps on fiber cable for campus wide network.
- ✦ STS-48 - 2.2 Gbps on fiber cable on a MAN.
- ✦ STS-192 - 8.8 Gbps on fiber cable on intercity long distance. This is normally used by phone companies.

- Synchronous Optical Network (SONET)—A physical layer standard that defines voice, data, and video delivery methods over fiber optic media. It defines data rates in terms of optical carrier (OC) levels. The transmission rate of OC-1 is 51.8 Mbps. Each level runs at a multiple of the first. The OC-5 data rate is 5 times 51.8 Mbps which is 259 Mbps. SONET also defines synchronous transport signals (STS) for copper media which use the same speed scale of OC levels. STS-3 runs at the same speed of OC-3. Mesh or ring topology is used to support SONET.

SONET uses multiplexing. The ITU has incorporated SONET into their Synchronous Digital Hierarchy (SDH) recommendations

WAN Technology Comparisons

Technology	Speed	Characteristics
Switched 56	56Kbps	Switched line, not dedicated
X.25	64Kbps	Packet switching, error correction, store and foreward, with round trip delay
Frame Relay	56Kbps to 1.544Mbps	Varying length frames with permanent virtual circuit
SMDS	1.533 to 45Mbps	Fixed cell length with no error checking
T1	1.544Mbps	24 Multiplexed channels
T3	44.736Mbps	672 Multiplexed channels
SONET	51.8Mbps (OC-1)	OC2 is 2X OC1, OC3 is 3X OC1
ATM	155Mbps to 622 Mbps	Fixed length packets. works on SONET and T carrier lines. Uses virtual circuits

3.5 Frame Relay

Frame Relay is a service for people, who want an absolute bare bones connection oriented way to move bits from A to B at reasonable speed and low cost.

Twenty years ago, communication using telephone lines was slow, analog and unreliable and computers were slow and expensive. As a result, complex protocols were required to mask errors and the user's computers were too expensive to have them to do this work.

The leased lines (leased telephone lines) are now fast, digital and reliable, and computers are fast and inexpensive. This suggests the use of simple protocols with must of the work being done by the user's computers, rather than by the network.

Frame Relay can be thought of as a virtual leased line. The customer leases a permanent virtual circuit between two points and then send Frames (*i.e.*, packets) of upto 1600 bytes between them. It is also possible to lease permanent virtual circuits between a given site and multiple other sits, so each frame carries a 10 bit number telling which virtual circuit to use.

Frame Relay Networks are often qualified as virtual private networks. They share a public infrastructure but implement virtual circuits between the senders and the receivers, similar to actual circuits. It is therefore a connection oriented network.

The difference between an actual leased line and a virtual leased line is that with an actual one, the user can send traffic all day long at the maximum speed with a virtual one, data bursts may be sent at full speed, but the long term average usage must be below a predetermined level.

In addition to competition with leased lines, frame relay also competes with X.25 Permanent virtual circuits, excepts that it operates at higher speeds usually 1.5 Mbps. Frame Relay provides a minimal services.

3.6 Switched Multimegabit Data Services (SMDS)

Switched Multimegabit Data Service (SMDS) is a Connectionless, high speed, packet switched data service. SMDS is used to interconnect distribute corporate LANs and WANs through the public Networks, because it is connectionless, SMDS elements, the need for carrier switches to establish a call path between two points of data transmission.

SMDS uses the IEEE 802.6 protocol, which has developed as a Metropolitan- area-network. The IEEE 802.6 standard is often described as a cell relay Technology. The IEEE 802.6 pockets called cells have a fixed size of 53 octets, 48 octets for data and 5 octets for the address header.

SMDS access devices pass 53 byte cells to a carrier switch. The switch reads addresses and forwards cells one by one over any available path to the desired endpoint.

Advantage (Benefits)

i) Reduce the need for precise traffic flow predictions over the entire networks.
ii) Relies only on connections between fixed locations.
iii) No need for a pre defined path between devices.
iv) Data can travel over the least congested routers.
v) Providing faster transmission
vi) Increased security.
vii) Greater flexibility to add or drop network sites.

SMDS defines a three-tiered Architecture

i) A switching infrastructure comprising SMDS compatible switches.
ii) A delivery system made up of T-1 and T-3 circuits called subscriber Network interfaces (SNIs)
iii) An Access control system for users to connect to the switching infrastructure.

Note : Connecting a LAN to an SMDS Network requires only a router and an SMDS compatible network interface card.

3.7 ATM in the Wide Area Network

ATM scheme is widely used for data communication network. ATM Network uses the ATM switch, which receives the requests for data transfer from different computers. The ATM switch facilitates the data Transmission in Asynchronous mode. Various computers are connected to the ATM switch, the ATM switch connects the sender's and receiver's computers and transfer the packets to destination at a high speed. ATM Network is similar to star Network.

NOTE : ATM Network (Switch) is more reliable or suitable for multimedia data transfer, which contains the text audio and video. The speed of communication between the computers and ATM switch is 155 Mbps.

The basic idea behind ATM is to transmit all information in small fixed size packets called cells. The cells are 53 bytes long of which 5 bytes are header and 48 bytes for data. The ATM uses cell switching technology and is also known as cell (switching) relay service.

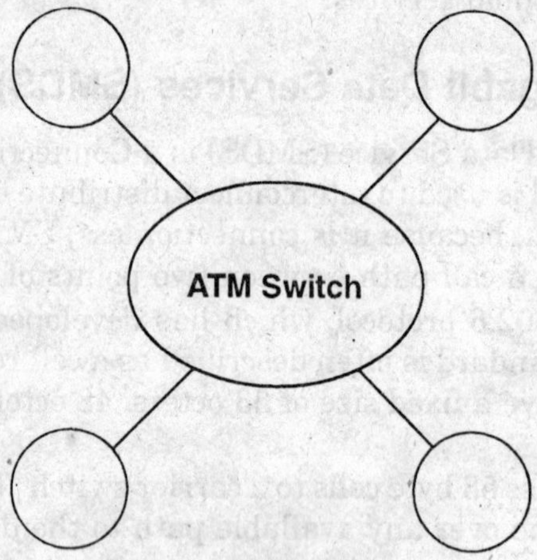

Fig. 3.8 ATM Switch

The cell switching technology has got the following advantages on traditional circuit switching technology:

i) It is highly flexible and can handle both fixed rate and variable rate traffic equally well.

ii) At the high speed envisioned, digital switching of cells is easier than using traditional multiplexing techniques.

iii) For Television distribution broad casting is essential, cell switching can provide this and circuit switching can not. ATM networks are connection-oriented making call require First sending a message to set up the connection; After that subsequent calls are follow the same path to the destination. Cell delivery is not guaranteed but their order is guaranteed.

The intended speeds for ATM networks are 155 Mbps and 622 Mbps. The speed 155 Mbps are chosen because this is the speed needed to transmit high definition television. ATM appears to be future of high speed networking for several business and technical reasons. ATM has been designed to be independent of the transmission medium.

3.8 ISDN—Integrated Services Digital Network

ISDN stands for integrated services digital network. It is the forerunner of B-ISDN. ISDN was designed to utilize the pre-existing copper wiring that runs from the telephone exchange. To telephones on the customer premises. ISDN operates by increasing the calling capacity of the existing telephone lines. Three types of ISDN channels are defined B, D and H.

B—Channel

It is a 64 kbps clear channel that can carry any digitized data and voice. A Clear channel means that no signaling information is sent and is meant to be an open communication line. There are two b channels on each ISDN lines and so two kind's information can be exchanged simultaneously.

D—Channel

D-channel used for signaling information, can operate at either 16 kbps for 64 kbps, the D channel can be used for what is known as communication signaling useful for synchronization, monitoring and alarm signals. This channel can also transport digital data at speed upto 9600 bits/second. This channel uses X.25 format for data transfer.

H—Channel

Three H channels all providing higher speed transmission than D channel. The Ho channel operates at 384 kbps and can be used for video conferencing, high speed fax or packet switched data.

Upto four Ho channels can be multiplexed into a single H1 Channel, which operates at 1.55 Mbps. The H1 channel is used for high speed data communications or LAN inter connections, The H2 channel operates at 1.9 Mbps is available only in Europe.

ISDN is used to transmit and receive data at high speeds. ISDN can provide high quality and performance services for remote access to a LAN.

B—ISDN

The B-ISDN stand for broad band integrated service digital network. The main goal of B-ISDN is integration of voice and non-voice (i.e. Audio and Video) data communication services.

3.9 Network Management

When Applications reside on a single central processor, the issues of network management assume great importance but often can be addressed by attentive operations staff. With the movement of client/server applications, processors may reside away from this attentiveness.

If the data or application logic necessary to run the business resides at a location remote from the glass house central computer room, these resources must be visible to some network managers. The provision of a network control center to manage all resources in a distributed network is the major challenge facing most large organizations today. Many organizations view this issue as the most significant obstacle to successful rollout of client/ server applications.

The key layers in the management system architecture:

i) Presentation describes the management console environment and the tools used there.
ii) Reduction refers to distributed intelligence which acts as an intermediary for the

network management interface. Reduction enables information to be consolidated and filtered and allowing the presentation service to delegate's tasks through the use of an emerging distributed program services such as RPC.

iii) Gathering of information is done by device agents. These device agents provide detailed diagnostics, detailed statistics and precise control.

There are five key OSI management areas

- Fault Management
- Performance Management
- Inventory Management
- Accounting Management
- Configuration Management

What Is Network Management?

Network management means different things to different people. In some cases, it involves a solitary network consultant monitoring network activity with an outdated protocol analyzer. In other cases, network management involves a distributed database, autopolling of network devices, and high-end workstations generating real-time graphical views of network topology changes and traffic. In general, network management is a service that employs a variety of tools, applications, and devices to assist human network managers in monitoring and maintaining networks.

A Historical Perspective

The early 1980s saw tremendous expansion in the area of network deployment. As companies realized the cost benefits and productivity gains created by network technology, they began to add networks and expand existing networks almost as rapidly as new network technologies and products were introduced. By the mid-1980s, certain companies were experiencing growing pains from deploying many different (and sometimes incompatible) network technologies.

The problems associated with network expansion affect both day-to-day network operation management and strategic network growth planning. Each new network technology requires its own set of experts. In the early 1980s, the staffing requirements alone for managing large, heterogeneous networks created a crisis for many organizations. An urgent need arose for automated network management (including what is typically called network capacity planning) integrated across diverse environments.

Network Management Architecture

Most network management architectures use the same basic structure and set of relationships. End stations (managed devices), such as computer systems and other network devices, run software that enables them to send alerts when they recognize problems (for example, when one or more user-determined thresholds are exceeded). Upon receiving these alerts, management entities are programmed to react by executing one, several, or a group of actions, including operator notification, event logging, system shutdown, and automatic attempts at system repair.

Management entities also can poll end stations to check the values of certain variables. Polling can be automatic or user-initiated, but agents in the managed devices respond to all polls. Agents are software modules that first compile information about the managed devices in which they reside, then store this information in a management database, and finally provide it (proactively or reactively) to management entities within network management systems (NMSs) via a network management protocol. Well-known network management protocols include the Simple Network Management Protocol (SNMP) and Common Management Information Protocol (CMIP). Management proxies are entities that provide management information on behalf of other entities. Figure 3.9 depicts a typical network management architecture.

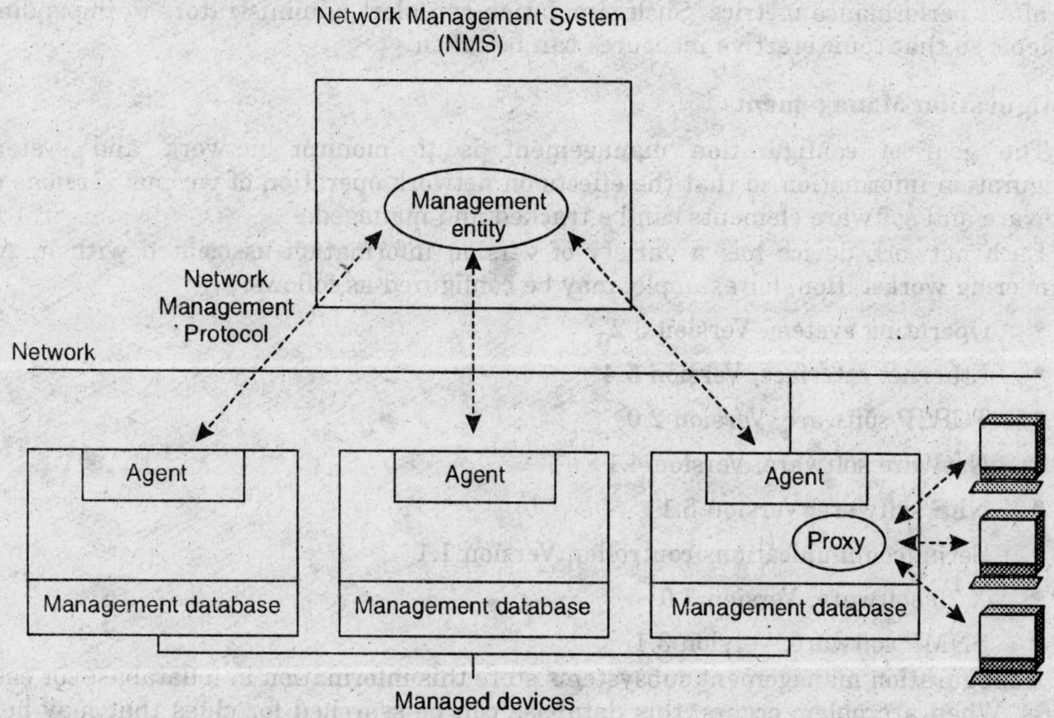

Figure 3.9 A Typical Network Management Architecture Maintains Many Relationships

ISO Network Management Model

The ISO has contributed a great deal to network standardization. Its network management model is the primary means for understanding the major functions of network management systems. This model consists of five conceptual areas.

Performance Management

The goal of performance management is to measure and make available various aspects of network performance so that internetwork performance can be maintained at an acceptable level. Examples of performance variables that might be provided include network throughput, user response times, and line utilization.

Performance management involves three main steps. First, performance data is gathered on variables of interest to network administrators. Second, the data is analyzed to determine normal (baseline) levels. Finally, appropriate performance thresholds are determined for each important variable so that exceeding these thresholds indicates a network problem worthy of attention.

Management entities continually monitor performance variables. When a performance threshold is exceeded, an alert is generated and sent to the network management system.

Each of the steps just described is part of the process to set up a reactive system. When performance becomes unacceptable because of an exceeded user-defined threshold, the system reacts by sending a message. Performance management also permits proactive methods: For example, network simulation can be used to project how network growth will affect performance metrics. Such simulation can alert administrators to impending problems so that counteractive measures can be taken.

Configuration Management

The goal of configuration management is to monitor network and system configuration information so that the effects on network operation of various versions of hardware and software elements can be tracked and managed.

Each network device has a variety of version information associated with it. An engineering workstation, for example, may be configured as follows:

- Operating system, Version 3.2
- Ethernet interface, Version 5.4
- TCP/IP software, Version 2.0
- NetWare software, Version 4.1
- NFS software, Version 5.1
- Serial communications controller, Version 1.1
- X.25 software, Version 1.0
- SNMP software, Version 3.1

Configuration management subsystems store this information in a database for easy access. When a problem occurs, this database can be searched for clues that may help solve the problem.

Accounting Management

The goal of accounting management is to measure network utilization parameters so that individual or group uses on the network can be regulated appropriately. Such regulation minimizes network problems (because network resources can be apportioned based on resource capacities) and maximizes the fairness of network access across all users.

As with performance management, the first step toward appropriate accounting management is to measure utilization of all important network resources. Analysis of the results provides insight into current usage patterns, and usage quotas can be set at this point. Some correction, of course, will be required to reach optimal access practices. From this point, ongoing measurement of resource use can yield billing information as well as information used to assess continued fair and optimal resource utilization.

Fault Management

The goal of fault management is to detect, log, notify users of, and (to the extent possible) automatically fix network problems to keep the network running effectively. Because faults can cause downtime or unacceptable network degradation, fault management is perhaps the most widely implemented of the ISO network management elements.

Fault management involves first determining symptoms and isolating the problem. Then the problem is fixed and the solution is tested on all-important subsystems. Finally, the detection and resolution of the problem is recorded.

Security Management

The goal of security management is to control access to network resources according to local guidelines so that the network cannot be sabotaged (intentionally or unintentionally) and sensitive information cannot be accessed by those without appropriate authorization. A security management subsystem, for example, can monitor users logging on to a network resource and can refuse access to those who enter inappropriate access codes.

Security management subsystems work by partitioning network resources into authorized and unauthorized areas. For some users, access to any network resource is inappropriate, mostly because such users are usually company outsiders. For other (internal) network users, access to information originating from a particular department is inappropriate. Access to Human Resource files, for example, is inappropriate for most users outside the Human Resources department.

Security management subsystems perform several functions. They identify sensitive network resources (including systems, files, and other entities) and determine mappings between sensitive network resources and user sets. They also monitor access points to sensitive network resources and log inappropriate access to sensitive network resources.

3.10 TCP/IP Protocol Suite

The TCP/IP Protocol suite is composed of following protocols, which are abide with certain services either N/W locally (LAN) or on WAN or with internet. The TCP/IP protocol suite is now being used in many commercial applications. It is particularly evident in inter networking between different LAN environments. TCP/IP is specially designed to handle communications through networks of inter connected networks.

i) Internet Protocol
ii) Transport Protocol
iii) Telnet
iv) File Transfer Protocol (FTP)
v) Simple Network Management Protocol (SNMP)
vi) Network File System Protocol
vii) Simple Mail Transfer Protocol

3.10.1 Internet Protocol (IP's)

Internet protocol represents the network layer and is equivalent to open system inter-connecting internet protocol. A unique network address is assigned to every system whether the system is connected to LAN or WAN. The system interacts with its associated routing protocols and lower level functions such as network to physical address resolution protocol (ARP). Commonly the routing protocol used on LAN or WAN to coordinate the IP is RIP (Routing Internet Protocol).

3.10.2 Transport Protocol

TCP provides the transport services over IP. It is a connection oriented *i.e.*, a session to be set up between the two parties (two workstation) to provide a service. The major role of transport protocol are transport the services, ensure end to end data transmission. Ordering of data and flow control of the data and also the error recovery. TCP provides the kind of communications the users and programs expect to have in locally connected sessions.

UDP provides connectionless transport services and is used in very specific applications that do not require end to end reliability such as that provided by TCP.

3.10.3 Telnet

Telnet is an application which provides some services using TCP. It provides terminal connection services and also supports the terminal to host connection over an internet work. It is measurely composed by client entity and server entity. Client entity provides services to access host and server entity provides services to be access by clients. Every workstation operating systems such as OS/2 and windows can provides telnet server supports using telnet application.

3.10.4 File Transfer Protocol (FTP)

FTP uses TCP services to provide file transfer services to applications. FTP includes a client and server portions. The server FTP for a session initiation sends the direction to the clients FTP, when request is made from the clients to downloaded certain files from the server. In a similar manner, In reverse order, process will carry on when a file is uploaded from client to server.

3.10.5 Simple N/W Management Protocol

SNMP provides intelligence and services to effectively manage an internet work. This protocol measurely uses in hubs that preferred to use a technology to monitor and manage the information between two connective workstations.

3.10.6 Network File System Protocol

The network file system protocol use IP services by server to share the disk space or the files either by the LAN manager network or LAN application. This protocol is useful in the environment in which the servers are running different operating systems.

3.10.7 Simple Mail Transfer Protocol

SMTP user TCP services connections to transfer the text oriented electronic mail among the user on the same host or among host over the network. Most electronic mail system now a days provides some form of SMTP gateway to let user connected globally.

3.11 OSI (Open System Inter Connection) Model

This model is based on proposal developed by the international standards organization (ISO) as a first step towards the international standardization of protocol used in various layer.This model is called the OSI (Open System Interconnection) reference model because it deals with connecting open system i.e. the systems that are open for communication with other systems.

The OSI model has seven layers as application, presentation, session, transport, network, data link and physical layer. The principles that were applied to arrive at the seven layers are as follows :

i) The layer should be created where a different level of abstraction is needed.
ii) Each layer should perform well defined functions.
iii) The functions of each layer should be chosen with an eye toward defining internationally standardized protocols.
iv) The layer boundaries should be chosen to minimize the information flow across the interface.
v) The sequence of layers is to be followed from lower level to the high level layer *i.e.*, physical to application at the receiving end, whereas, the same is reversed at the sending end.

Physical Layer

Physical layer is the lowest level layer of the OSI model and it covers the physical interface between devices i.e. the physical and the electrical characteristic of the connection that make up the network. It includes such things as interface specification as well as detailed specification. For the use of twisted pair, fiber optic and coaxial cable.

Data Link Layer

Data Link Layer is responsible for establishing an error free communication path between two terminals.

Network Layer

Network Layer set up a logical path between source and destination and also responsible for switching and routing messages to their proper destination. It coordinates for addressing and the delivering messages.

Transport Layer

The Transport Layer splits the messages into smaller units and the sequencing of the messages and is also responsible for ensuring whether the message has been delivered successfully or not.

Session Layer

Session Layer provides the means of establishing, maintaining and terminating a session between two users. For example—once we are dealing with rediffmail Inbox and incase if we do not hit the Inbox continuously for 20 minutes then automatically a protocol which is we invoke when there is no hitting of the inbox in 20 minutes sends the information to the other terminals *i.e.*, the server and the session for the user is terminated. This session is the facilities given by the server. In case a user wants to use inbox further, he has to login again.

Presentation Layer

Presentation layer provides the facilities to converts, encoded, transmitted data into a displayable form.

Application Layer

Application layer is the user oriented layer (*i.e.*, the facility of the application at the user terminal). It provides a service that directly supports the end user of network. In simple words we can say, it deals with application programming interface (API's).

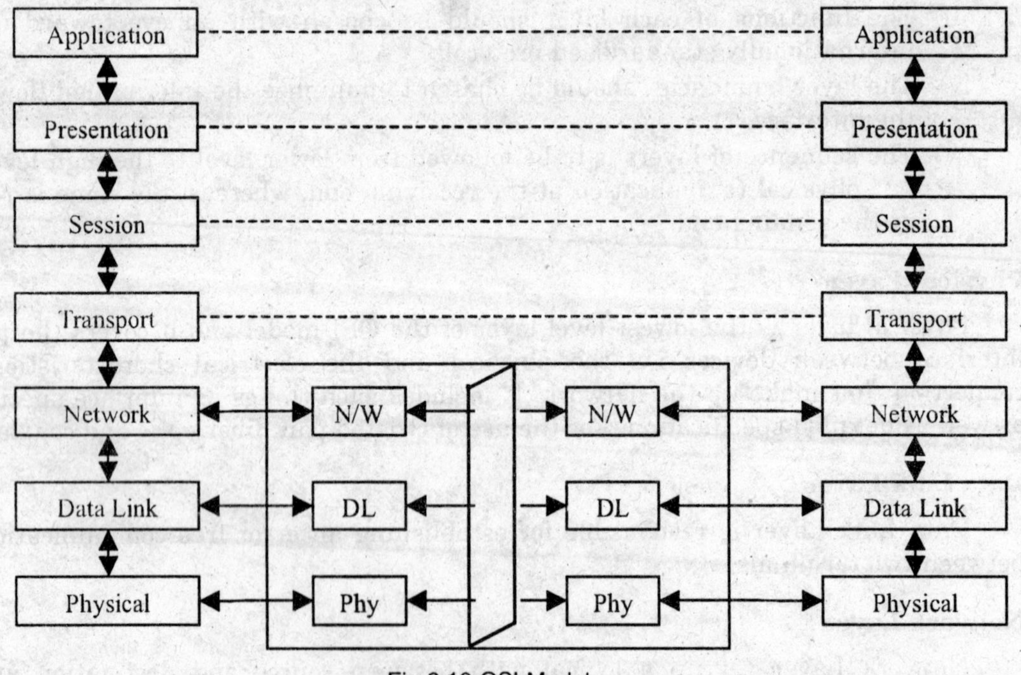

Fig 3.10 OSI Model

3.12 Summary

- Connectivity is the unbiased transport of packets between two end points. This is also the essential definition of "IP" (Internet Protocol).
- Inter-Process Communication (IPC) is a set of techniques for the exchange of data

between two or more threads in one or more processes. Processes may be running on one computer or on two or more computers connected by a network. IPC techniques are divided into methods for message passing, synchronization, shared memory, and remote procedure calls (RPC).

- A wide area network or WAN, spans a large geographical area, often a country or continent. It contains a collection of machines intended for running user (*i.e.*, application) programs.
- Switched Multimegabit Data Service (SMDS) is a Connectionless, high speed, packet switched data service. SMDS is used to interconnect distribute corporate LANs and WANs through the public Networks, because it is connectionless, SMDS elements, the need for carrier switches to establish a call path between two points of data transmission.
- ATM scheme is widely used for data communication network. ATM Network uses the ATM switch, which receives the requests for data transfer from different computers. The ATM switch facilitates the data Transmission in Asynchronous mode.
- ISDN stands for integrated services digital network. It is the forerunner of B-ISDN. ISDN was designed to utilize the pre-existing copper wiring that runs from the telephone exchange. To telephones on the customer premises.

REVIEW QUESTIONS

1. Name the different areas of network management.

   [**Ans.** Configuration, accounting, fault, security, and performance.]

2. What are the goals of performance management?

   [**Ans.** Measure and make available various aspects of network performance so that internetwork performance can be maintained at an acceptable level.]

3. What are the goals of configuration management?

   [**Ans.** Monitor network and system configuration information so that the effects on network operation of various versions of hardware and software elements can be tracked and managed.]

4. What are the goals of accounting management?

   [**Ans.** Measure network utilization parameters so that individual or group uses on the network can be regulated appropriately.]

5. What are the goals of fault management?

   [**Ans.** Detect, log, notify users of, and automatically fix network problems to keep the network running effectively.]

6. What are the goals of security management?

   [**Ans.** Control access to network resources according to local guidelines so that the network cannot be sabotaged and so that sensitive information cannot be accessed by those without appropriate authorization.]

Chapter 4

Client/Server System Development Software

4.1 Business Process Reengineering

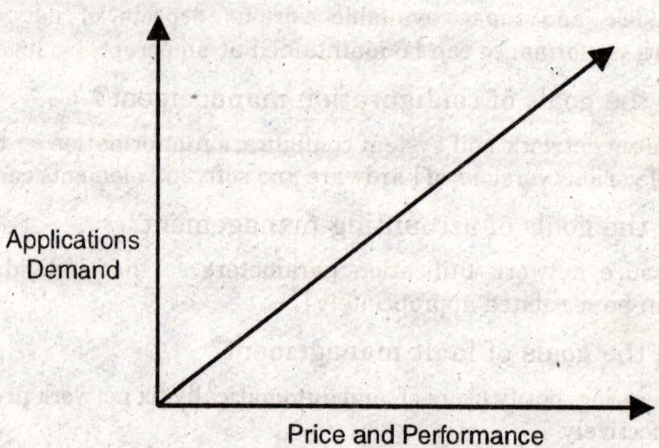

Fig 4.1 Systems Development Demand

The Software processes are mainly classified into two activities as software development and software maintenance. The Software development process (SDLC) gives a direction of flow of activities, requirement analysis, Software design, implementation and testing.

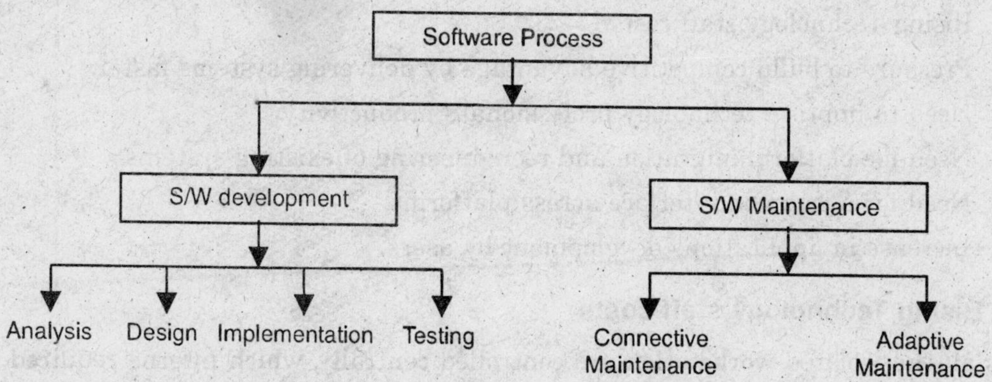

To avoid the maintenance at the most usually two kinds of special testing are performed, *i.e.*, α-testing (the testing by the team of the organization, which is not the part of Software development) and β-testing (the testing by the friendly client, so that the chances of occurring the error at the part of client testing should be minimum). One another process which is as important is processed in the reverse direction of Software engineering from implementation to Software design to requirement analysis to Software design to implementation. So that the maintenance can be avoided is known as business process reengineering or Software reengineering on the basis of cost and customer services.

Business process re-engineering technologies helps organizations achieve competitive advantage through substantive improvements in quality, customer services and costs. BPR must be aligned with technology strategy to be effective. Organizations must use technology to enable the business change defined by the BPR effect.

The optimized ratio is B/D where 3 are for Software development and 7 for the Software maintenance. The 3/7 is not preferred because in these situations Software goes in corrective maintenance i.e. we can say that in this case the chances are higher to goes into corrective maintenance and also adoptive maintenance. The best ratio for Sofware processes is 4/6 in which 4 is for Software development and 6 is for Software maintenance.

4.2 Factors Driving Demand for Application Software Development

Following are the major Driving forces which enforce the development of client/server Application Software, because it has got numerous benefits in terms of cost saving time to market new products (has the numerous client and workstation are connected, so the productivity services flayered rapidly) customer satisfaction and so on. The one of the prominent reason to develop the centrally existing application is TQM (Total Quality Management). Once we talk about isolated workstation, the facility of the developed product, the provided interface upto certain extent depends upon the composition of Hardware and existing Software of the workstation, but once we talk about server orientation (central node) the features of the developed Software are coordinating with only one system which is configured with dense Hardware and sensitive Software. With the help of this universally common interface and the customer services, facilities of software can be shared globally.

- Rising Technology staff costs.
- Pressure to build competitive advantage by delivering systems faster.
- Need to improve technology professional's productivity.
- Need for platform migration and reengineering of existing systems.
- Need for a common interface across platforms.
- Increase in applications development by users.

4.2.1 Rising Technology staff costs

As all the isolated workstation are controlled centrally, which interns required less number of qualified staff particularly toward the developed software i.e. the professionals are required to deal with the server, sub server and further sub server to the sub server. In this way total quality management can be maintained with few and highly qualified technology professionals.

4.2.2 Pressure to Build Competitive Advantage by Delivering Systems Faster

The major objective of centrally developed software is towards the services provided to client and customers that is why more and more vendors are releasing their client server version with having more and new facility with their upcoming versions.

A major example of this kind of system delivery is the time of .com era when with in 3 months, the vendor Microsoft release 3 versions of their product internet explorer with updated and required facility either from market or customers.

4.2.3 Need to Improve Technology Professional's Productivity

The Computer Aided Software Development Engineering (CASE) tools and other technologies that speed up S/W development are being used 70% of the top IT executives has been maintained by a survey. The CASE market is growing at the rate of 30% per year just to enhance the productivity of the professionals.

4.2.4 Need for Platform Migration and Reengineering of Existing Systems

BPR attempts to reduce business process cost and complexity by moving decision making responsibility to those individuals who first encounter the customer or problem. Organizations are using the client/server to bring information to the workplace of empoered employees.

4.2.5 Need for Common Interface Across Platforms

According to the single system Image concept A common user interface across all platforms is twice as important as the next most important criteria as a purchasing criterion for software.

The single system image concept is that every user from every workstation have access to every application for which they have a need and right without regard to or awareness of the technology.

4.2.6 Increase in Applications Development by Users

The trend towards application development by end-users will create disasters. Without a consistent, disciplined approach that makes the developer insensitive to the underlying components of the technology. End user application developers also must understand the Intricacies of languages and Interfaces.

The next and necessary step is to determine how the tools will be used within your organization. This step involves the creation of your SDE without the integration of an SDE methodology; organizations will be unable to achieve the benefits of client/server computing. Discipline and Standards are essential to create platform Independent systems. With the uncertainly over which technologies will survive as standards, the isolation of application from their computing platform is an essential Insurance policy.

4.3 Client / Server Systems Development Methodology

The purpose of a methodology is to describe a disciplined process through which technology can be applied to achieve the business objectives. The client/server system development methodology defines the following factors as System Integration Life Cycle (SILC).

i) System Planning.
ii) Project Initiation
iii) Architecture Definition
iv) Analysis
v) Design
vi) Development
vii) Engineering
viii) Implementation
ix) Post Implementation Support

4.3.1 System Planning

- Initiate Systems Planning
- Gather Data
- Identify Current Situation
- Describe Existing Systems
- Define Requirements
- Analyse Applications and Data Architectures
- Analyse Technology Platforms
- Prepare Implementation Plan

The system planning defines the Scopes of the system, the methodology we are going to use, identification of the tasks, estimation of the systems in terms of cost schedule and quality. Quality is measure on the basis of quality parameter like product transition, product revision and product operation, which takes care of the concept like platform independenceness, integrity, inter operability, flexibility, maintainability, interactive ness, correctness, efficiency (in terms of response time, through put and sickness time) and also establishing the appropriate staff and their organizing.

System Planning densely takes care about the project schedule (the schedule in term of time duration for the different subsystem and the modules of the subsystem of a system) and milestones (the task i.e. functions to be achieved with in that duration).

NOTE : The major activity of the system planning are describing the existing system, identifying the current situation, framing the requirement gathering the data for requirement start the system planning onwards and finally analyzing the data architecture.

4.3.2 Project Initiation

- Identify Relationship to long range systems plan.
- Initiate Project.
- Prepare plan for next phase.

The project initiation focuses on preparing the plan of the different phases, the activity of the system, subsystem and identification the relationship among the different subsystems.

4.3.3 Architecture Definition

- Gather Data.
- Expand the requirements to the next level of detail.
- Conceptualize alternative solutions.
- Develop proposed conceptual architecture.
- Select specific products and vendors.

In the architecture definition phase, the cost of different operations, the response time of the system i.e. what is the real speed of the system, the interactiveness (user friendly), and the availability of the assisting component (Sophisticated H/W & S/W). The security of the system i.e. How the authorization should be given and the flexibility of the system ie. How easily it can be maintained (updated).

The major architecture definition phase takes care about the expansion of the requirement to the next level of detail. The conceptual alternative solution, the data gathering of alternative solution.

4.3.4 Analysis

- Gather Data
- Develop a logical model of the new application system.
- Define general information system requirements.
- Prepare external system design.

The major responsibility of the Analysis phase are developing the logical model (blue prints) of new application system identifying the general requirements of the information system in terms of their's facilities.

4.3.5 Design

- Perform Preliminary Design.
- Perform Detailed Design.
- Design System Test.
- Design user Aids.
- Design Conversion System.

In the design phase the logical flow of the information is represented by either system design or detailed design. Detailed design sometimes also called as architecture design.

The system design simply takes of the integration of the subsystem of a system and the integration of modules of any subsystem whereas architecture design takes of the linear and non linear data structure used. The algorithmic structure followed, the languages used for different used data structures.

4.3.6 Development

- Set up the Development Environment.
- Code Modules.
- Develop User Aids.
- Conduct System Test.

The next phase is the development phase. The development phase, focuses on, setting up the developing interfaces the functionality of the different modules.

4.3.7 Facilities Engineering

- Gather Data.
- Conduct Site Survey.
- Document Facility Requirements.
- Design Data Center.
- Plan Site Preparation.
- Prepare Site
- Plan Hardware Installation.
- Install and Test Hardware.

The facilities Engineering phase deals with grater data, conduct site survey and Design data center. It also emphasizes on plan site preparation, prepare site and Plan hardware installation and also install and test Hardware. This phase majorly focuses on the H/W and S/W coordination.

4.3.8 Implementation

- Develop Contingency Procedures.

- Develop Maintenance and Release Procedures.
- Train System Users.
- Ensure that Production Environment is ready.
- Convert Existing Data.
- Install Application System.
- Provide Warranty Supports.

The implementation phase deals with develop contingency procedures, develop maintenance and release procedures, Train the system users and ensure that production environment is ready. It also emphasizes on Install application system and provide warranty supports. It majorly focuses on coding structure & case tools.

4.3.9 Post-Implementation Support

- Initiate support and maintenance services.
- Support Hardware and communication configuration.
- Support Software.
- Perform other project completion tasks as appropriate.

The next phase i.e. last is the post implementation support. The post implementation support takes care about aspected feature which may be the part of the adaptive maintenance.

This phase deals with initiate the support and maintenance services, support Hardware, Software and communication configuration. It majorly focuses on perform other project completion tasks as appropriate.

4.4 Client / Server Development-Hardware

1. Hardware / Network.
2. Different Processing.
   v) PC level processing units.
   vi) Macintosh.
   vii) Note Books.
   viii) Pen
3. Server and Workstation
   iii) UNIX
   iv) X-terminals
4. Server Hardware
5. Data Storage
   viii) Magnetic Disk.
   ix) Mirrored Disk.
   x) Tape.
   xi) RAID.
   xii) Optical Disk.

xiii) CD-Rom.

xiv) WORM.

6. Power Protection Devices

iii) UPS

iv) Surge (Stream) protectors (CVT)

7. N/W Interfaces

i) NIC's (Network Interface Cards).

ii) Token Ring

iii) Ethernet

iv) FDDI

v) CDDI.

4.4.1 Hardware / Network

By selecting client hardware for end users, most organizations define the standards for classes of users and accordingly the selection of the hardware takes place. This set of standards simplifies the appropriate hardware for the user and it also allow boss to make the purchasing agreement (the needs of the hardware for a specific tasks) so that in future if the specific kind of activity is performed, the same type of hardware is supposed to be.

There are number of issues to consider while selecting the client workstation

i) Processor type.

ii) Co-processor capabilities.

iii) Internal Bus structure.

iv) The size of the base units.

Analyzing the above, the client workstation is fixed with certain hardware requirement. Out of these issues, one important factor is also considered which is responsible for clients workstation interface i.e. graphical user interface (GUI). GUI applications requires better screen drivers and other hardware and software composition accordingly.

As screens larger than 15″ PC standards are required for only those users who normally at a time deals with more than two three active windows. In such cases we require monitors having more than 15″ screens. As GUI concerned the use of images, graphics, full motion videos one required with inturns requires the high resolution adaptors.

If regular access of LAN data is required. A router base internetworking implementation is required and if only occasional off line access is required, then bridges can be used. The benefits of using router is providing the addition advantage of support of Multiprotocol internet working these routers usually installed mostly in Ethernet or Token Ring Environment.

4.4.2 Different Processing

(i) PC level Processing Unit

The client/server processing requirement and input output demands vary with the server and client hosted application. In general, the client that supports protected mode addressing should be purchased for an organization. While UNIX N/W Client/Server system is there. This implies for the better coordination the existence of 32 bit processors at the server workstation. As it does not coordinates effectively with the 16 bits processors systems.

Likewise, lot more hardware and the application orientations of the clients workstation and sever workstation are checked their priority are monitored and accordingly the best setup is hosted.

(ii) Macintosh

The Mac system 7 operating system is visually intuitive and provides the best productivity when response time to GUI operations is secondary. The Motorola 68040, 8Mb Ram, 12 MB disk is recommended. By early 1995. The availability of power PC technology and the integration of system 7 with AIX and windows means that users will need considerably more processor capacity. The powerful PC will provide this for the same or lower cost then the existing Motorola technology.

(iii) Note Books

Notebooks computer is a lessly graphical user interface but highly time complexed computer systems. This usually use the Intel PC based technology as the centrally server workstation. This hardware technology coordinate with remote chip based system which less equipped with graphical images and other graphics facilities, but they are useful as they are rough preview of the graphics which are daimly important as informatics as all web enabled cell phone specially Reliance.

(iv) Pen

Mostly pen technology are bearing laser technology and register diffusing technology which makes its impact on the screen and on the basis of impact, the central processor system is monitoring the data input. Sometime it is also known as personal digital assistant or packet size computing. Example, Digital Diary. The screen resolution is kept usually very high. So that the minor digital signal impact can felt easily.

4.4.3 Server and Workstation

(i) UNIX Work Station

UNIX client workstations are used when the client processing needs are intensive. In many applications requiring UNIX, X-terminals connected to a UNIX presentation server will be the clients of choice. A UNIX client workstation will then have more processing power than a PC client.

The introduction of S/W from sun soft, insignia solutions and locus computing that supports the execution of DOS and windows 3.x applications in a UNIX window makes the UNIX desktop available to users requiring software from both environments. The power PC and spare technologies will battle for this market place.

The UNIX workstation provides the capability to perform presentation services, processing services, database services, communication services and application services.

(ii) X—Terminals

X—Terminals provide the capability to perform only presentation services at the workstation. Processing services are provided by another UNIX, window 3.x, NT, OS/2 or VMS server. Database communications and application services are provided by the same or other servers in the network. The minimum memory configuration requirement for an x-terminal used in a client / server application is 4-8 MB RAM, depending on the number of open windows.

4.4.4 Server Hardware

Server requirements vary according to the complexity of the application and the distribution of work. Because servers are multi user devices, the number of active users is also a major sizing factor. Servers that provide for 32 bit preemptive multitasking operating systems with storage protection are preferred in the multi-user environment.

Intel based power PCs and symmetric multi processors (SMPs) are commonly used for workgroup LANs with file and application service requirements.

SMP products are provided by vendors such as IBM, Compaq and Net Frame. The Traditional UNIX Vendors, such as SUN, IBM provides server Hardware for applications requiring UNIX stability and capacity for database and application servers and large workgroup file services.

The SMP products, in conjunction with RAID disk technology can be configured to provide mainframe level reliability for client/server applications. It is critical that the server be architected as part of the systems management support strategy to achieve this reliability.

4.4.5 Data Storage

Permanent storage requirements are very application specific. In addition to quantity of disk storage, the issues of performance and reliability must be considered; software and large reports distributed to a large number of users are good candidates for this media. CD ROM is also more Reliable for shipping and distribution than magnetic disks or tape.

(i) Magnetic Disk

Disk storage devices should use the SCS1-2 standard controller interface. This provides the best performance in a standards based environments. Many vendors provide high-capacity, high performance and highly reliable disk storage devices for this controller. The use of high capacity cache storage dramatically improves performance. The use of compression software can easily double this capacity with the increasing size of GUI software and the introduction of multimedia applications, the demand for disk capacity will increase rapidly.

(ii) Mirrored Disk

Mirrored disks are designed to provide high data availability by automatically maintaining identical information on two partner disks. When an application writes to a disk, disk mirroring causes the information to be written to both drive partners. Applications running on the system are unaware that disk mirroring is present.

Mirrored disk are used for the reliable data storage. There are the Hardware technologies which creates the backup of data at every movement. So that in case if the primary disk data is get corrupted, the original data can be retrieved from the minored disk.

(iii) RAID—Redundant Array of Inexpensive Drives

These enabled data files to be spread across several physical devices i.e. a execution at the same workstation are being also copies on the physical devices of the remote workstation, some times it is also called as Raid disk Array. It is a server to sub server process. High capacity caches must be used in conjunction with RAID to achieve optimum performance. The SBC will be identified as part of the architecture definition.

In computing, the acronym RAID (originally redundant array of inexpensive disks, now also known as redundant array of independent disks) refers to a data storage scheme using multiple hard drives to share or replicate data among the drives. Depending on the configuration of the RAID (typically referred to as the RAID level), the benefit of RAID is one or more of increased data integrity, fault-tolerance, throughput or capacity compared to single drives. In its original implementations, its key advantage was the ability to combine multiple low-cost devices using older technology into an array that offered greater capacity, reliability, speed, or a combination of these things, than was affordably available in a single device using the newest technology.

At the very simplest level, RAID combines multiple hard drives into a single logical unit. Thus, instead of seeing several different hard drives, the operating system sees only one. RAID is typically used on server computers, and is usually (but not necessarily) implemented with identically sized disk drives. With decreases in hard drive prices and wider availability of RAID options built into motherboard chipsets, RAID is also being found and offered as an option in more advanced personal computers. This is especially true in computers dedicated to storage-intensive tasks, such as video and audio editing.

The original RAID specification suggested a number of prototype "RAID levels", or combinations of disks. Each had theoretical advantages and disadvantages. Over the years, different implementations of the RAID concept have appeared. Most differ substantially from the original idealized RAID levels, but the numbered names have remained. This can be confusing, since one implementation of RAID 5, for example, can differ substantially from another. RAID 3 and RAID 4 are often confused and even used interchangeably.

The very definition of RAID has been argued over the years. The use of the term redundant leads many to object to RAID 0 being called a RAID at all. Similarly, the change from inexpensive to independent confuses many as to the intended purpose of RAID. There are even some single-disk implementations of the RAID concept.

(iv) Magnetic Tape

Magnetic tape is a non-volatile storage medium consisting of a magnetic coating on a thin plastic strip. Nearly all recording tape is of this type, whether used for video, audio storage or general purpose digital data storage using a computer.

Magnetic-optical and optical tape storage products have been developed using many of the same concepts as magnetic storage, but have achieved little commercial success.

Tape is a very popular form of low cost magnetic storage and is used primarily for backup purposes. The standard backup tape device today is digital audio tape (DAT). These tapes provides approximately 1.2 GB of storage on a standard cartridge-size cassette tape. Tape is sequential medium and does not adequately support direct (random) access to information. If an organization standardizes on a single tap form at and technology, distribution of information by mailing tape can be a cost effective communications mechanism for large quantities of information that do not require real time transmission.

(v) Optimal Disks

In computing, sound reproduction, and video, an optical disc is a flat, circular, usually polycarbonate disc where data is stored in the form of pits (or bumps) within a flat surface. This data is generally accessed when a special material on the disc (often aluminum) is illuminated with a laser diode. The pits distort the reflected laser light.

The promotion of standardised optical storage is undertaken by the Optical Storage Technology Association (OSTA). The information on an optical disc is stored sequentially on a continuous spiral track from the innermost track to the outermost track.

Erasable optical drives are used as an alternative to standard magnetic disk drives when speed of access is not important and the volume of data stored is large. They can be used for image, multimedia, back up or high volume, low activity storage.

(vi) CD ROM

CD-ROM (an abbreviation of "Compact Disc Read-Only Memory") is a compact disc that contains data accessible by a computer. While the compact disc format was originally designed for music storage and playback, the format was later adapted to hold any form of binary data. CD-ROMs are popularly used to distribute computer software, including games and multimedia applications, though any data can be stored (up to the capacity limit of a disc). Some CDs hold both computer data and audio with the latter capable of being played on a CD player, whilst data (such as software or digital video) is only usable on a computer. These are called Enhanced CDs.

Although many people use lowercase letters in this acronym, proper presentation is in all capital letters with a hyphen between CD and ROM. Compact disk read only memory optical drives are used for storage of information that is distributed for read only use. A singly CD can hold upto 800 MB of information.

All software and documentation will be distributed only on CD ROM. The advent of multimedia applications and the resulting storage requirements will further drive the demand for CD ROM.

(vii) WORM (Write Once Read Many)

These are the optical drives are used to store information that is to be written to the disk just once and being read by number of remote workstations. (This is the client workstation through sub server process). Traffic ticket issued by police departments are scanned and stored on WORM drives for reference on payment or non payment. The WORM technology guarantees that the image can not be tampered with.

A magnetic drive can be used to store an index into the data on the WORM drive. Data can be effectively erased from a WORM by removing reference to it from the Index. This can be useful when a permanent audit trail of changes is required.

4.4.6 Power Protection Devices

There are some devices that are specially dedicating to help your business objectives.

The power protection devices are as such type of services. The major power protection devices are:

- UPS (Uninterruptible Power Supply)
- Surge Protectors.

(i) UPS (Uninterruptible Power Supply)

An **uninterruptible power supply (UPS), uninterruptible power source** or sometimes called a **battery backup** is a device which maintains a continuous supply of electric power to connected equipment by supplying power from a separate source when utility power is not available.

A UPS is inserted between the source of power (typically commercial utility power) and the load it is protecting. When a power failure or abnormality occurs, the UPS will effectively switch from utility power to its own power source almost instantaneously.

While not limited to any particular type of equipment, a UPS is typically used to protect computers, telecommunication equipment or other electrical equipment where an unexpected power disruption could cause injuries, fatalities, serious business disruption or data loss. UPS units come in sizes ranging from units which will back up a single computer without monitor (around 200 VA) to units which will power entire data centers or buildings (several megawatts). Larger UPS units typically work in conjunction with generators.

Historically, UPS units were very expensive and were most likely to be used on expensive computer systems and in areas where the power supply is interrupted frequently. However, UPS units are now more affordable, and have become an essential piece of equipment for data centers and business computers, but are also used for personal computers, entertainment systems and more.

In North America in particular, the electrical grid is under increasing strain particularly during heavy demand periods such as summer when air conditioning use is at its highest. In order to prevent blackouts, electrical utilities will sometimes use a process called load shedding, which involves cutting the power to large groups of customers for short periods of time. The single biggest event that brought attention to the need for UPS power backup units was the 2003 North America blackout in the north-eastern US and eastern Canada.

A UPS is not to be confused with a standby generator, which does not provide protection from a momentary power interruption and may result in an interruption when it is switched into service, whether manually or automatically. However, such generators are typically placed before the UPS to provide cover for lengthy outages.

Common Power Problems

There are nine common power problems that UPS units are used to correct. They are as follows:

1. Power failure—Total loss of utility power

2. Power sag—Short term under-voltage
3. Power surge (spike)—Quick burst of over-voltage
4. Under-voltage (brownout)—Low line voltages for an extended period of time
5. Over-voltage—Increased voltages for an extended period of time
6. Line noise—Distortions superimposed on the power waveform.
7. Frequency—Variation of the power waveform.
8. Switching transient—Under-voltage or over-voltage for up to a few nanoseconds.
9. Harmonic Distortion—Multiples of power frequency superimposed on the power waveform.

UPS units are divided into categories based on which of the above problems their UPS units address

UPS Designs

The general categories of modern UPS systems are on-line, off-line and standby. The traditional definition of an on-line UPS was one that continuously powered the load from a DC bus that was supplied by two sources: batteries, and DC rectified from the incoming AC. In a standby UPS, the load is powered by the source until the power fails and then it quickly switches on a battery source and a DC-to-AC converter. Since 2004, the majority of units sold below 1 kVA are standby UPS. Fuel cell UPS have also been developed in recent years using hydrogen and a fuel cell as a power source potentially providing long runtimes in a small space.

Rotary

Rotary uninterruptible power supply equipment contain a motor-generator system with a large flywheel that keeps the generator rotating and producing electric power while an auxiliary generator is started at the moment of power interruption. Sometimes the flywheel itself is used to start the generator. These systems can typically cover a 30 second interruption until the auxiliary motor starts. Rotary UPS equipment may be more tolerant of lightning strikes than static equipment.

Standby (Offline)

With this design, the UPS simply passes utility power through to the load until either a power failure, sag or spike occurs, at which point, the UPS switches the load onto battery power and disconnects the utility power until it returns to an acceptable level. In this design, the UPS unit only charges the battery when it is running on utility power. This design is the most cost effective and typically makes use of a square wave or modified square wave inverter. These units are typically found in units 600 VA and below and designed for home use. This design solves problems 1—3, however the disadvantage of this is that any of the power problems numbered 4 - 9 will cause the UPS to switch to battery, and may cause it to completely drain the battery and shut off even though line voltage is still present.

Line-interactive

Line interactive UPS units are designed so that the inverter is always connected to the output of the UPS. When line power is present, the inverter operates in reverse to charge the battery. When utility power fails, the UPS reverses the power flow from the inverter and provides power to the load. This design provides better filtering than a standby unit because the inverter is always connected to the load.

Line interactive units typically will incorporate an automatic voltage regulator. AVR allows the UPS to effectively step-up or step-down the incoming line voltage without switching to battery power. This allows the UPS to correct most long term over-voltages or under-voltages without draining the batteries. Another advantage is that it reduces the number of transfers to battery which extends the lifetime of the batteries.

Line-interactive UPS units are the most common design for units in the 0.5 kVA to 5 kVA range. They are typically used in small server environments.

Delta Conversion Online

Delta conversion is a new concept online technology. Unlike offline technology, no “switch on” time is required. Like other True-Online technology, a continuous separation of load and primary power is offered except the frequency (#7). With Delta Conversion, frequency is synchronized with main input. The reason for this technology (which all True-Online UPS have) is to synchronize the frequency with the main input (normal operation mode). This is necessary when UPS transfers from normal mode to bypass mode. It will request a frequency synchronize between input/output for a successful transfer. In fact, other True-Online UPS will supply separation frequency only when bypass mode is disabled. With the UPS, bypass mode is very important. Like brakes or air bags in a car, it is a "fail safe"; it will help to supply continuous power in case of UPS fault, overload, etc. Within the same range, Delta coversion is cheaper than other True-Online and is efficient up to 97%.

Dual Conversion Online

Dual conversion uninterruptible power supplies operate by converting incoming utility AC power to DC and then convert the DC back to AC to power the connected equipment. This is also called "double conversion." The batteries are directly connected to the DC level, which provides an excellent filter for removing line noise. Effectively, this design isolates the load from the incoming power and regenerates the sine wave. This yields many benefits. First, this design will protect against all 9 of the common power problems. It allows the UPS to use almost any incoming power, including generators. Second, this design allows the UPS to change incoming voltages and even frequencies easily. Third, because the load is always powered by the inverter, when power fails, there is no transfer time while the UPS switches from line power to battery power. While for most computer applications the switching time is not a problem, some industrial equipment can be harmed (air conditioner compressors for example), making this a better solution. These units are not quite as efficient as line interactive or standby units, however efficiencies do reach as high as 94%.

Online units are typically used in environments with sensitive equipment or environments where a generator is used to provide backup power to the UPS. Almost all UPS units 5 kVA and above are online, although they can be found in capacities as small as 1000VA.

Because the AC output must be constantly generated by the UPS inverter, any failure of this inverter could potentially cause an interruption to the connected load. This is the very thing that the UPS is designed to avoid in the first place. As a measure of reliability, nearly all double conversion UPS units have a sophisticated monitoring system on the output that senses when the voltage or current goes out of specification. A solid state based bypass is then activated to shunt incoming AC directly to the attached load without interruption. This can be due to UPS output inverter failure, input rectifier failure (and eventual battery discharge) or other internal UPS failure. By detecting and shunting raw incoming AC directly to the load, these failures can be avoided. Another mode that requires bypass is fault clearing mode. A fault on the connected load, such as a short circuit in a power distribution panel or computer server power supply, may require more current than the UPS inverter can produce, in order for a fuse to blow, or a breaker to trip. During this mode of operation, bypass current is supplied directly to the output until the fault condition is resolved, usually in a matter of milliseconds. Without bypass modes, all of the other attached loads could lose power if even one experiences a fault. In addition to a high speed electronic bypass, most large (greater than 10KVA) UPS units have one or more layers of switches and/or breakers connected to the input and output to allow the entire unit to be bypassed, shut down, and isolated for maintenance without the connected loads being affected.

The ability for a UPS to bypass itself during abnormal conditions drastically increases the reliability of its output. Double online UPSes have their frequency and phase synchronized with its input (normal operation mode). It's very neccessary when a UPS transfers from normal mode to bypass mode not to disturb the power in any way, including not abruptly changing phase or frequency.

Larger UPSes are expensive but are often a better value. Fewer larger UPSes tend to be more reliable than many smaller units (that don't contain bypass circuits). These units may be marketed as Power conditioners. In data centers, multiple sets of UPS units may run in parallel providing dual sources of conditioned power to static switches that then send power to server loads. In such a system, a complete UPS failure can occur without the loads connected to the switches being affected.

Ferro-resonant

Ferro-resonant units operate in the same way as a standby UPS unit with the exception that a ferro-resonant transformer is used to filter the output. This transformer is designed to hold energy long enough to cover the time between switching from line power to battery power and effectively eliminates the transfer time. Because the transformer typically gives off a lot of heat, these units are typically large, bulky, and inefficient.

While this used to be the dominant type of UPS, they are no longer used for common applications. Power factor correcting equipment found in newer computer systems interacts with the transformer, causing potentially damaging oscillations, and the transformer itself can create distortions which yield power less acceptable than poor quality line AC. These units are still used in some industrial settings, but have mostly disappeared from use with general computer equipment.

DC Systems

Many systems used in telecommunications use DC power (often 48 V). Rather than converting AC to DC to charge batteries, then DC to AC and then convert it back to DC again, some equipment accepts 48 V DC power directly. By simply converting AC power to DC power and adding batteries to the DC side, one or more conversion steps can be saved. There has been much experimentation with DC power for computer servers, in the hope of reducing the likelihood of failure and the cost of equipment. Because there is more current to transfer the same amount of energy at the lower DC voltage, larger conductors are needed, and more energy is lost as heat. On the surface, eliminating a conversion step may seem more reliable, but the ability of online double conversion AC systems to entirely remove themselves from operation and transfer to bypass mode during certain UPS failures and maintenance allows for the connected servers to continue to function on unconditioned AC power while the UPS is repaired. DC-based power systems do not have this luxury, as it requires that all equipment has special DC power inputs that cannot utilize AC voltages in the event of a main DC rectifier or power distribution failure. DC has typically been the dominant power source for telecommunications, and AC has typically been the dominant source for computers and servers. Higher voltage DC (370 volts), however, may find an eventual use in data center applications.

Internal UPS

Internal UPS are a group of uninterruptible power supplies (UPS) designed to be placed inside computer chasses. There are two types of Internal UPS. First type is miniaturized regular UPS that are made small enough to fit into a 5.25" CD-ROM slot bay of a regular computer chassis. The other type is re-engineered switching power supplies that utilize dual power sources of AC and/or DC as power inputs and have an AC-DC built-in switching management control units.

The first type often requires extra connection wires between the internal UPS and computer's power supply. Some internal UPS of this group output high voltage (110 V - 220 V) direct current (DC) and some output nine-step table wave AC. Neither design is safe or energy efficient. As of 2006, there are only couple companies still selling this type of internal UPS in Asia and some part of Europe

The second group of internal UPS replaces the regular switching power supplies. There are three main design mechanisms:

1. Optic-coupling that imitates AC during AC outages. This mechanism was first introduced by American Advanced Power of USA and Magnum Power of UK in 1997, as well as Apollo Power of Taiwan in 1998. This design provides a low-cost solution but its efficiency is low and it has a very low overall wattage (, W) limit.
2. An analog-circuitry-controlled AC-DC switching mechanism. This design also provides a low-cost solution. However, because of the bulky component circuit board, little space is available for increasing wattage output. Plus, the final products are very sensitive to factors such as local heat and causing frequent operational errors. Nevertheless, because of its low cost, it is still popular in China. Most Asian internal UPS manufacturers belong to this category.
3. A CPU controlled AC-DC switching mechanism. This design was first introduced by American Advanced Power Inc. of USA and Amsdeli of Canada. It provides error-free switching control and a complicated communication protocol between the power supply and computer.

Using a UPS

Choosing a UPS

Besides choosing a UPS design, there are 2 key ratings to be aware of when choosing a UPS unit. The first is the VA and wattage ratings. Both the VA (volt amp) and wattage ratings represent the maximum amount of load that can be plugged into a UPS in different ways. The connected load typically should not exceed 80% of either UPS rating. Special considerations must be made when connecting certain equipment such as printers or any type of motorized load. The second factor in deciding which unit to puachase is the amount of runtime the unit will be able to provide when the power fails. This number will vary with the load amount that is plugged into the UPS. For example, a unit may run a single computer for 30 minutes, but with 2 computers plugged in, it might only last 12 minutes. Larger units typically can provide more runtime for the same load than smaller units, however that is not always the case. Some UPS units are designed to provide extended runtime or have the ability to have external battery packs connected.

Replacing batteries

In order to provide the desired protection, UPS units must be properly maintained. Sealed lead/acid batteries have a useful lifetime of 3-5 years. In determining when to replace batteries, it is important to remember that the batteries can be completely bad after 3-5 years and lose their ability to hold a charge gradually over that time. If a UPS started with 1 hour of runtime for the connected load, after 1 year, it may only provide 45 minutes and after 2 years, it may only provide 20 minutes. Some UPS units have user replaceable batteries, but some require a qualified technician or electrician to replace the batteries.

Disposing of UPS batteries

UPS units contain sealed lead-acid batteries and electronics which can be detrimental to the environment.

In the United States, it is illegal to dispose of lead-acid batteries in a landfill, and they must be properly recycled. Sealed lead-acid batteries are recycled in the same manner as car batteries, so any auto shop that accepts used car batteries for recycling will also accept sealed lead acid batteries.

Some Manufacturers

- Alpha—Manufacturer of UPS, surge suppressors, enclosures, batteries, and powering accessories. http://www.alpha.com
- American Power Conversion—Manufacturer of UPS , Power management software, and power system accessories. http://www.apcc.com
- Belkin
- Chloride Power—Manufacture of UPS, Static Transfer Switches, Power Conditioners, DC Power Systems, Industrial Systems power management software.
- Clary Corporation

- Cyber Power Systems—Manufacturer of Standby UPS, Line Interactive UPS, Double Conversion UPS, DC UPS, Surge Protection, and Power Management Software.
- Energy Technologies—Manufacturers **UPS, power and frequency conditioning for** military vehicle and defence areas.
- Euro-Diesel—Manufacturer of dynamic UPS (200 to 2000 kVA). http://www.euro-diesel.com
- General Electric—GE offers static online double conversion UPS systems rating from 250 upto 4.000.000 VA under the Digital Energy brand name.
- Hitec Power Protection—Manufacturer of Rotating UPS and Power conditioning Systems.
- Leviton Manufacturing—Standby, line-interactive and online UPS, power distribution units (PDU's) and surge protective devices (SPD's or TVSS).
- Liebert—A Division of Emerson Network Power.
- MGE UPS Systems—Manufacture of UPS, power distribution units, complete power supply solutions for VoIP and Wi-Fi, static transfer switches, harmonic filters, surge suppressors.
- Mitsubishi Electric **Automation**
- OPTI-UPS—Manufacturers of standby, line-interactive, and online UPS systems.
- Power Innovations International—Makers of online UPS systems.
- Powerware (Eaton Powerware)—Power quality products, UPS, DC power systems, software, services.
- Riello UPS—European manufacturer of single and three phase UPS in the range 400 VA to 6400 kVA.
- Socomec Sicon UPS—Global Supplier and Manufacturer of Power quality products, UPS, DC power systems, software, services http://www.socomec.com/
- TrippLite—Power Protection and Connectivity Products
- Trust - Dutch producer of cheap UPSs for home use.

TSi Power Corporation—Power protection; special equipment input power requirements, including precision voltage regulation.

Prices for UPS have declined to the point where they are Widely used for LAN server protection. These units contain battery backups to enable at least a graceful power down sequence. All busters can be purged and files closed so that no information is lost. Other units provide 15-90 minutes of power backup to handle most powerful failure situations.

(ii) Surge Protectors

A surge protector is an appliance designed to protect electrical devices from power surges and voltage spikes. Surge protectors attempt to regulate the voltage supplied to an electric device by either blocking or shorting to ground voltage above a safe threshold.Surge protectors can be built with one or more of the following electronic components:

- A fuse burns out or a circuit breaker trips when excessive power is being consumed and fed to a device within the designed time lag and current rating. These can protect both from surges caused by the device itself and from external surges that last long enough.
- An iron poor transformer can transmit AC power similar to a normal iron core transformer (although less efficiently), but will be unable to transmit sudden surges that saturate the small iron core.
- A metal oxide varistor (MOV) is a small device that will short when presented with a voltage above its rated "clamping voltage", passing the surge to ground through the MOV rather than through the protected device, provided the current rating (joule) is not exceeded. If the surge exceeds the joule rating, the MOV will be destroyed. Even if not destroyed, MOVs also deteriorate each time they receive a voltage spike, and thus stop working after some time. Some surge protectors have a light to tell you when this stage has been reached.
- A zener diode is a small diode designed to protect against normal spikes in a circuit, especially motor controller circuits. These are sometimes paired as a transient voltage suppression diode.
- A gas discharge tube is used much like a MOV, except that it relies on a trapped gas to become ionized to pass the voltage. This has the advantage of being able to pass much more power without self destructing, but with the disadvantage of reacting to the high voltage more slowly.
- A quarter-wave coaxial surge arrestor is used in RF signal transmission routes. It features a tuned quarter-wavelength short-circuit stub that makes it pass a relatively narrow band of characteristic radio frequencies, but presents a short to any other signals, especially down towards DC. Quarter-wave coax surge arrestors have coaxial terminals, compatible with common coax cable connectors (N, BNC or F types). They provide the strongest available protection for narrow-band RF signals, much better than gas discharge cells typically used in the universal/broadband coax surge arrestors. Very useful for WiFi base band at 2.4 or 5 GHz, not much use for TV/SAT/CaTV, nor for systems sending phantom power for an LNB up the coax downlink.
- An inductor resists sudden changes in current flow. Surge protectors using inductors are sometimes called "series mode" surge protectors, because the inductor is connected in series with the load, rather than diverting current to neutral or ground as with MOVs and diodes.
- A capacitor resists sudden changes in voltage, and acts as a low pass filter, reducing spikes and noise.
- Devices having several outlets with surge protectors described may have all or some outlets protected. The better ones have higher ratings and offer more modes of protection against surges between the phase and neutral and grounding conductors; maybe for telephone and coax cable connections. (The best have insurance policies paying for damages from surges.)
- A UPS of the flywheel type seldom pass surges. The battery variety may absorb spikes much like a capacitor acts as a low pass filter. The battery ones also have

protectors described above. "On line" UPSs provide the best protection. The electronics in computer systems are affected by power fluctuations. Protection can be obtained through the use of surge protection equipment. Every client and server processor and all peripherals should be wired through a surge protector. Most UPS Systems include Integrated surge protectors.

4.5 Summary

- Business process re-engineering technologies helps organizations achieve competitive advantage through substantive improvements in quality, customer services and costs. BPR must be aligned with technology strategy to be effective. Organizations must use technology to enable the business change defined by the BPR effect.
- The major objective of centrally developed S/W is towards the services provided to client and customers that is why more and more vendors are releasing their client server version with having more and new facility with their upcoming versions.
- The purpose of a methodology is to describe a disciplined process through which technology can be applied to achieve the business objectives.
- The client/server processing requirement and input output demands vary with the server and client hosted application. In general, the client that supports protected mode addressing should be purchased for an organization. While UNIX N/W Client/Server system is there.
- Mirrored disks are designed to provide high data availability by automatically maintaining identical information on two partner disks. When an application writes to a disk, disk mirroring causes the information to be written to both drive partners. Applications running on the system are unaware that disk mirroring is present.
- In computing, the acronym RAID (originally redundant array of inexpensive disks, now also known as redundant array of independent disks) refers to a data storage scheme using multiple hard drives to share or replicate data among the drives.
- Magnetic tape is a non-volatile storage medium consisting of a magnetic coating on a thin plastic strip. Nearly all recording tape is of this type, whether used for video, audio storage or general purpose digital data storage using a computer.
- A magnetic drive can be used to store an index into the data on the WORM drive. Data can be effectively erased from a WORM by removing reference to it from the Index. This can be useful when a permanent audit trail of changes is required.
- An uninterruptible power supply (UPS), uninterruptible power source or sometimes called a battery backup is a device which maintains a continuous supply of electric power to connected equipment by supplying power from a separate source when utility power is not available.

REVIEW QUESTIONS

1. Explain the Business Process Reengineering in details.
2. Explain the advantages of Business Process Reengineering.
3. Explain the Factors Driving Demand for Application Software Development.
4. Discuss the Client / Server Systems Development Methodology
5. Discuss the Client / Server Development-Hardware.
6. Write short notes o:

(xv) Magnetic Disk. (xvi) Mirrored Disk.
(xvii) Tape. (xviii) RAID.
(xix) Optical Disk. (xx) CD-Rom.
(xxi) WORM.

Chapter 5

Network Interfaces

In telecommunications and computer networking, a network interface is one of:

1. The point of interconnection between a user terminal and a private or public network.
2. The network card on a computer (in casual usage).
3. The point of interconnection between a public switched telephone network and a privately owned terminal. In the United States, the Code of Federal Regulations, Title 47, part 68, stipulates the interface parameters.

The point of interconnection between one network and another network.

5.1 Network Interface Cards (NICS)

A network card, network adapter or NIC (network interface controller) is a piece of computer hardware designed to allow computers to communicate over a computer network. It is an OSI model layer 2 item because it has a MAC address. It allows users to connect to each other either by using cables or wirelessly.

Every network card has a unique 48-bit serial number called a MAC address, which is written to ROM carried on the car. Every computer on a network must have a card with a unique MAC address. No two cards ever manufactured should share the same address. This is because the Institute of Electrical and Electronics Engineers (The IEEE) is responsible for assigning unique MAC addresses to the vendors of network interface controllers.

Whereas network cards used to be expansion cards that plug into a computer bus, the low cost and ubiquity of the Ethernet standard means that most newer computers have a network interface built into the motherboard. These motherboards either have Ethernet capabilities intergrated into the motherboard chipset, or implemented via a low cost dedicated ethernet chip, connected through the PCI (or the newer PCIe bus). A separate network card is not required unless multiple interfaces are needed or some other type of network is used. Even newer motherboards may have built-in dual network (ethernet) interfaces.

The card implements the electronic circuitry required to communicate using a specific physical layer and data link layer standard such as ethernet or token ring. This provides a base for a full network protocol stack, allowing communication among small groups of computers on the same LAN and large-scale network communications through routable protocols, such as IP.

There are four techniques used for transfer of data, the NIC may use one or more of these techniques.

- Polling is where the microprocessor examines the status of the peripheral under program control.
- Programmed I/O is where the microprocessor alerts the designated peripheral by applying its address to the system's address bus.
- Interrupt-driven I/O is where the peripheral alerts the microprocessor that it's ready to transfer data.
- DMA is where the intelligent peripheral assumes control of the system bus to access memory directly. This removes load from the CPU but requires a separate processor on the card.

A network card typically has a twisted pair, BNC, or AUI socket where the network cable is connected, and a few LEDs to inform the user of whether the network is active, and whether or not there is data being transmitted on it. The Network Cards are typically available in 10/100/1000 Mbits/s(Mbps). This means they can support a transfer rate of 10 or 100 or 1000 Megabits per second.

Client and servers processors are attached to the LAN through NICs. These provide physical connectivity to the wire and protocol support to send / receive messages.

Connectivity and Interoperability between the client workstation and the server are achieved through a combination of physical cables and devices and software's that implements communication protocols. The most popular network protocols are Token ring, Ethernet and FDDI.

5.2 Token Ring

The Token Ring network was originally developed by IBM in the 1970s. It is still IBM's primary local-area network (LAN) technology. The related IEEE 802.5 specification is almost identical to and completely compatible with IBM's Token Ring network. In fact, the IEEE 802.5 specification was modeled after IBM Token Ring, and it continues to shadow IBM's Token Ring development. The term Token Ring generally is used to refer to both IBM's Token Ring network and IEEE 802.5 networks.

Token Ring and IEEE 802.5 networks are basically compatible, although the specifications differ in minor ways. IBM's Token Ring network specifies a star, with all end stations attached to a device called a multistation access unit (MSAU). In contrast, IEEE 802. does not specify a topology, although virtually all IEEE 802.5 implementations are based on a star. Other differences exist, including media type (IEEE 802.5 does not specify a media type, although IBM Token Ring networks use twisted-pair wire) and routing information field size. Figure 9-1 summarizes IBM Token Ring nd IEEE 802.5 specifications.

Figure 5.1 Although Dissimilar in Some Respects, IBM's Token Ring Network and IEEE 802.5 Are Generally Compatible

	IBM Token Ring Network	IEEE 802.5
Data rates	4.16 Mbps	4.16 Mbps
Stations segment	250	250
Topology	Star	Not specitied
Media	Tested pair	Not specitied
Signaling	Basetend	Basetend
Access method	Token possing	Token possing
Enoding	Differential manchester	Differential manchester

Fig. 5.1. Disimilar between token ring and IEEE 802.5

Physical Connections

IBM Token Ring network stations are directly connected to MSAUs, which can be wired together to form one large ring (see Figure 5.2). Patch cables connect MSAUs to

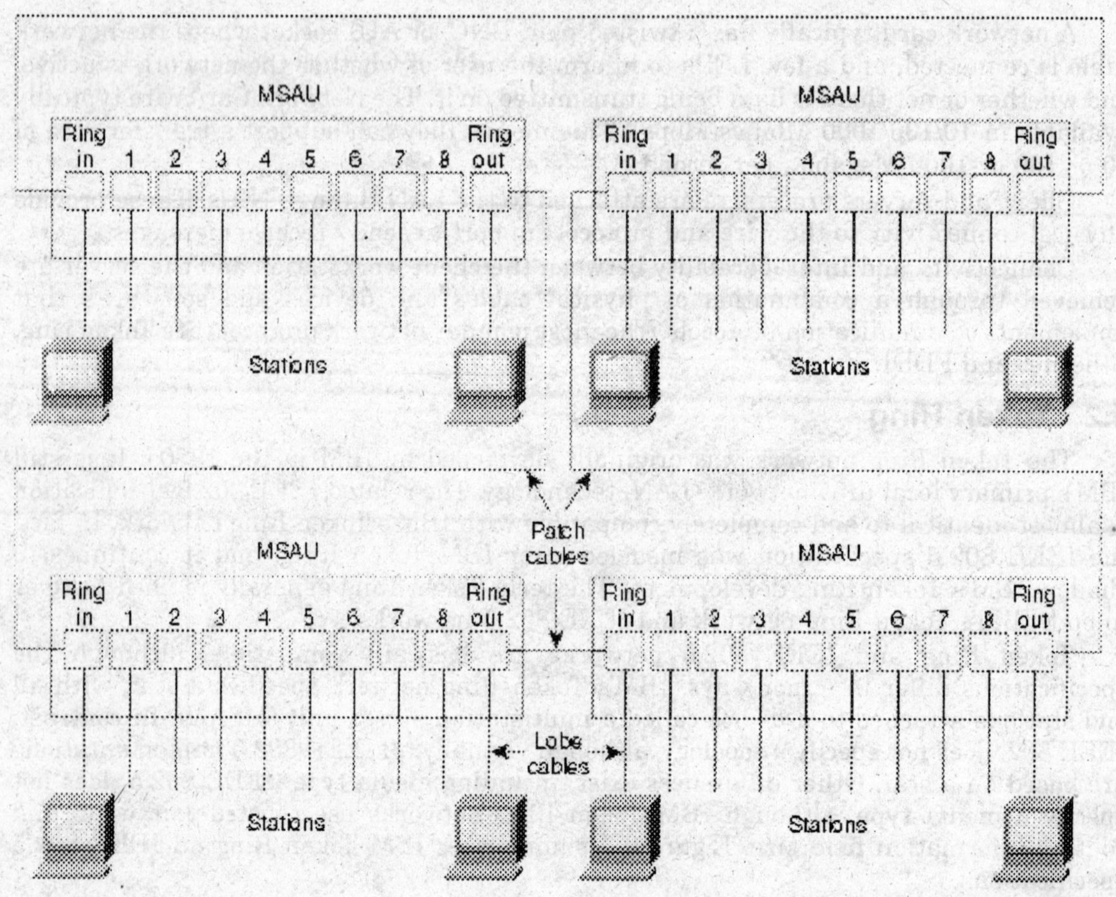

Fig. 5.2

adjacent MSAUs, while lobe cables connect MSAUs to stations. MSAUs include bypass relays for removing stations from the ring.

Figure 5.2 MSAUs Can Be Wired Together to Form One Large Ring in an IBM Token Ring Network

Token Ring Operation

Token Ring and IEEE 802.5 are two principal examples of token-passing networks (FDDI is the other). Token-passing networks move a small frame, called a token, around the network. Possession of the token grants the right to transmit. If a node receiving the token has no information to send, it passes the token to the next end station. Each station can hold the token for a maximum period of time.

If a station possessing the token does have information to transmit, it seizes the token, alters 1 bit of the token (which turns the token into a start-of-frame sequence), appends the information that it wants to transmit, and sends this information to the next station on the ring. While the information frame is circulating in the ring, no token is on the network (unless the ring supports early token release), which means that other stations wanting to transmit must wait. Therefore, collisions cannot occur in Token Ring networks. If early token release is supported, a new token can be released when frame transmission is complete.

The information frame circulates the ring until it reaches the intended destination station, which copies the information for further processing. The information frame continues to circle the ring and is finally removed when it reaches the sending station. The sending station can check the returning frame to see whether the frame was seen and subsequently copied by the destination.

Unlike CSMA/CD networks (such as Ethernet), token-passing networks are deterministic, which means that it is possible to calculate the maximum time that will pass before any end station will be capable of transmitting. This feature and several reliability features, which are discussed in the section "Fault-Management Mechanisms," later in this chapter, make Token Ring networks ideal for applications in which delay must be predictable and robust network operation is important. Factory automation environments are examples of such applications.

Priority System

Token Ring networks use a sophisticated priority system that permits certain user-designated, high-priority stations to use the network more frequently. Token Ring frames have two fields that control priority: the priority field and the reservation field. Only stations with a priority equal to or higher than the priority value contained in a token can seize that token. After the token is seized and changed to an information frame, only stations with a priority value higher than that of the transmitting station can reserve the token for the next pass around the network. When the next token is generated, it includes the higher priority of the reserving station. Stations that raise a token's priority level must reinstate the previous priority after their transmission is complete.

Fault-Management Mechanisms

Token Ring networks employ several mechanisms for detecting and compensating for network faults. For example, one station in the Token Ring network is selected to be the active monitor. This station, which potentially can be any station on the network, acts as a centralized source of timing information for other ring stations and performs a variety of ring-maintenance functions. One of these functions is the removal of continuously circulating frames from the ring. When a sending device fails, its frame may continue to circle the ring. This can prevent other stations from transmitting their own frames and essentially can lock up the network. The active monitor can detect such frames, remove them from the ring, and generate a new token.

The IBM Token Ring network's star topology also contributes to overall network reliability. Because all information in a Token Ring network is seen by active MSAUs, these devices can be programmed to check for problems and selectively remove sations from the ring, if necessary.

A Token Ring algorithm called beaconing detects and tries to repair certain network faults. Whenever a station detects a serious problem with the network (such as a cable break), it sends a beacon frame, which defines a failure domain. This domain includes the station reporting the failure, its nearest active upstream neighbor (NAUN), and everything in between. Beaconing initiates a process called autoreconfiguration, in which nodes within the failure domain automatically perform diagnostics in an attempt to reconfigure the network around the failed areas. Physically, the MSAU can acomplish this through electrical reconfiguration.

Frame Format

Token Ring and IEEE 802.5 support two basic frame types: tokens and data/command frames. Tokens are 3 bytes in length and consist of a start delimiter, an access control byte, and an end delimiter. Data/command frames vary in size, depending on the size of the Information field. Data frames carry information for upper-layer protocols, while command frames contain control information and have no data for upper-layer protocols. Both formats are shown in Figure 5.3.

Figure 5-3 IEEE 802.5 and Token Ring Specify Tokens and Data/Command Frames.

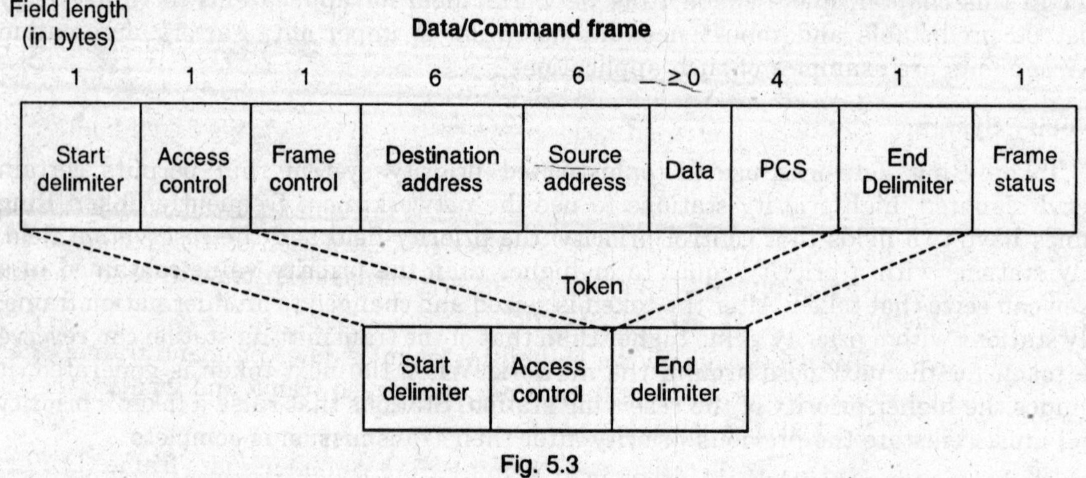

Fig. 5.3

Token Frame Fields

The three token frame fields illustrated in Figure 5.3 are summarized in the descriptions that follow:

- **Start delimiter**—Alerts each station of the arrival of a token (or data/command frame). This field includes signals that distinguish the byte from the rest of the frame by violating the encoding scheme used elsewhere in the frame.
- **Access-control byte**—Contains the Priority field (the most significant 3 bits) and the Reservation field (the least significant 3 bits), as well as a token bit (used to differentiate a token from a data/command frame) and a monitor bit (used by the active monitor to determine whether a frame is circling the ring endlessly). End delimiterSignals the end of the token or data/command frame. This field also contains bits to indicate a damaged frame and identify the frame that is the last in a logical sequence.

Data/Command Frame Fields

Data/command frames have the same three fields as Token Frames, plus several others. The Data/command frame fields illustrated in Figure 5.3 are described in the following summaries:

- **Start Delimiter**—Alerts each station of the arrival of a token (or data/command frame). This field includes signals that distinguish the byte from the rest of the frame by violating the encoding scheme used elsewhere in the frame.
- **Access-Control Byte**—Contains the Priority field (the most significant 3 bits) and the Reservation field (the least significant 3 bits), as well as a token bit (used to differentiate a token from a data/command frame) and a monitor bit (used by the active monitor to determine whether a frame is circling the ring endlessly).
- **Frame-Control Bytes**—Indicates whether the frame contains data or control information. In control frames, this byte specifies the type of control information.
- **Destination and Source Addresses**—Consists of two 6-byte address fields that identify the destination and source station addresses.
- **Data**—Indicates that the length of field is limited by the ring token holding time, which defines the maximum time a station can hold the token.
- **Frame-Check Sequence (FCS)**—Is filed by the source station with a calculated value dependent on the frame contents. The destination station recalculates the value to determine whether the frame was damaged in transit. If so, the frame is discarded.
- **End Delimiter**—Signals the end of the token or data/command frame. The end delimiter also contains bits to indicate a damaged frame and identify the frame that is the last in a logical sequence.
- **Frame Status**—Is a 1-byte field terminating a command/data frame. The Frame Status field includes the address-recognized indicator and frame-copied indicator.

5.3 Ethernet

The term Ethernet refers to the family of local-area network (LAN) products covered by the IEEE 802.3 standard that defines what is commonly known as the CSMA/CD protocol. Three data rates are currently defined for operation over optical fiber and twisted-pair cables:

- 10 Mbps10Base-T Ethernet
- 100 MbpsFast Ethernet
- 1000 MbpsGigabit Ethernet

10-Gigabit Ethernet is under development and will likely be published as the IEEE 802.3 supplement to the IEEE 802.3 base standard in late 2001 or early 2002.

Other technologies and protocols have been touted as likely replacements, but the market has spoken. Ethernet has survived as the major LAN technology (it is currently used for approximately 85 percent of the world's LAN-connected PCs and workstations) because its protocol has the following characteristics:

- Is easy to understand, implement, manage, and maintain
- Allows low-cost network implementations
- Provides extensive topological flexibility for network installation
- Guarantees successful interconnection and operation of standards-compliant products, regardless of manufacturer

Ethernet A Brief History

The original Ethernet was developed as an experimental coaxial cable network in the 1970s by Xerox Corporation to operate with a data rate of 3 Mbps using a carrier sense multiple access collision detect (CSMA/CD) protocol for LANs with sporadic but occasionally heavy traffic requirements. Success with that project attracted early attention and led to the 1980 joint development of the 10-Mbps Ethernet Version 1.0 specification by the three-company consortium: Digital Equipment Corporation, Intel Corporation, and Xerox Corporation.

The original IEEE 802.3 standard was based on, and was very similar to, the Ethernet Version 1.0 specification. The draft standard was approved by the 802.3 working group in 1983 and was subsequently published as an official standard in 1985 (ANSI/IEEE Std. 802.3-1985). Since then, a number of supplements to the standard have been defined to take advantage of improvements in the technologies and to support additional network media and higher data rate capabilities, plus several new optional network access control features.

Ethernet Network Elements

Ethernet LANs consist of network nodes and interconnecting media. The network nodes fall into two major classes:

- **Data terminal equipment (DTE)**—Devices that are either the source or the destination of data frames. DTEs are typically devices such as PCs, workstations, file servers, or print servers that, as a group, are all often referred to as end stations.
- **Data communication equipment (DCE)**—Intermediate network devices that receive and forward frames across the network. DCEs may be either standalone devices such as repeaters, network switches, and routers, or communications interface units such as interface cards and modems.

Throughout discussion, standalone intermediate network devices will be referred to as either intermediate nodes or DCEs. Network interface cards will be referred to as NICs.

The current Ethernet media options include two general types of copper cable: unshielded twisted-pair (UTP) and shielded twisted-pair (STP), plus several types of optical fiber cable.

Ethernet Network Topologies and Structures

LANs take on many topological configurations, but regardless of their size or complexity, all will be a combination of only three basic interconnection structures or network building blocks.

The simplest structure is the point-to-point interconnection, shown in Figure 5.4. Only two network units are involved, and the connection may be DTE-to-DTE, DTE-to-DCE, or DCE-to-DCE. The cable in point-to-point interconnections is known as a network link. The maximum allowable length of the link depends on the type of cable and the transmission method that is used.

Fig. 5.4 Example Point-to-Point Interconnection

The original Ethernet networks were implemented with a coaxial bus structure, as shown in Figure 5.5 Segment lengths were limited to 500 meters, and up to 100 stations could be connected to a single segment. Individual segments could be interconnected with repeaters, as long as multiple paths did not exist between any two stations on the network and the number of DTEs did not exceed 1024. The total path distance between the most-distant pair of stations was also not allowed to exceed a maximum prescribed value.

Although new networks are no longer connected in a bus configuration, some older bus-connected networks do still exist and are still useful.

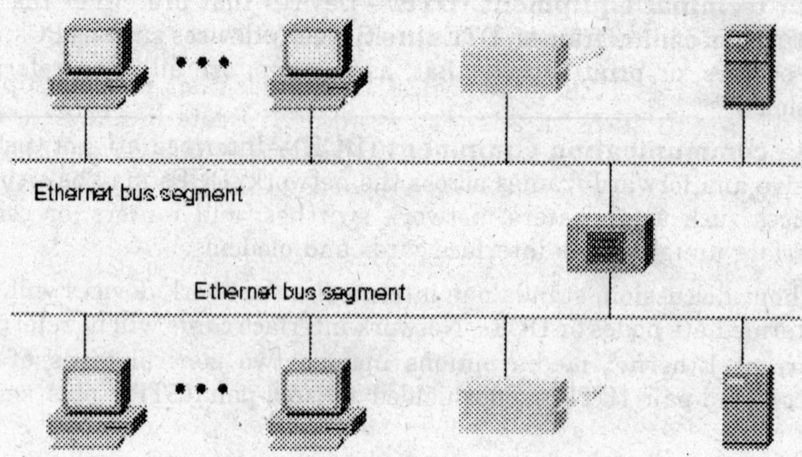

Fig. 5.5 Example Coaxial Bus Topology

Since the early 1990s, the network configuration of choice has been the star-connected topology, shown in Figure 5-6, The central network unit is either a multiport repeater (also known as a hub) or a network switch. All connections in a star network are point-to-point links implemented with either twisted-pair or optical fiber cable.

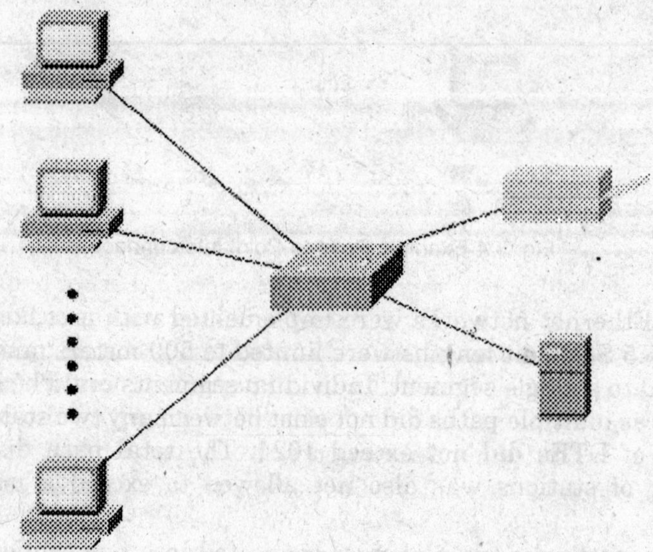

Fig. 5.6 Example Star-Connected Topology

The IEEE 802.3 Logical Relationship to the ISO Reference Model

Figure 5.7 shows the IEEE 802.3 logical layers and their relationship to the OSI reference model. As with all IEEE 802 protocols, the ISO data link layer is divided into two IEEE 802 sublayers, the Media Access Control (MAC) sublayer and the MAC-client sublayer. The IEEE 802.3 physical layer corresponds to the ISO physical layer.

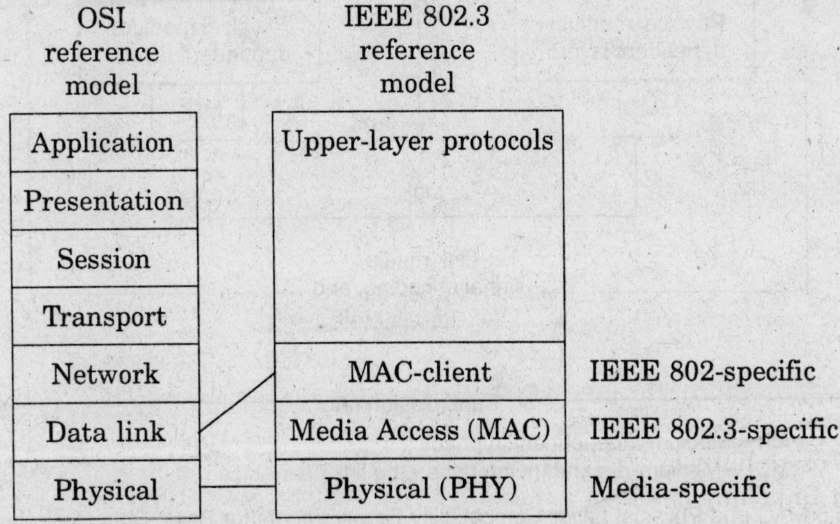

Fig. 5.7 Ethernet's Logical Relationship to the ISO Reference Model

The MAC-client sublayer may be one of the following:

- Logical Link Control (LLC), if the unit is a DTE. This sublayer provides the interface between the Ethernet MAC and the upper layers in the protocol stack of the end station. The LLC sublayer is defined by IEEE 802.2 standards.
- Bridge entity, if the unit is a DCE. Bridge entities provide LAN-to-LAN interfaces between LANs that use the same protocol (for example, Ethernet to Ethernet) and also between different protocols (for example, Ethernet to Token Ring). Bridge entities are defined by IEEE 802.1 standards. Because specifications for LLC and bridge entities are common for all IEEE 802 LAN protocols, network compatibility becomes the primary responsibility of the particular network protocol. Figure 5-8 shows different compatibility requirements imposed by the MAC and physical levels for basic data communication over an Ethernet link.

The MAC layer controls the node's access to the network media and is specific to the individual protocol. All IEEE 802.3 MACs must meet the same basic set of logical requirements, regardless of whether they include one or more of the defined optional protocol extensions. The only requirement for basic communication (communication that does not require optional protocol extensions) between two network nodes is that both MACs must support the same transmission rate.

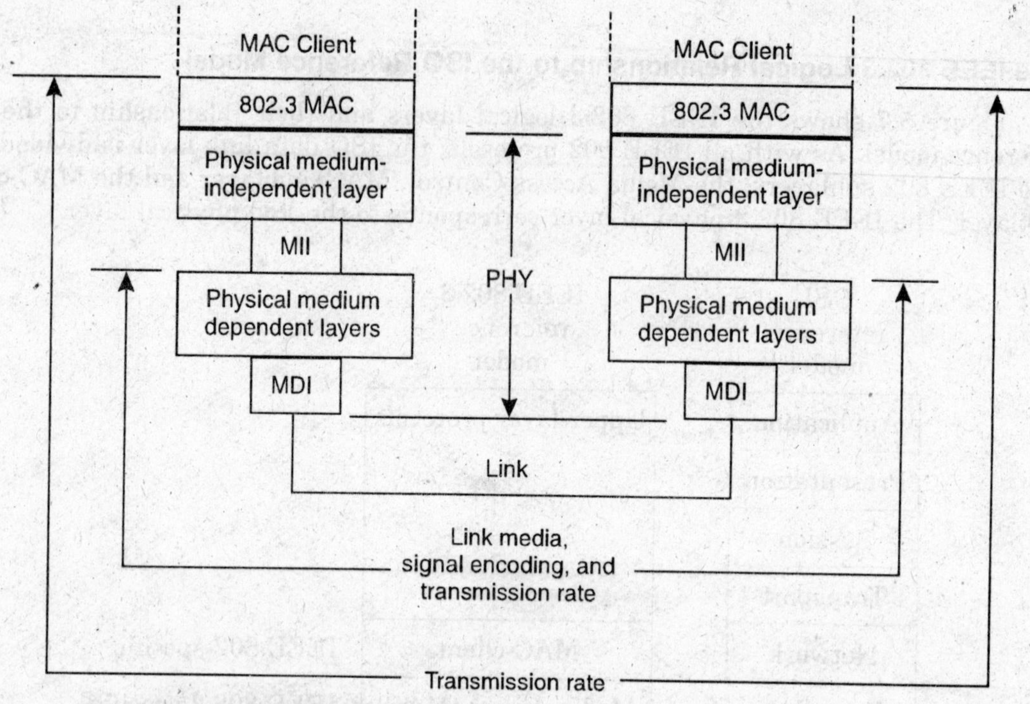

Fig. 5.8 MAC and Physical Layer Compatibility Requirements for Basic Data Communication

The 802.3 physical layer is specific to the transmission data rate, the signal encoding, and the type of media interconnecting the two nodes. Gigabit Ethernet, for example, is defined to operate over either twisted-pair or optical fiber cable, but each specific type of able or signal-encoding procedure requires a different physical layer implementation.

The Ethernet MAC Sublayer

The MAC sublayer has two primary responsibilities:

- Data encapsulation, including frame assembly before transmission, and frame parsing/error detection during and after reception
- Media access control, including initiation of frame transmission and recovery from transmission failure

The Basic Ethernet Frame Format

The IEEE 802.3 standard defines a basic data frame format that is required for all MAC implementations, plus several additional optional formats that are used to extend the protoco's basic capability. The basic data frame format contains the seven fields shown in Figure 5.9.

- **Preamble (PRE)**—Consists of 7 bytes. The PRE is an alternating pattern of ones and zeros that tells receiving stations that a frame is coming, and that provides a means to synchronize the frame-reception portions of receiving physical layers with the incoming bit stream.

- **Start-of-frame delimiter (SOF)**—Consists of 1 byte. The SOF is an alternating pattern of ones and zeros, ending with two consecutive 1-bits indicating that the next bit is the left-most bit in the left-most byte of the destination address.
- **Destination address (DA)**—Consists of 6 bytes. The DA field identifies which station(s) should receive the frame. The left-most bit in the DA field indicates whether the address is an individual address (indicated by a 0) or a group address (indicated by a 1). The second bit from the left indicates whether the DA is globally administered (indicated by a 0) or locally administered (indicated by a 1). The remaining 46 bits are a uniquely assigned value that identifies a single station, a defined group of stations, or all stations on the network.
- **Source addresses (SA)**—Consists of 6 bytes. The SA field identifies the sending station. The SA is always an individual address and the left-most bit in the SA field is always 0.
- **Length/Type**—Consists of 2 bytes. This field indicates either the number of MAC-client data bytes that are contained in the data field of the frame, or the frame type ID if the frame is assembled using an optional format. If the Length/Type field value is less than or equal to 1500, the number of LLC bytes in the Data field is equal to the Length/Type field value. If the Length/Type field value is greater than 1536, the frame is an optional type frame, and the Length/Type field value identifies the particular type of frame being sent or received.
- **Data**—Is a sequence of n bytes of any value, where n is less than or equal to 1500. If the length of the Data field is less than 46, the Data field must be extended by adding a filler (a pad) sufficient to bring the Data field length to 46 bytes.
- **Frame check sequence (FCS)**—Consists of 4 bytes. This sequence contains a 32-bit cyclic redundancy check (CRC) value, which is created by the sending MAC and is recalculated by the receiving MAC to check for damaged frames. The FCS is generated over the DA, SA, Length/Type, and Data fields.

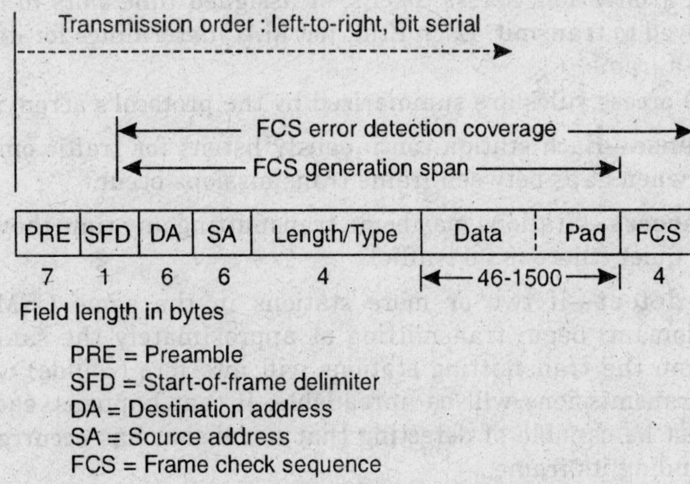

Fig. 5.9 The Basic IEEE 802.3 MAC Data Frame Format

NOTE : Individual addresses are also known as unicast addresses because they refer to a single MAC and are assigned by the NIC manufacturer from a block of addresses allocated by the IEEE. Group addresses (a.k.a. multicast addresses) identify the end stations in a workgroup and are assigned by the network manager. A special group address (all 1sthe broadcast address) indicates all stations on the network.

Frame Transmission

Whenever an end station MAC receives a transmit-frame request with the accompanying address and data information from the LLC sublayer, the MAC begins the transmission sequence by transferring the LLC information into the MAC frame buffer.

- The preamble and start-of-frame delimiter are inserted in the PRE and SOF fields.
- The destination and source addresses are inserted into the address fields.
- The LLC data bytes are counted, and the number of bytes is inserted into the Length/Type field.
- The LLC data bytes are inserted into the Data field. If the number of LLC data bytes is less than 46, a pad is added to bring the Data field length up to 46.
- An FCS value is generated over the DA, SA, Length/Type, and Data fields and is appended to the end of the Data field.

After the frame is assembled, actual frame transmission will depend on whether the MAC is operating in half-duplex or full-duplex mode.

The IEEE 802.3 standard currently requires that all Ethernet MACs support half-duplex operation, in which the MAC can be either transmitting or receiving a frame, but it cannot be doing both simultaneously. Full-duplex operation is an optional MAC capability that allows the MAC to transmit and receive frames simultaneously.

Half-Duplex Transmission—The CSMA/CD Access Method

The CSMA/CD protocol was originally developed as a means by which two or more stations could share a common media in a switch-less environment when the protocol does not require central arbitration, access tokens, or assigned time slots to indicate when a station will be allowed to transmit. Each Ethernet MAC determines for itself when it will be allowed to send a frame.

The CSMA/CD access rules are summarized by the protocol's acronym:

- **Carrier sense**—Each station continuously listens for traffic on the medium to determine when gaps between frame transmissions occur.
- **Multiple access**—Stations may begin transmitting any time they detect that the network is quiet (there is no traffic).
- **Collision detect**—If two or more stations in the same CSMA/CD network (collision domain) begin transmitting at approximately the same time, the bit streams from the transmitting stations will interfere (collide) with each other, and both transmissions will be unreadable. If that happens, each transmitting station must be capable of detecting that a collision has occurred before it has finished sending its frame.

Each must stop transmitting as soon as it has detected the collision and then must wait a quasirandom length of time (determined by a back-off algorithm) before attempting to retransmit the frame.

The worst-case situation occurs when the two most-distant stations on the network both need to send a frame and when the second station does not begin transmitting until just before the frame from the first station arrives. The collision will be detected almost immediately by the second station, but it will not be detected by the first station until the corrupted signal has propagated all the way back to that station. The maximum time that is required to detect a collision (the collision window, or "slot time") is approximately equal to twice the signal propagation time between the two most-distant stations on the network.

This means that both the minimum frame length and the maximum collision diameter are directly related to the slot time. Longer minimum frame lengths translate to longer slot times and larger collision diameters; shorter minimum frame lengths correspond to shorter slot times and smaller collision diameters.

The trade-off was between the need to reduce the impact of collision recovery and the need for network diameters to be large enough to accommodate reasonable network sizes. The compromise was to choose a maximum network diameter (about 2500 meters) and then to set the minimum frame length long enough to ensure detection of all worst-case collisions.

The compromise worked well for 10 Mbps, but it was a problem for higher data-rate Ethernet developers. Fast Ethernet was required to provide backward compatibility with earlier Ethernet networks, including the existing IEEE 802.3 frame format and error-detection procedures, plus all applications and networking software running on the 10-Mbps networks.

Although signal propagation velocity is essentially constant for all transmission rates, the time required to transmit a frame is inversely related to the transmission rate. At 100 Mbps, a minimum-length frame can be transmitted in approximately one-tenth of the defined slot time, and any collision that occurred during the transmission would not likely be detected by the transmitting stations. This, in turn, meant that the maximum network diameters specified for 10-Mbps networks could not be used for 100-Mbps networks. The solution for Fast Ethernet was to reduce the maximum network diameter by approximately a factor of 10 (to a little more than 200 meters).

The same problem also arose during specification development for Gigabit Ethernet, but decreasing network diameters by another factor of 10 (to approximately 20 meters) for 1000-Mbps operation was simply not practical. This time, the developers elected to maintain approximately the same maximum collision domain diameters as 100-Mbps networks and to increase the apparent minimum frame size by adding a variable-length nondata extension field to frames that are shorter than the minimum length (the extension field is removed during frame reception).

Fig. 5.10 shows the MAC frame format with the gigabit extension field, and Table

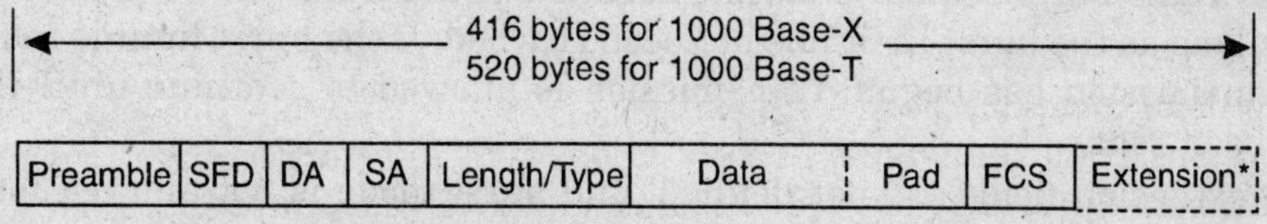

Fig. 5.10 MAC Frame with Gigabit Carrier Extension

5.1 shows the effect of the trade-off between the transmission data rate and the minimum frame size for 10-Mbps, 100-Mbps, and 1000-Mbps Ethernet.

Table 5.1 Limits for Half-Duplex Operation

Parameter	10 Mbps	100 Mbps	1000 Mbps
Minimum frame size	64 bytes	64 bytes	520 bytes1 (with extension field added)
Maximum collision diameter, DTE to DTE	100 meters UTP	100 meters UTP 412 meters fiber	100 meters UTP 316 meters fiber
Maximum collision diameter with repeaters	2500 meters	205 meters	200 meters
Maximum number of repeaters in network path	5	2	1

520 bytes applies to 1000Base-T implementations. The minimum frame size with extension field for 1000Base-X is reduced to 416 bytes because 1000Base-X encodes and transmits 10 bits for each byte.

Another change to the Ethernet CSMA/CD transmit specification was the addition of frame bursting for gigabit operation. Burst mode is a feature that allows a MAC to send a short sequence (a burst) of frames equal to approximately 5.4 maximum-length frames without having to relinquish control of the medium. The transmitting MAC fills each interframe interval with extension bits, as shown in Figure 5-11, so that other stations on the network will see that the network is busy and will not attempt transmission until after the burst is complete.

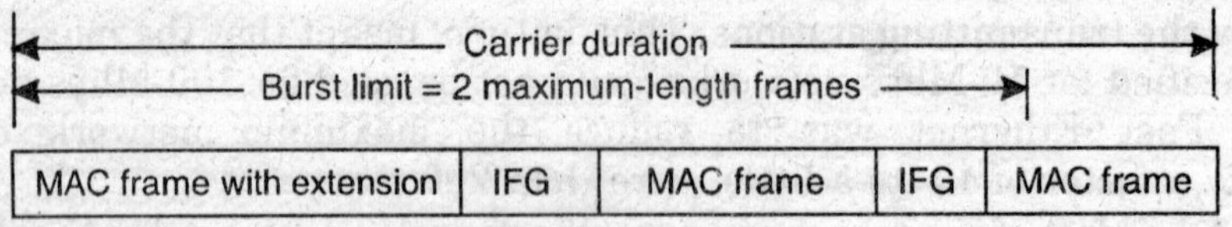

Fig. 5.11 A Gigabit Frame-Burst Sequence

If the length of the first frame is less than the minimum frame length, an extension field is added to extend the frame length to the value indicated in Table 5-1. Subsequent frames in a frame-burst sequence do not need extension fields, and a frame burst may continue as long as the burst limit has not been reached. If the burst limit is reached after a frame transmission has begun, transmission is allowed to continue until that entire frame has been sent.

Frame extension fields are not defined, and burst mode is not allowed for 10 Mbps and 100 Mbps transmission rates.

Full-Duplex Transmission—An Optional Approach to Higher Network Efficiency

Full-duplex operation is an optional MAC capability that allows simultaneous two-way transmission over point-to-point links. Full duplex transmission is functionally much simpler than half-duplex transmission because it involves no media contention, no collisions, no need to schedule retransmissions, and no need for extension bits on the end of short frames. The result is not only more time available for transmission, but also an effective doubling of the link bandwidth because each link can now support full-rate, simultaneous, two-way transmission.

Transmission can usually begin as soon as frames are ready to send. The only restriction is that there must be a minimum-length interframe gap between successive frames, as shown in Figure 5.12, and each frame must conform to Ethernet frame format standards.

Figure 5.12 Full Duplex Operation Allows Simultaneous Two-Way Transmission on the Same Link.

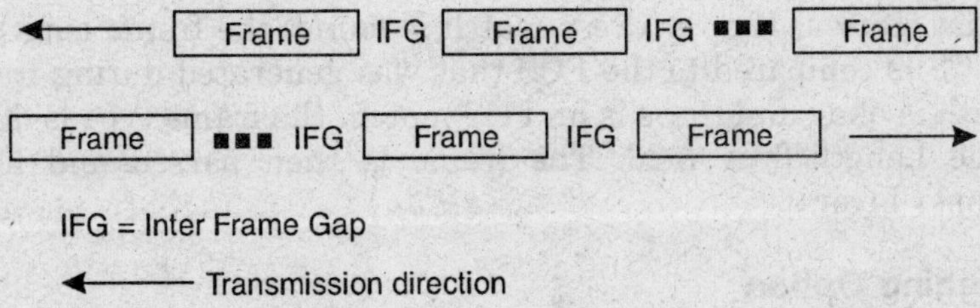

Flow Control

Full-duplex operation requires concurrent implementation of the optional flow-control capability that allows a receiving node (such as a network switch port) that is becoming congested to request the sending node (such as a file server) to stop sending frames for a selected short period of time. Control is MAC-to-MAC through the use of a pause frame that is automatically generated by the receiving MAC. If the congestion is relieved before the requested wait has expired, a second pause frame with a zero time-to-wait value can be sent to request resumption of transmission. An overview of the flow control operation is shown in Figure 5.13.

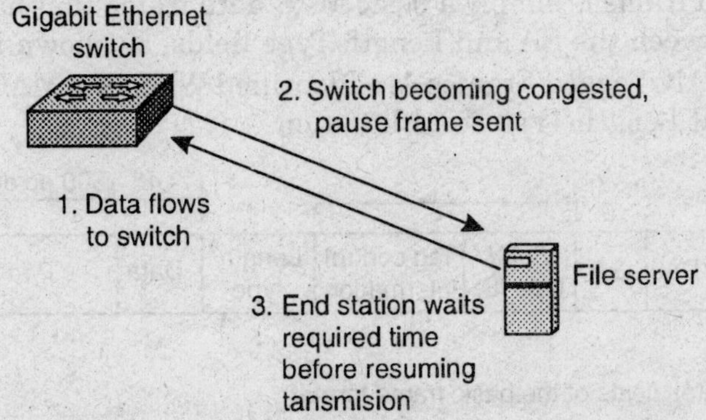

Fig. 5.13 An Overview of the IEEE 802.3 Flow Control Sequence

The full-duplex operation and its companion flow control capability are both options for all Ethernet MACs and all transmission rates. Both options are enabled on a link-by-link basis, assuming that the associated physical layers are also capable of supporting full-duplex operation.

Pause frames are identified as MAC control frames by an exclusive assigned (reserved) length/type value. They are also assigned a reserved destination address value to ensure that an incoming pause frame is never forwarded to upper protocol layers or to other ports in a switch.

Frame Reception

Frame reception is essentially the same for both half-duplex and full-duplex operations, except that full-duplex MACs must have separate frame buffers and data paths to allow for simultaneous frame transmission and reception.

Frame reception is the reverse of frame transmission. The destination address of the received frame is checked and matched against the station's address list (its MAC address, its group addresses, and the broadcast address) to determine whether the frame is destined for that station. If an address match is found, the frame length is checked and the received FCS is compared to the FCS that was generated during frame reception. If the frame length is okay and there is an FCS match, the frame type is determined by the contents of the Length/Type field. The frame is then parsed and forwarded to the appropriate upper layer.

The VLAN Tagging Option

VLAN tagging is a MAC option that provides three important capabilities not previously available to Ethernet network users and network managers:

- Provides a means to expedite time-critical network traffic by setting transmission priorities for outgoing frames.
- Allows stations to be assigned to logical groups, to communicate across multiple LANs as though they were on a single LAN. Bridges and switches filter destination addresses and forward VLAN frames only to ports that serve the VLAN to which the traffic belongs.
- Simplifies network management and makes adds, moves, and changes easier to administer.

A VLAN-tagged frame is simply a basic MAC data frame that has had a 4-byte VLAN header inserted between the SA and Length/Type fields, as shown in Figure 5.14.

Figure 5-14 VLAN-Tagged Frames Are Identified When the MAC Finds the LAN Type Value in the Normal Length/Type Field Location

46-1500 octets

Pre	SFD	DA	SA	VLAN type ID	Tag control information	Length/ type	Data	Pad	FCS	Ext
*	*	*	*			*	*		*	

* Indicates fields of the basic frame format

The VLAN header consists of two fields:

- A reserved 2-byte type value, indicating that the frame is a VLAN frame
- A two-byte Tag-Control field that contains both the transmission priority (0 to 7, where 7 is the highest) and a VLAN ID that identifies the particular VLAN over which the frame is to be sent The receiving MAC reads the reserved type value, which is located in the normal Length/Type field position, and interprets the received frame as a VLAN frame. Then the following occurs:
- If the MAC is installed in a switch port, the frame is forwarded according to its priority level to all ports that are associated with the indicated VLAN identifier.
- If the MAC is installed in an end station, it removes the 4-byte VLAN header and processes the frame in the same manner as a basic data frame.

VLAN tagging requires that all network nodes involved with a VLAN group be equipped with the VLAN option.

The Ethernet Physical Layers

Because Ethernet devices implement only the bottom two layers of the OSI protocol stack, they are typically implemented as network interface cards (NICs) that plug into the host device's motherboard. The different NICs are identified by a three-part product name that is based on the physical layer attributes.

The naming convention is a concatenation of three terms indicating the transmission rate, the transmission method, and the media type/signal encoding. For example, consider this:

- 10Base-T = 10 Mbps, baseband, over two twisted-pair cables.
- 100Base-T2 = 100 Mbps, baseband, over two twisted-pair cables.
- 100Base-T4 = 100 Mbps, baseband, over four-twisted pair cables.
- 1000Base-LX = 100 Mbps, baseband, long wavelength over optical fiber cable.

A question sometimes arises as to why the middle term always seems to be "Base". Early versions of the protocol also allowed for broadband transmission (for example, 10Broad), but broadband implementations were not successful in the marketplace. All current Ethernet implementations use baseband transmission.

Encoding for Signal Transmission

In baseband transmission, the frame information is directly impressed upon the link as a sequence of pulses or data symbols that are typically attenuated (reduced in size) and distorted (changed in shape) before they reach the other end of the link. The receiver's task is to detect each pulse as it arrives and then to extract its correct value before transferring the reconstructed information to the receiving MAC.

Filters and pulse-shaping circuits can help restore the size and shape of the received waveforms, but additional measures must be taken to ensure that the received signals are sampled at the correct time in the pulse period and at same rate as the transmit clock:

- The receive clock must be recovered from the incoming data stream to allow the receiving physical layer to synchronize with the incoming pulses.

- Compensating measures must be taken for a transmission effect known as baseline wander.

Clock recovery requires level transitions in the incoming signal to identify and synchronize on pulse boundaries. The alternating 1s and 0s of the frame preamble were designed both to indicate that a frame was arriving and to aid in clock recovery. However, recovered clocks can drift and possibly lose synchronization if pulse levels remain constant and there are no transitions to detect (for example, during long strings of 0s).

Baseline wander results because Ethernet links are AC-coupled to the transceivers and because AC coupling is incapable of maintaining voltage levels for more than a short time. As a result, transmitted pulses are distorted by a droop effect similar to the exaggerated example shown in Figure 5-15. In long strings of either 1s or 0s, the droop can become so severe that the voltage level passes through the decision threshold, resulting in erroneous sampled values for the affected pulses.

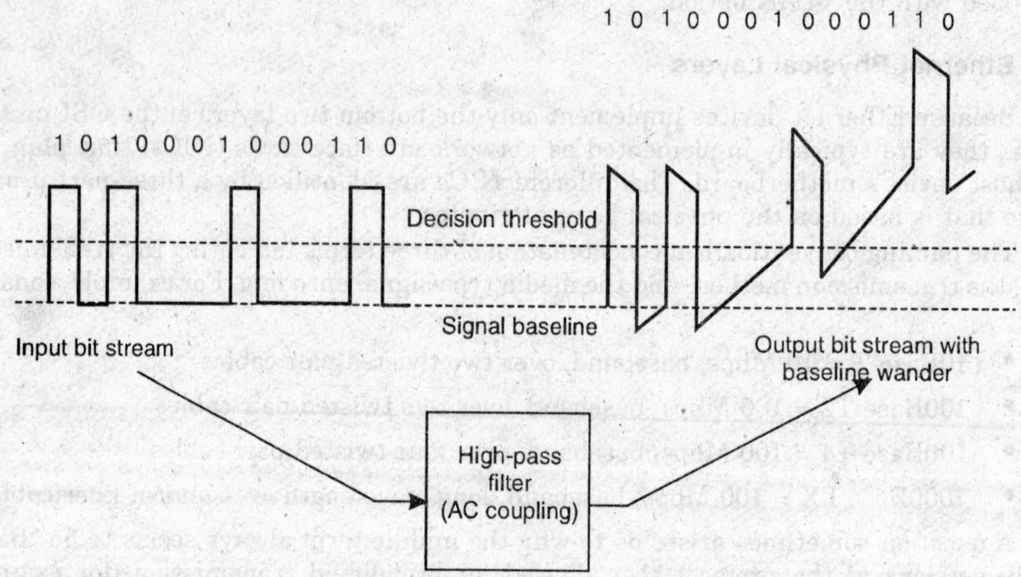

Fig. 5.15 A Concept Example of Baseline Wander

Fortunately, encoding the outgoing signal before transmission can significantly reduce the effect of both these problems, as well as reduce the possibility of transmission errors. Early Ethernet implementations, up to and including 10Base-T, all used the Manchester encoding method, shown in Figure 5-16. Each pulse is clearly identified by the direction of the midpulse transition rather than by its sampled level value.

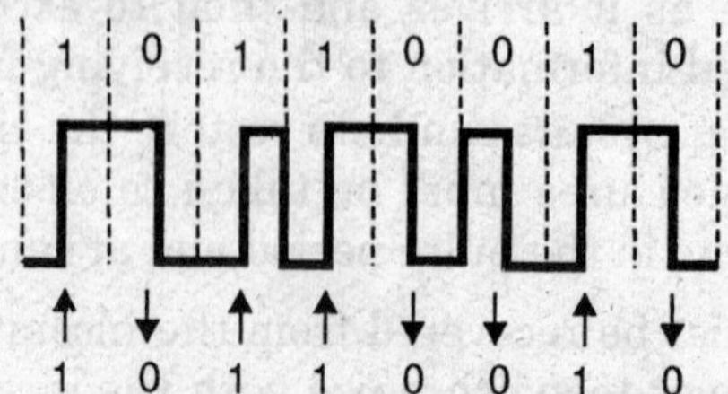

Fig. 5.16 Transition-Based Manchester Binary Encoding

Unfortunately, Manchester encoding introduces some difficult frequency-related problems that make it unsuitable for use at higher data rates. Ethernet versions subsequent to 10Base-T all use different encoding procedures that include some or all of the following techniques:

- **Using Data Scrambling**—A procedure that scrambles the bits in each byte in an orderly (and recoverable) manner. Some 0s are changed to 1s, some 1s are changed to 0s, and some bits are left the same. The result is reduced run-length of same-value bits, increased transition density, and easier clock recovery.
- **Expanding the Code Space**—A technique that allows assignment of separate codes for data and control symbols (such as start-of-stream and end-of-stream delimiters, extension bits, and so on) and that assists in transmission error detection.
- **Using Forward Error-Correcting Codes**—An encoding in which redundant information is added to the transmitted data stream so that some types of transmission errors can be corrected during frame reception.

NOTE : Forward error-correcting codes are used in 1000Base-T to achieve an effective reduction in the bit error rate. Ethernet protocol limits error handling to detection of bit errors in the received frame. Recovery of frames received with uncorrectable errors or missing frames is the responsibility of higher layers in the protocol stack.

The 802.3 Physical Layer Relationship to the ISO Reference Model

Although the specific logical model of the physical layer may vary from version to version, all Ethernet NICs generally conform to the generic model shown in Figure 5.17

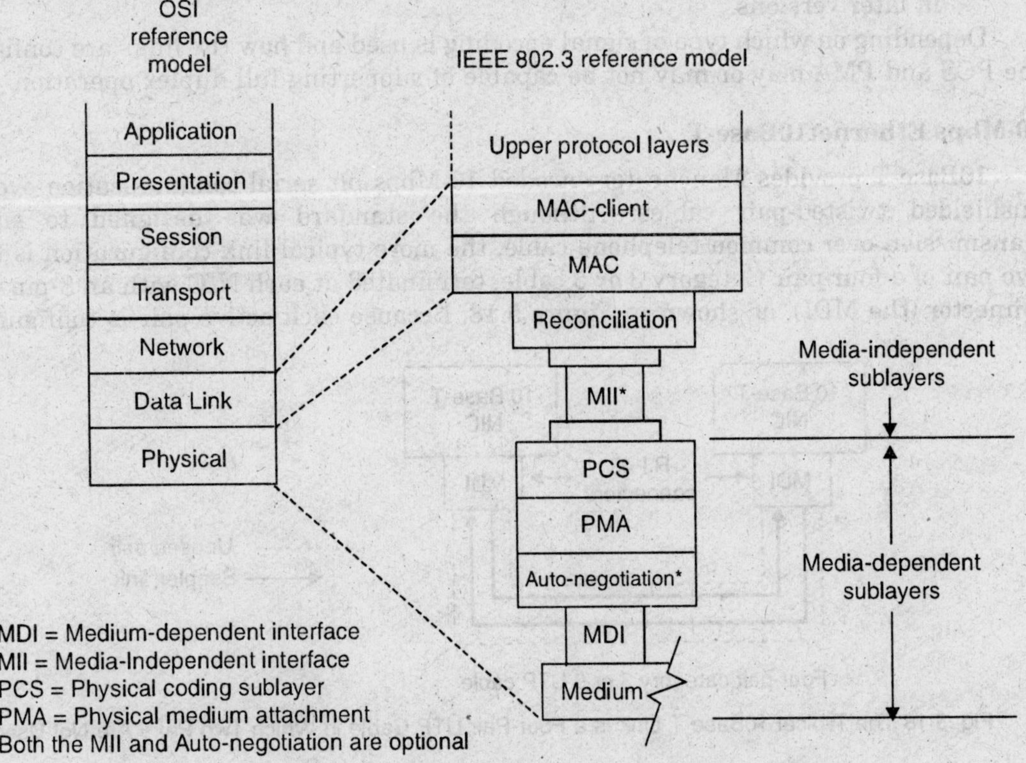

Fig. 5.17 The Generic Ethernet Physical Layer Reference Model

The physical layer for each transmission rate is divided into sublayers that are independent of the particular media type and sublayers that are specific to the media type or signal encoding.

- The reconciliation sublayer and the optional media-independent interface (MII in 10-Mbps and 100-Mbps Ethernet, GMII in Gigabit Ethernet) provide the logical connection between the MAC and the different sets of media-dependent layers. The MII and GMII are defined with separate transmit and receive data paths that are bit-serial for 10-Mbps implementations, nibble-serial (4 bits wide) for 100-Mbps implementations, and byte-serial (8 bits wide) for 1000-Mbps implementations. The media-independent interfaces and the reconciliation sublayer are common for their respective transmission rates and are configured for full-duplex operation in 10Base-T and all subsequent Ethernet versions.
- The media-dependent physical coding sublayer (PCS) provides the logic for encoding, multiplexing, and synchronization of the outgoing symbol streams as well symbol code alignment, demultiplexing, and decoding of the incoming data.
- The physical medium attachment (PMA) sublayer contains the signal transmitters and receivers (transceivers), as well as the clock recovery logic for the received data streams.
- The medium-dependent interface (MDI) is the cable connector between the signal transceivers and the link.
- The Auto-negotiation sublayer allows the NICs at each end of the link to exchange information about their individual capabilities, and then to negotiate and select the most favorable operational mode that they both are capable of supporting. Auto-negotiation is optional in early Ethernet implementations and is mandatory in later versions.

Depending on which type of signal encoding is used and how the links are configured, the PCS and PMA may or may not be capable of supporting full-duplex operation.

10-Mbps Ethernet10Base-T

10Base-T provides Manchester-encoded 10-Mbps bit-serial communication over two unshielded twisted-pair cables. Although the standard was designed to support transmission over common telephone cable, the more typical link configuration is to use two pair of a four-pair Category 3 or 5 cable, terminated at each NIC with an 8-pin RJ-45 connector (the MDI), as shown in Figure 5.18. Because each active pair is configured as

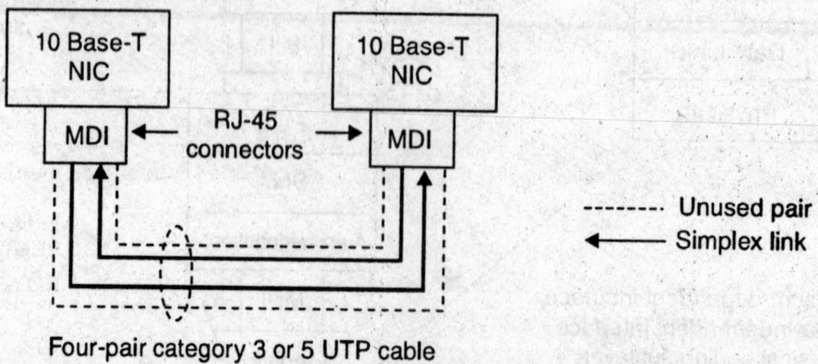

Fig. 5.18 The Typical 10Base-T Link Is a Four-Pair UTP Cable in Which Two Pairs Are Not Used

a simplex link where transmission is in one direction only, the 10Base-T physical layers can support either half-duplex or full-duplex operation.

Although 10Base-T may be considered essentially obsolete in some circles, it is included here because there are still many 10Base-T Ethernet networks, and because full-duplex operation has given 10BaseT an extended life.

10Base-T was also the first Ethernet version to include a link integrity test to determine the health of the link. Immediately after powerup, the PMA transmits a normal link pulse (NLP) to tell the NIC at the other end of the link that this NIC wants to establish an active link connection.

- If the NIC at the other end of the link is also powered up, it responds with its own NLP.
- If the NIC at the other end of the link is not powered up, this NIC continues sending an NLP about once every 16 ms until it receives a response.

The link is activated only after both NICs are capable of exchanging valid NLPs.

100 MbpsFast Ethernet

Increasing the Ethernet transmission rate by a factor of ten over 10Base-T was not a simple task, and the effort resulted in the development of three separate physical layer standards for 100 Mbps over UTP cable: 100Base-TX and 100Base-T4 in 1995, and 100Base-T2 in 1997. Each was defined with different encoding requirements and a different set of media-dependent sublayers, even though there is some overlap in the link cabling. Table 7.2 compares the physical layer characteristics of 10Base-T to the various 100Base versions.

Table 5.2 Summary of 100Base-T Physical Layer Characteristics

Ethernet Version	Transmit Symbol Rate1	Encoding	Cabling	Full-Duplex Operation
10Base-T	10 MBd	Manchester	Two pairs of UTP Category -3 or better	Supported
100Base-TX	125 MBd	4B/5B	Two pairs of UTP Category -5 or Type 1 STP	Supported
100Base-T4	33 MBd	8B/6T	Four pairs of UTP Category -3 or better	Not supported
100Base-T2	25 MBd	PAM5x5	Two pairs of UTP Category -3 or better	Supported

Note : 1 One baud = one transmitted symbol per second, where the transmitted symbol may contain the equivalent value of 1 or more binary bits.

Although not all three 100-Mbps versions were successful in the marketplace, all three have been discussed in the literature, and all three did impact future designs. As such, all three are important to consider here.

100Base-X

100Base-X was designed to support transmission over either two pairs of Category 5 UTP copper wire or two strands of optical fiber. Although the encoding, decoding, and clock recovery procedures are the same for both media, the signal transmission is differentelectrical pulses in copper and light pulses in optical fiber. The signal transceivers that were included as part of the PMA function in the generic logical model of Figure 5.17 were redefined as the separate physical media-dependent (PMD) sublayers shown in Figure 5.19.

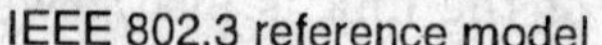

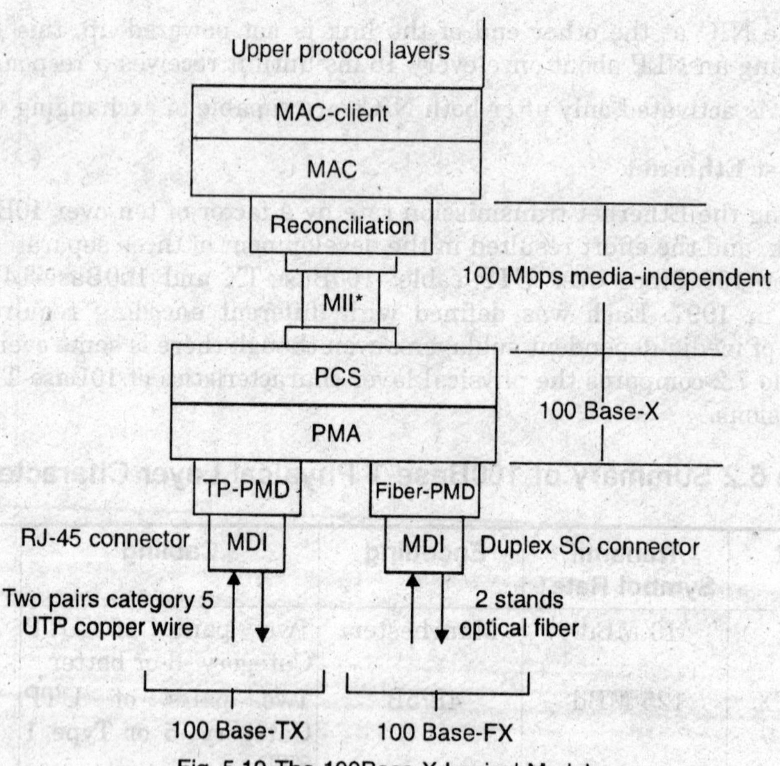

Fig. 5.19 The 100Base-X Logical Model

The 100Base-X encoding procedure is based on the earlier FDDI optical fiber physical media-dependent and FDDI/CDDI copper twisted-pair physical media-dependent signaling standards developed by ISO and ANSI. The 100Base-TX physical media-dependent sublayer (TP-PMD) was implemented with CDDI semiconductor transceivers and RJ-45 connectors; the fiber PMD was implemented with FDDI optical transceivers and the Low Cost Fibre Interface Connector (commonly called the duplex SC connector).

The 4B/5B encoding procedure is the same as the encoding procedure used by FDDI, with only minor adaptations to accommodate Ethernet frame control. Each 4-bit data nibble (representing half of a data byte) is mapped into a 5-bit binary code-group that is transmitted bit-serial over the link. The expanded code space provided by the 32 5-bit code-groups allow separate assignment for the following:

- The 16 possible values in a 4-bit data nibble (16 code-groups).
- Four control code-groups that are transmitted as code-group pairs to indicate the start-of-stream delimiter (SSD) and the end-of-stream delimiter (ESD). Each MAC frame is "encapsulated" to mark both the beginning and end of the frame. The first byte of preamble is replaced with SSD code-group pair that precisely identifies the frame's code-group boundaries. The ESD code-group pair is appended after the frame's FCS field.
- A special IDLE code-group that is continuously sent during interframe gaps to maintain continuous synchronization between the NICs at each end of the link. The receipt of IDLE is interpreted to mean that the link is quiet.
- Eleven invalid code-groups that are not intentionally transmitted by a NIC (although one is used by a repeater to propagate receive errors). Receipt of any invalid code-group will cause the incoming frame to be treated as an invalid frame.

Figure 5.20 shows how a MAC frame is encapsulated before being transmitted as a 100Base-X code-group stream.

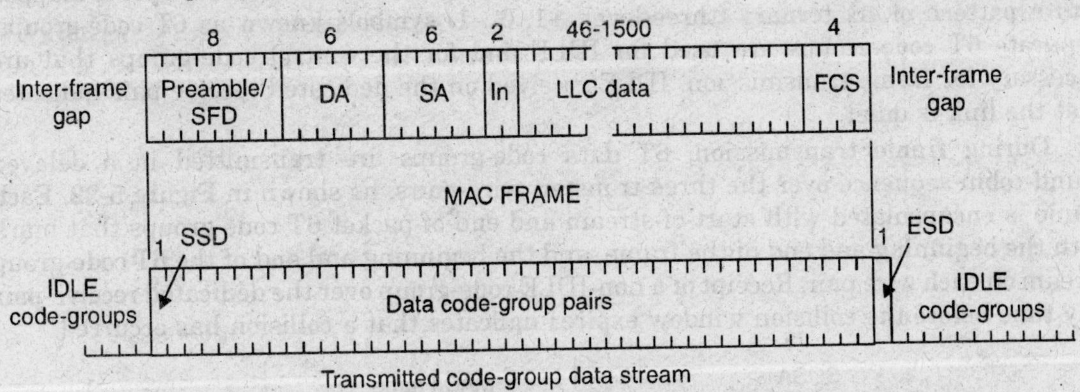

Fig. 5.20 The 100Base-X Code-Group Stream with Frame Encapsulation

100Base-TX transmits and receives on the same link pairs and uses the same pin assignments on the MDI as 10Base-T. 100Base-TX and 100Base-FX both support half-duplex and full-duplex transmission.

100Base-T4

100Base-T4 was developed to allow 10BaseT networks to be upgraded to 100-Mbps operation without requiring existing four-pair Category 3 UTP cables to be replaced with the newer Category 5 cables. Two of the four pairs are configured for half-duplex operation and can support transmission in either direction, but only in one direction at a time. The other two pairs are configured as simplex pairs dedicated to transmission in one direction only. Frame transmission uses both half-duplex pairs, plus the simplex pair that is appropriate for the transmission direction, as shown in Figure 5-21. The simplex pair for the opposite direction provides carrier sense and collision detection. Full-duplex operation cannot be supported on 100Base-T4.

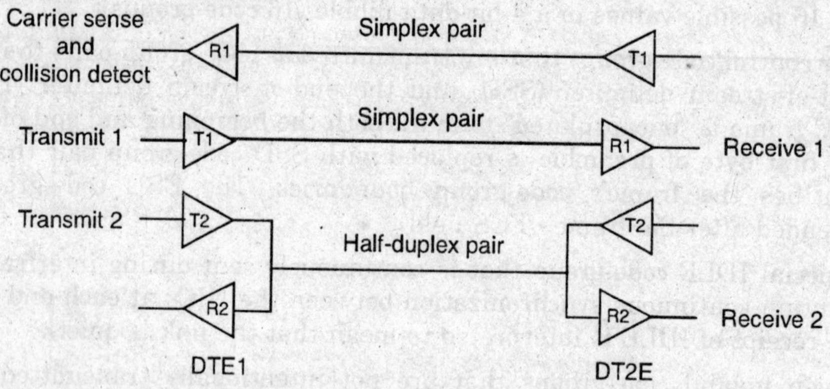

Fig. 5.21 The 100Base-T4 Wire-Pair Usage During Frame Transmission

100Base-T4 uses an 8B6T encoding scheme in which each 8-bit binary byte is mapped into a pattern of six ternary (three-level: +1, 0, -1) symbols known as 6T code-groups. Separate 6T code-groups are used for IDLE and for the control code-groups that are necessary for frame transmission. IDLE received on the dedicated receive pair indicates that the link is quiet.

During frame transmission, 6T data code-groups are transmitted in a delayed round-robin sequence over the three transmit wire-pairs, as shown in Figure 5-22. Each frame is encapsulated with start-of-stream and end-of-packet 6T code-groups that mark both the beginning and end of the frame, and the beginning and end of the 6T code-group stream on each wire pair. Receipt of a non-IDLE code-group over the dedicated receive-pair any time before the collision window expires indicates that a collision has occurred.

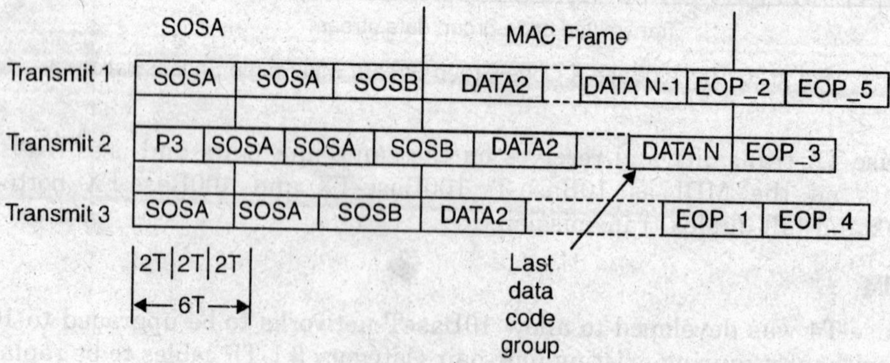

Fig. 5.22 The 100Base-T4 Frame Transmission Sequence

100Base-T2

The 100Base-T2 specification was developed as a better alternative for upgrading networks with installed Category 3 cabling than was being provided by 100Base-T4. Two important new goals were defined:

- To provide communication over two pairs of Category 3 or better cable.
- To support both half-duplex and full-duplex operation.

100Base-T2 uses a different signal transmission procedure than any previous twisted-pair Ethernet implementations. Instead of using two simplex links to form one full-duplex link, the 100Base-T2 dual-duplex baseband transmission method sends encoded symbols simultaneously in both directions on both wire pairs, as shown in Figure 5.23. The term "TDX:2" indicates the 2 most significant bits in the nibble before encoding and transmission. "RDX:2" indicates the same 2 bits after receipt and decoding.

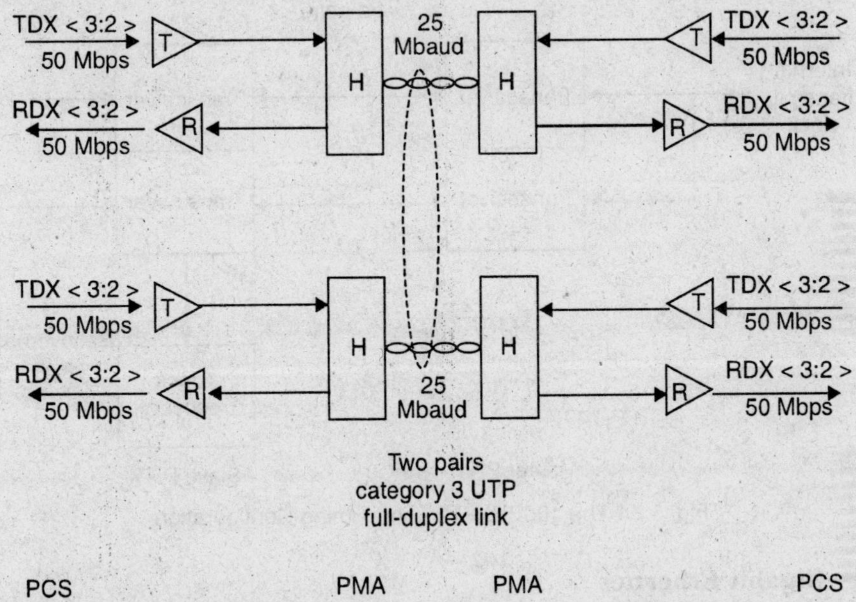

H = Hybrid canceller transceiver
T = Transmit encoder
R = Receive decoder
Two PAM5 code symbols = One nibble

Fig. 5.23 The 100Base-T2 Link Topology

Dual-duplex baseband transmission requires the NICs at each end of the link to be operated in a master/slave loop-timing mode. Which NIC will be master and which will be slave is determined by autonegotiation during link initiation. When the link is operational, synchronization is based on the master NIC's internal transmit clock. The slave NIC uses the recovered clock for both transmit and receive operations, as shown in Figure 5.24.

Each transmitted frame is encapsulated, and link synchronization is maintained with a continuous stream of IDLE symbols during interframe gaps.

The 100Base-T2 encoding process first scrambles the data frame nibbles to randomize the bit sequence. It then maps the two upper bits and the two lower bits of each nibble into two five-level (+2, +1, 0, -1, -2) pulse amplitude-modulated (PAM5) symbols that are simultaneously transmitted over the two wire pairs (PAM5x5). Different scrambling procedures for master and slave transmissions ensure that the data streams traveling in opposite directions on the same wire pair are uncoordinated.

Signal reception is essentially the reverse of signal transmission. Because the signal on each wire pair at the MDI is the sum of the transmitted signal and the received signal, each receiver subtracts the transmitted symbols from the signal received at the MDI to recover the symbols in the incoming data stream. The incoming symbol pair is then decoded, unscrambled, and reconstituted as a data nibble for transfer to the MAC.

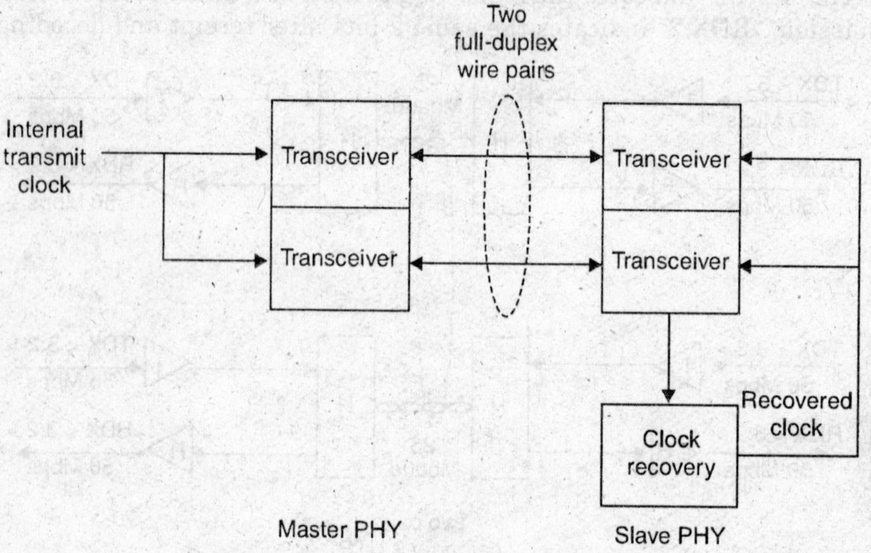

Fig. 5.24 The 100Base-T2 Loop Timing Configuration

1000 Mbps—Gigabit Ethernet

The Gigabit Ethernet standards development resulted in two primary specifications: 1000Base-T for UTP copper cable and 1000Base-X STP copper cable, as well as single and multimode optical fiber (see Figure 5.25).

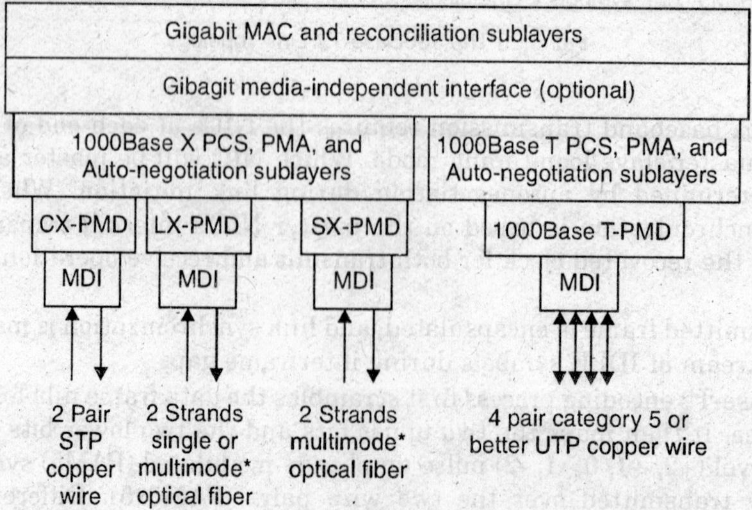

Fig. 5.25 Gigabit Ethernet Variations

1000Base-T

1000Base-T Ethernet provides full-duplex transmission over four-pair Category 5 or better UTP cable. 1000Base-T is based largely on the findings and design approaches that led to the development of the Fast Ethernet physical layer implementations:

- 100Base-TX proved that binary symbol streams could be successfully transmitted over Category 5 UTP cable at 125 MBd.

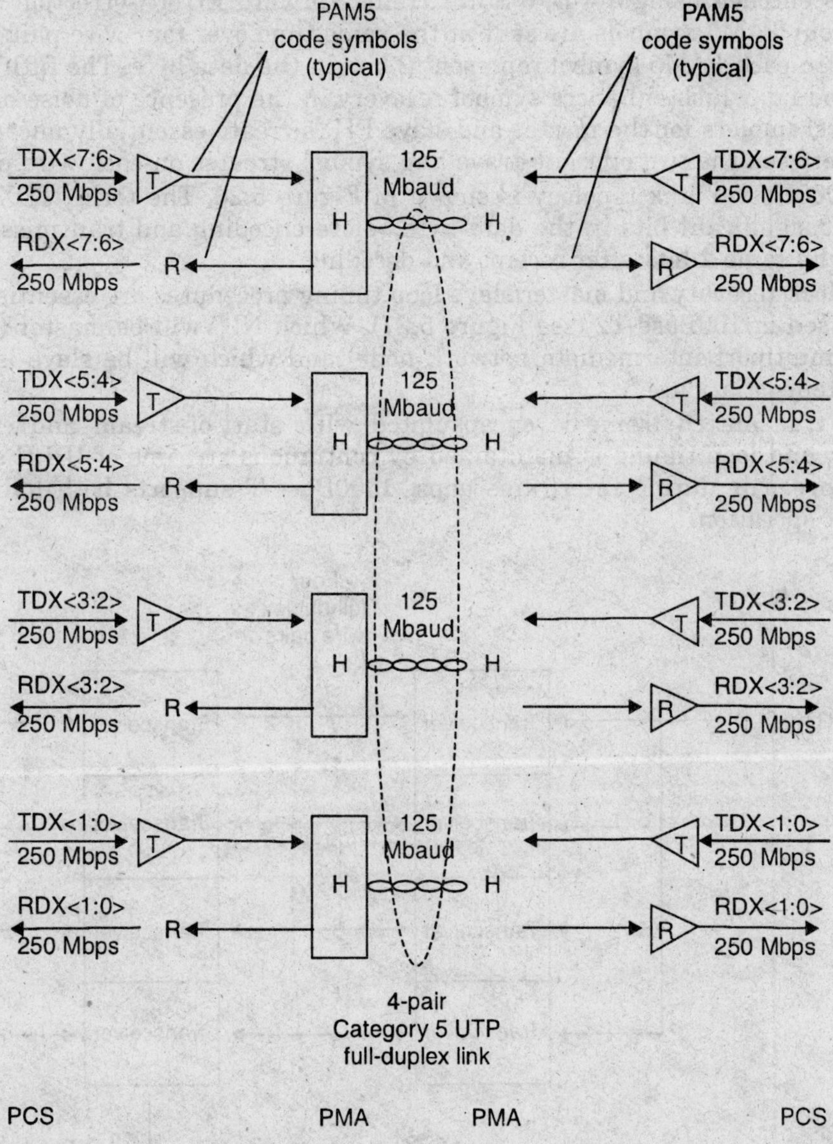

Fig. 5.26 The 1000Base-T Link Topology

- 100Base-T4 provided a basic understanding of the problems related to sending multilevel signals over four wire pairs.
- 100Base-T2 proved that PAM5 encoding, coupled with digital signal processing, could handle both simultaneous two-way data streams and potential crosstalk problems resulting from alien signals on adjacent wire pairs.

1000Base-T scrambles each byte in the MAC frame to randomize the bit sequence before it is encoded using a 4-D, 8-State Trellis Forward Error Correction (FEC) coding in which four PAM5 symbols are sent at the same time over four wire pairs. Four of the five levels in each PAM5 symbol represent 2 bits in the data byte. The fifth level is used for FEC coding, which enhances symbol recovery in the presence of noise and crosstalk. Separate scramblers for the master and slave PHYs create essentially uncorrelated data streams between the two opposite-travelling symbol streams on each wire pair.

The1000Base-T link topology is shown in Figure 5.26. The term "TDX:6" indicates the 2 most significant bits in the data byte before encoding and transmission. "RDX:6" indicates the same 2 bits after receipt and decoding.

The clock recovery and master/slave loop timing procedures are essentially the same as those used in 100Base-T2 (see Figure 5.27). Which NIC will be master (typically the NIC in a multiport intermediate network node) and which will be slave is determined during autonegotiation.

Each transmitted frame is encapsulated with start-of-stream and end-of-stream delimiters, and loop timing is maintained by continuous streams of IDLE symbols sent on each wire pair during interframe gaps. 1000Base-T supports both half-duplex and full-duplex operation.

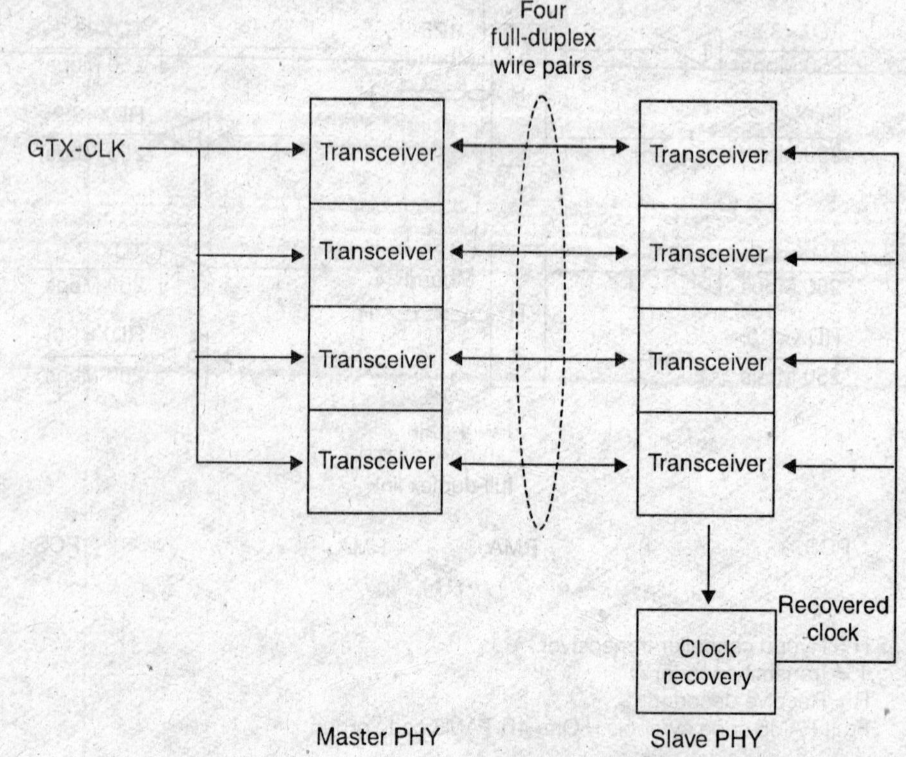

Fig. 5.27 1000Base-T Master/Slave Loop Timing Configuration

1000Base-X

All three 1000Base-X versions support full-duplex binary transmission at 1250 Mbps over two strands of optical fiber or two STP copper wire-pairs, as shown in Figure 5.28. Transmission coding is based on the ANSI Fibre Channel 8B/10B encoding scheme. Each 8-bit data byte is mapped into a 10-bit code-group for bit-serial transmission. Like earlier Ethernet versions, each data frame is encapsulated at the physical layer before transmission, and link synchronization is maintained by sending a continuous stream of IDLE code-groups during interframe gaps. All 1000Base-X physical layers support both half-duplex and full-duplex operation.

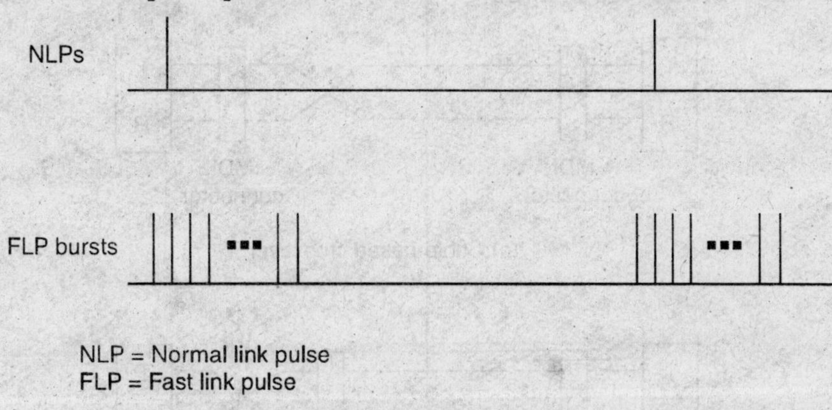

Fig. 5.28 1000Base-X Link Configuration

The principal differences among the 1000Base-X versions are the link media and connectors that the particular versions will support and, in the case of optical media, the wavelength of the optical signal (see Table 5.3).

Table 5.3 1000Base-X Link Configuration Support

Link Configuration	1000Base-CX	1000Base-SX (850 nm Wavelength)	1000Base-LX (1300 nm Wavelength)
150 W STP copper	Supported	Not supported	Not supported
125/62.5 mm multimode optical fiber[1]	Not supported	Supported	Supported
125/50 mm multimode optical fiber	Not supported	Supported	Supported
125/10 mm single mode optical fiber	Not supported	Not supported	Supported
Allowed connectors	IEC style 1 or Fibre Channel style 2	SFF MT-RJ or Duplex SC	SFF MT-RJ or Duplex SC

The 125/62.5 mm specification refers to the cladding and core diameters of the optical fiber.

Network Cabling—Link Crossover Requirements

Link compatibility requires that the transmitters at each end of the link be connected to the receivers at the other end of the link. However, because cable connectors at both ends of the link are keyed the same, the conductors must cross over at some point to ensure that transmitter outputs are always connected to receiver inputs.

Unfortunately, when this requirement first came up in the development of 10Base-T, IEEE 802.3 chose not to make a hard rule as to whether the crossover should be implemented in the cable as shown in Figure 5.29(a) or whether it should be implemented internally as shown in Figure 5.29(b).

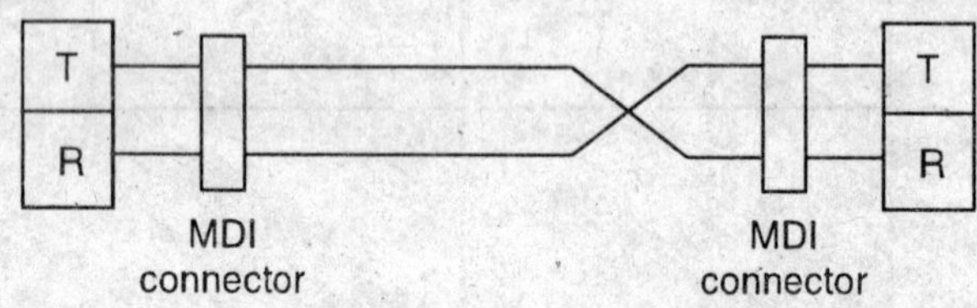

(a) Cable-based crossover

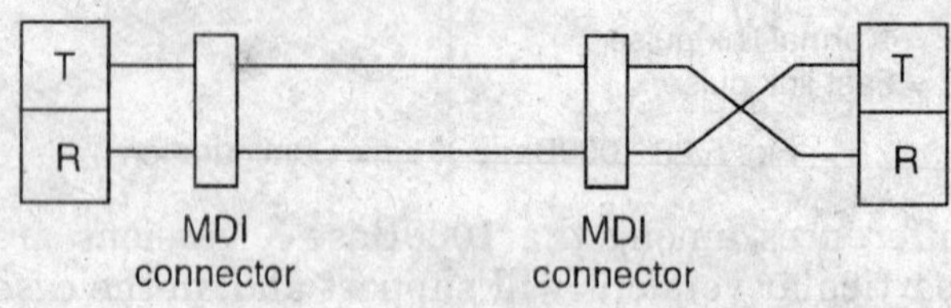

(b) Internal crossover

Fig. 5.29 Alternative Ways for Implementing the Link Crossover Requirement

Instead, IEEE 802.3 defined two rules and made two recommendations:

- There must be an odd number of crossovers in all multiconductor links.
- If a PMD is equipped with an internal crossover, its MDI must be clearly labeled with the graphical X symbol.
- Implementation of an internal crossover function is optional.
- When a DTE is connected to a repeater or switch (DCE) port, it is recommended that the crossover be implemented within the DCE port.

The eventual result was that ports in most DCEs were equipped with PMDs that contained internal crossover circuitry and that DTEs had PMDs without internal crossovers. This led to the following oft-quoted de facto "installation rule"

- Use a straight-through cable when connecting DTE to DCE. Use a crossover cable when connecting DTE to DTE or DCE to DCE.

Unfortunately, the de facto rule does not apply to all Ethernet versions that have been developed subsequent to 10Base-T. As things now stand, the following is true:

- All fiber-based systems use cables that have the crossover implemented within the cable.
- All 100Base systems using twisted-pair links use the same rules and recommendations as 10Base-T.
- 1000Base-T NICs may implement a selectable internal crossover option that can be negotiated and enabled during autonegotiation. When the selectable crossover option is not implemented, 10Base-T rules and recommendations apply.

System Considerations

Given all the choices discussed previously, it might seem that it would be no problem to upgrade an existing network or to plan a new network. The problem is twofold. Not all the choices are reasonable for all networks, and not all Ethernet versions and options are available in the market, even though they may have been specified in the standard.

Choosing UTP-Based Components and Media Category

It should be obvious that UTP-based NICs are available for 10-Mbps, 100-Mbps, and 1000-Mbps implementations. The choice is relatively simple for both 10-Mbps and 1000-Mbps operation: 10Base-T and 1000Base-T. From the previous discussions, however, it would not seem to be that simple for 100-Mbps implementations. Although three UTP-based NICs are defined for 100 Mbps, the market has effectively narrowed the choice to just 100Base-TX, which became widely available during the first half of 1995:

- By the time 100Base-T4 products first appeared on the market, 100Base-TX was well entrenched, and development of the full-duplex option, which 100Base-T4 could not support, was well underway.
- The 100Base-T2 standard was not approved until spring 1997, too late to interest the marketplace. As a result, 100Base-T2 products were not even manufactured. Several choices have also been specified for UTP media: Category 3, 4, 5, or 5E.The differences are cable cost and transmission rate capability, both of which increase with the category numbers. However, current transmission rate requirements and cable cost should not be the deciding factors in choosing which cable category to install. To allow for future transmission rate needs, cables lower than Category 5 should not even be considered, and if gigabit rates are a possible future need, Category 5E should be seriously considered:
- Installation labor costs are essentially constant for all types of UTP four-pair cable.
- Labor costs for upgrading installed cable (removing the existing and installing new) are typically greater than the cost of the original installation. UTP cable is backward-compatible. Higher-category cable will support lower-category NICs, but not vice versa.
- The physical life of UTP cable (decades) is much longer than the useable life of the connected equipment.

Auto-negotiation—An Optional Method for Automatically Configuring Link Operational Modes

The purpose of autonegotiation is to find a way for two NICs that share a UTP link to communicate with each other, regardless of whether they both implemented the same Ethernet version or option set.

Autonegotiation is performed totally within the physical layers during link initiation, without any additional overhead either to the MAC or to higher protocol layers. Autonegotiation allows UTP-based NICs to do the following:

- Advertise their Ethernet version and any optional capabilities to the NIC at the other end of the link.
- Acknowledge receipt and understanding of the operational modes that both NICs share.
- Reject any operational modes that are not shared.
- Configure each NIC for highest-level operational mode that both NICs can support.

Autonegotiation is specified as an option for 10Base-T, 100Base-TX, and 100Base-T4, but it is required for 100Base-T2 and 1000Base-T implementations. Table 5-4 lists the defined selection priority levels (highest level = top priority) for UTP-based Ethernet NICs.

Table 5.4 The Defined Autonegotiation Selection Levels for UTP NICs

Selection Level	Operational Mode	Maximum Total Data Transfer Rate (Mbps)[1]
9	1000Base-T full-duplex	2000
8	1000Base-T half-duplex	1000
7	100Base-T2 full-duplex	200
6	100Base-TX full-duplex	200
5	100Base-T2 half-duplex	100
4	100Base-T4 half-duplex	100
3	100Base-TX half-duplex	100
2	10Base-T full-duplex	20
1	10Base-T half-duplex	10

Because full-duplex operation allows simultaneous two-way transmission, the maximum total transfer rate for full-duplex operation is double the half-duplex transmission rate.

The autonegotiation function in UTP-based NICs uses a modified 10Base-T link integrity pulse sequence in which the NLPs are replaced by bursts of fast link pulses (FLPs), as shown in Figure 5.30. Each FLP burst is an alternating clock/data sequence in which the data bits in the burst identify the operational modes supported by the transmitting NIC and also provide information used by the autonegotiation handshake mechanism. If the NIC at the other end of the link is a compatible NIC but does not have autonegotiation capability, a parallel detection function still allows it to be recognized. A NIC that fails to respond to FLP bursts and returns only NLPs is treated as a 10Base-T half-duplex NIC.

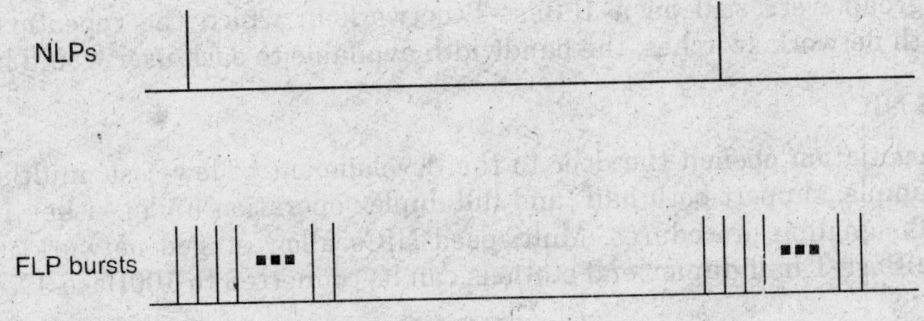

NLP = Normal link pulse
FLP = Fast link pulse

Fig. 5.30 Autonegotiation FLP Bursts Replace NLPs During Link Initiation

At first glance, it may appear that the autonegotiation process would always select the mode supported by the NIC with the lessor capability, which would be the case if both NICs use the same encoding procedures and link configuration. For example, if both NICs are 100Base-TX but only one supports full-duplex operation, the negotiated operational mode will be half-duplex 100Base-TX. Unfortunately, the different 100Base versions are not compatible with each other at 100 Mbps, and a 100Base-TX full-duplex NIC would autonegotiate with a 100Base-T4 NIC to operate in 10Base-T half-duplex mode.

Autonegotiation in 1000Base-X NICs is similar to autonegotiation in UTP-based systems, except that it currently applies only to compatible 1000Base-X devices and is currently constrained to negotiate only half-duplex or full-duplex operation and flow control direction.

Network Switches Provide a Second, and Often Better, Alternative to Higher Link Speeds in CSMA/CD Network Upgrades

Competitively priced network switches became available on the market shortly after the mid-1990s and essentially made network repeaters obsolete for large networks. Although repeaters can accept only one frame at a time and then send it to all active ports (except the port on which it is being received), switches are equipped with the following:

- MAC-based ports with I/O frame buffers that effectively isolate the port from traffic being sent at the same time to or from other ports on the switch.
- Multiple internal data paths that allow several frames to be transferred between different ports at the same time.

These may seem like small differences, but they produce a major effect in network operation. Because each port provides access to a high-speed network bridge (the switch), the collision domain in the network is reduced to a series of small domains in which the number of participants is reduced to two the switch port and the connected NIC. Furthermore, because each participant is now in a private collision domain, his or her available bandwidth has not only been markedly increased, it was also done without having to change the link speed.

Consider, for example, a 48-station workgroup with a couple of large file servers and several network printers on a 100-Mbps CSMA/CD network. The average available bandwidth, not counting interframe gaps and collision recovery, would be 100 3 50 = 2 Mbps (network print servers do not generate network traffic). On the other hand, if the same workgroup were still on a 10Base-T network in which the repeaters had been replaced with network switches, the bandwidth available to each user would be 10 Mbps.

Multispeed NICs

Auto-negotiation opened the door to the development of low-cost, multispeed NICs that, for example, support both half- and full-duplex operation under either 100Base-TX or 10Base-T signaling procedures. Multispeed NICs allow staged network upgrades in which the 10Base-T half-duplex end stations can be connected to 100Base-TX full-duplex

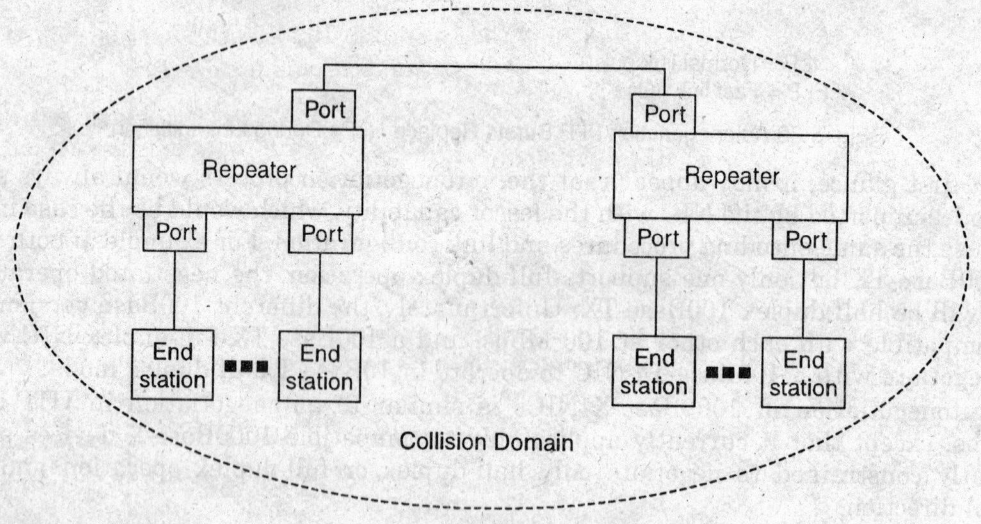

(a) Repeater-based CSMA/CD network

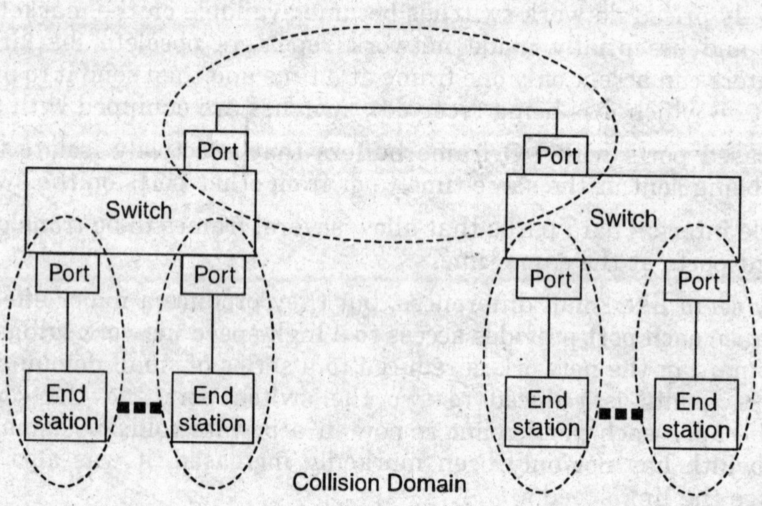

(b) Switch-based CSMA/CD network

Fig. 5.31 Replacing the Network Repeaters with Switches Reduces the Collision Domains to Two NICs Each

switch ports without requiring the NIC in the PC to be changed. Then, as more bandwidth is needed for individual PCs, the NICs in those PCs can be upgraded to 100Base-TX full-duplex mode.

Choosing 1000Base-X Components and Media

Although Table 7.3 shows that there is considerable flexibility of choice in the 1000Base-X link media, there is not total flexibility. Some choices are preferred over others:

- NICs at both ends of the link must be the same 1000Base-X version (CX, LX, or SX), and the link connectors must match the NIC connectors.
- The 1000Base-CX specification allows either style 1 or style 2 connectors, but style 2 is preferred because some style 1 connectors are not suitable for operation at 1250 Mbps. 1000Base-CX links are intended for patch-cord use within a communications closet and are limited to 25 meters.
- The 1000Base-LX and 1000Base-SX specifications allow either the small form factor SFF MT-RJ or the larger duplex SC connectors. Because SFF MT-RJ connectors are only about half as large as duplex SC connectors, and because space is a premium, it follows that SFF MT-RJ connectors may become the predominant connector.
- 1000Base-LX transceivers generally cost more than 1000Base-SX transceivers.
- The maximum operating range for optical fibers depends on both the transmission wavelength and the modal bandwidth (MHz.km) rating of the fiber. See Table 5.5.

Table 5.5 Maximum Operating Ranges for Common Optical Fibers

Fiber Core Diameter/ Modal Bandwidth	1000Base-SX (850 nm Wavelength)	1000Base-LX (1300 nm Wavelength)
62.5 mm multimode fiber (200/500) MHz.km	275 meters	550 meters[1]
50 mm multimode fiber (400/400) MHz.km	500 meters	550 meters[1]
50 mm multimode fiber (500/500) MHz.km	550 meters	550 meters[1]
10 mm single-mode fiber	Not supported	5000 meters

[1]1000Base-LX transceivers may also require use of an offset-launch, mode-conditioning patch cord when coupling to some existing multimode fibers.

The operating ranges shown in Table 5-5 are those specified in the IEEE 802.3 standard. In practice, however, the maximum operating range for LX transceivers over 62.5 mm multimode fiber is approximately 700 meters, and some LX transceivers have been qualified to support a 10,000-meter operating range over single-mode fiber.

Multiple-Rate Ethernet Networks

Given the opportunities shown by the example in the previous sections, it is not surprising that most large Ethernet networks are now implemented with a mix of transmission rates and link media, as shown in the cable model in Figure 5.6.

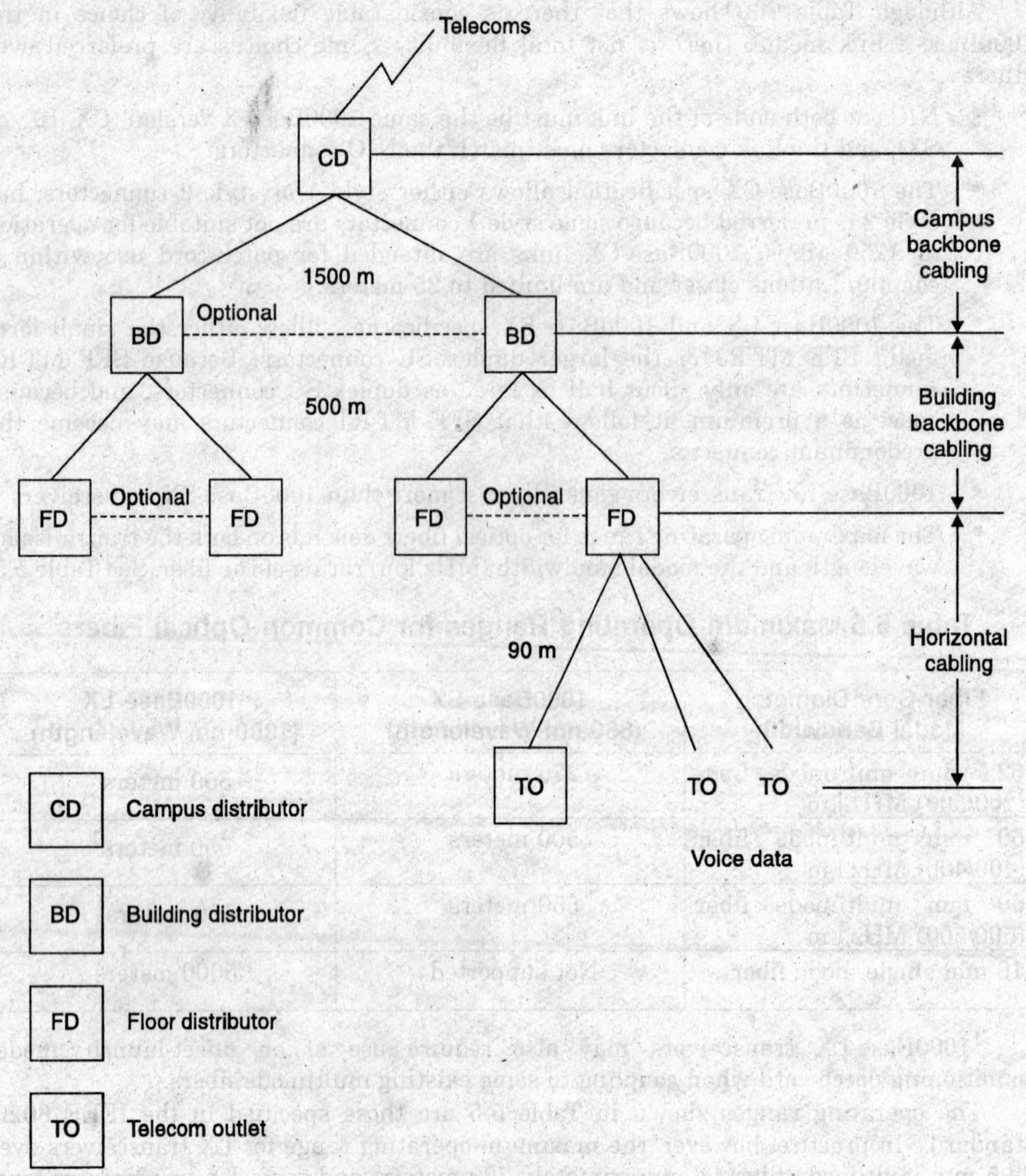

Fig. 5.32 An Example Multirate Network Topologythe ISO/IEC 11801 Cable Model

The ISO/IEC 11801 cable model is the network model on which the IEEE 802.3 standards are based:

- **Campus distributor**—The term campus refers to a facility with two or more buildings in a relatively small area. This is the central point of the campus backbone and the telecom connection point with the outside world. In Ethernet LANs, the campus distributor would typically be a gigabit switch with telecom interface capability.
- **Building distributor**—This is the building's connection point to the campus backbone. An Ethernet building distributor would typically be a 1000/100- or 1000/100/10-Mbps switch.
- **Floor distributor**—This is the floor's connection point to the building distributor. ISO/IEC 11801 recommends at least one floor distributor for every 1000 m2 of floor space in office environments, and, if possible, a separate distributor for each floor in the building. An Ethernet floor distributor would typically be a 1000/100/10- or 100/10-Mbps switch.
- **Telecom outlet**—This is the network connection point for PCs, workstations, and print servers. File servers are typically colocated with and directly connected to the campus, building, or floor distributors, as appropriate for their intended use. Campus backbone cablingThis is typically single- or multimode cable that interconnects the central campus distributor with each of the building distributors.
- **Building backbone cabling**—This is typically Category 5 or better UTP or multimode fiber cable that interconnects the building distributor with each of the floor distributors in the building.
- **Horizontal cabling**—This is predominantly Category 5 or better UTP cable, although a few installations are using multimode fiber.

As with UTP cable selection, the choice of link media and intermediate network nodes should always be made with an eye to future transmission rate needs and the life expectancy of the network elements, unpredictable though they may be. In the 1990s, LAN transmission rates increased 100 times and, by 2002, will increase yet another 10 times.

This does not mean that allow some even end stations and their interconnecting links will require gigabit capability. It does mean, however, that more central network nodes (such as most campus distributors and many building distributors) should be equipped with gigabit capability, and that all floor distributors should have at least 100 Mbps capability. It also means that all network switches should be nonblocking and that all ports should have full-duplex capability, and that any new campus backbone links should be installed with single-mode fiber.

Link Aggregation—Establishing Higher-Speed Network Trunks

Link aggregatio is a recent optional MAC capability that allows several physical links to be combined into one logical higher-speed trunk. It provides the means to increase the effective data rate between two network nodes in unit multiples of the individual link transmission rate rather than in an order-of-magnitude step.

Link aggregation can be a cost-effective way to provide higher-speed connections in Ethernet LANs that are reaching saturation with 100 Mbps transmission rates but that won't require gigabit capability, at least in the short term. For example, the maximum length for 62.5 mm multimode fiber links is 2000 meters at 100 Mbps, and multimode fiber has been often used for campus backbone links. The logical upgrade would seem to be to reuse these links for 1000 Mbps operation, but the maximum supportable length for multimode fiber is only 700 meters and only with 1000Base-LX. If the existing links are longer than 700 meters, aggregating n existing links will support an effective transmission rate of (100 n) Mbps.

Link aggregation should be viewed as a network configuration option that is primarily used in the few interconnections that require higher data rates than can be provided by single links, such as switch-to-switch and in switch-to-file server. It can also be used to increase the reliability of critical links. Aggregated links can be rapidly reconfigured (typically in about 1 second or less) in case of link failure, with low risk of duplicated o reordered frames.

Link aggregation does not affect either the IEEE 802.3 data frame format(s) or any higher layers in the protocol stack. It is backward-compatible with "aggregation-unaware" devices and can be used with any Ethernet data rate (although it does not make sense for 10 Mbps because it would likely cost less to procure a pair of 100-Mbps NICs). Link aggregation can be enabled only on parallel point-to-point links and those that support full-duplex same-speed operation.

Network Management

All higher-speed Ethernet specifications include definitions for managed objects and control agents that are compatible with Simple Network Management Protocol (SNMP) and that can be used to gather statistics about the operation of the network nodes and to assist in network management. Because user information is anecdotal at best and usually comes long after the fact, all larger networks should at least be configured with managed switches and network servers to ensure that potential problems and bottlenecks can be identified before they cause serious network deterioration.

Migrating to Higher-Speed Networks

By now, it should be apparent that upgrading existing networks typically does not require wholesale equipment or media changes, but it does require knowledge of the current network configuration and the network location of potential problems. This means that a network management system should be in place and that a cable plant database should be both available and accurate. It is time-consuming and often difficult to determine link type and availability after the cables have been pulled through conduit, buried in walls, and layered in cable trays.

Links are often the limiting factors in network upgrades. Existing Category 5 links should support all current Ethernet rates from 10 Mbps to 1000 Mbps, although they should be tested to ensure their capability to support gigabit rates. If the network is equipped with only Category 3 cable, some links will have to be replaced before upgrading to 1000 Mbps. A similar situation exists with single- and multimode fiber. Multimode fiber cannot be used for all backbone installations. Single-mode fiber, on the other hand, not only can support all backbone lengths up to 10,000 meters at 1000 Mbps, but it also willbe capable of supporting backbone use at 10-gigabit data rates in the future.

Switch replacement can begin as soon as the necessary links are available. Existing switches at the campus and building distributor levels can often be reused at the building or floor distributor level. NICs can generally be replaced to extend the useful life of end stations. And so on.

5.4 FDDI: Fiber Distributed Data Interchange

The Fiber Distributed Data Interface (FDDI) specifies a 100-Mbps token-passing, dual-ring LAN using fiber-optic cable. FDDI is frequently used as high-speed backbone technology because of its support for high bandwidth and greater distances than copper. It should be noted that relatively recently, a related copper specification, called Copper Distributed Data Interface (CDDI), has emerged to provide 100-Mbps service over copper. CDDI is the implementation of FDDI protocols over twisted-pair copper wire.

FDDI uses dual-ring architecture with traffic on each ring flowing in opposite directions (called counter-rotating). The dual rings consist of a primary and a secondary ring. During normal operation, the primary ring is used for data transmission, and the secondary ring remains idle. The primary purpose of the dual rings is to provide superior reliability and robustness. Figure 5.33 shows the counter-rotating primary and secondary FDDI rings.

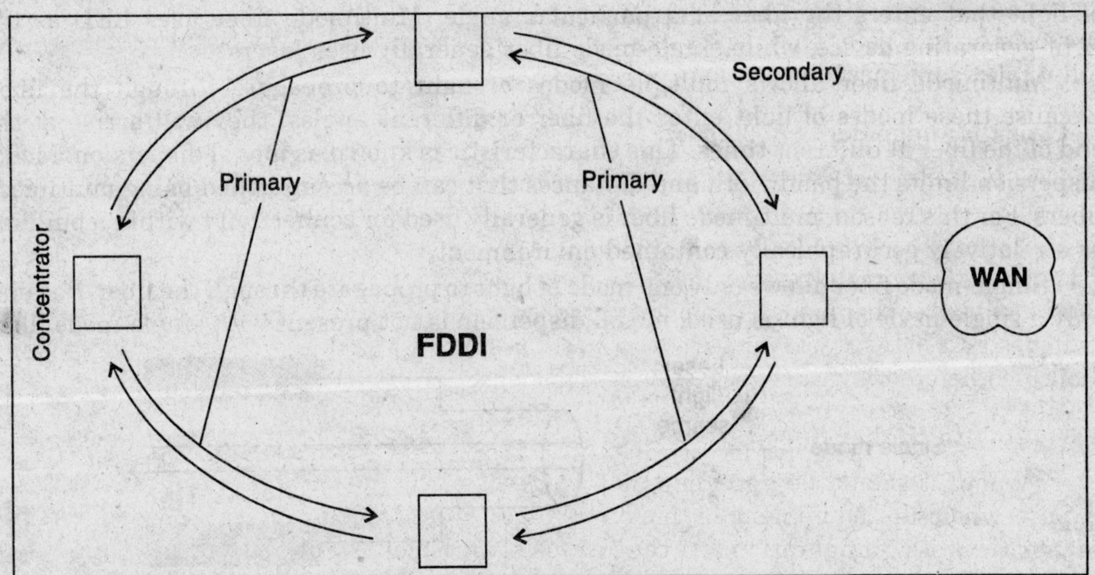

Fig. 5.33 FDDI Uses Counter-Rotating Primary and Secondary Rings

Standards

FDDI was developed by the American National Standards Institute (ANSI) X3T9.5 standards committee in the mid-1980s. At the time, high-speed engineering workstations were beginning to tax the bandwidth of existing local-area networks (LANs) based on Ethernet and Token Ring. A new LAN media was needed that could easily support these workstations and their new distributed applications. At the same time, network reliability had become an increasingly important issue as system managers migrated mission-critical applications from large computers to networks. FDDI was developed to fill these needs. After completing the FDDI specification, ANSI submitted FDDI to the International Organization for Standardization (ISO), which created an international version of FDDI that is completely compatible with the ANSI standard version.

FDDI Transmission Media

FDDI uses optical fiber as the primary transmission medium, but it also can run over copper cabling. As mentioned earlier, FDDI over copper is referred to as Copper-Distributed Data Interface (CDDI). Optical fiber has several advantages over copper media. In particular, security, reliability, and performance all are enhanced with optical fiber media because fiber does not emit electrical signals. A physical medium that does emit electrical signals (copper) can be tapped and therefore would permit unauthorized access to the data that is transiting the medium. In addition, fiber is immune to electrical interference from radio frequency interference (RFI) and electromagnetic interference (EMI). Fiber historically has supported much higher bandwidth (throughput potential) than copper, although recent technological advances have made copper capable of transmitting at 100 Mbps. Finally, FDDI allows 2 km between stations using multimode fiber, and even longer distances using a single mode.

FDDI defines two types of optical fiber: single-mode and multimode. A mode is a ray of light that enters the fiber at a particular angle. Multimode fiber uses LED as the light-generating device, while single-mode fiber generally uses lasers.

Multimode fiber allows multiple modes of light to propagate through the fiber. Because these modes of light enter the fiber at different angles, they will arrive at the end of the fiber at different times. This characteristic is known as modal dispersion. Modal dispersion limits the bandwidth and distances that can be accomplished using multimode fibers. For this reason, multimode fiber is generally used for connectivity within a building or a relatively geographically contained environment.

Single-mode fiber allows only one mode of light to propagate through the fiber. Because only a single mode of light is used, modal dispersion is not present with single-mode fiber.

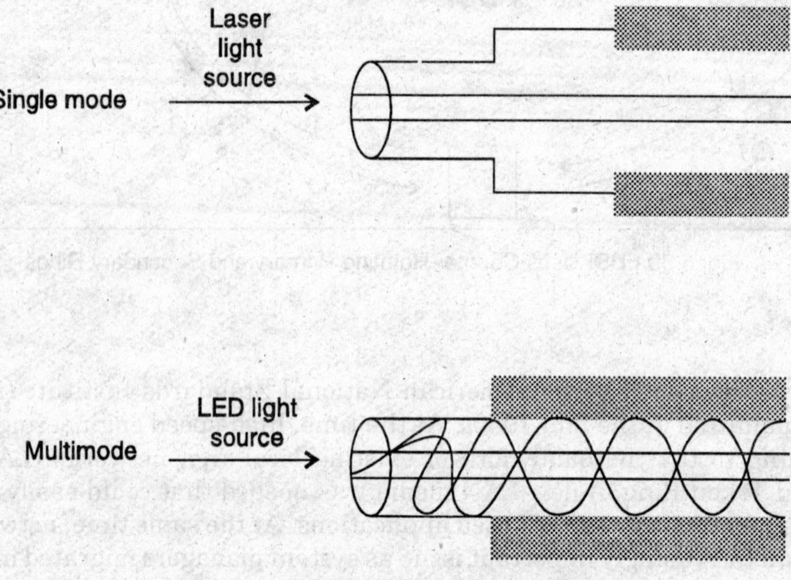

Fig. 5.34 Light Sources Differ for Single-Mode and Multimode Fibers

Therefore, single-mode fiber is capable of delivering considerably higher performance connectivity over much larger distances, which is why it generally is used for connectivity between buildings and within environments that are more geographically dispersed.

Figure 5.34 depicts single-mode fiber using a laser light source and multimode fiber using a light emitting diode (LED) light source.

FDDI Specifications

FDDI specifies the physical and media-access portions of the OSI reference model. FDDI is not actually a single specification, but it is a collection of four separate specifications, each with a specific function. Combined, these specifications have the capability to provide high-speed connectivity between upper-layer protocols such as TCP/IP and IPX, and media such as fiber-optic cabling.

FDDI's four specifications are the Media Access Control (MAC), Physical Layer Protocol (PHY), Physical-Medium Dependent (PMD), and Station Management (SMT) specifications. The MAC specification defines how the medium is accessed, including frame format, token handling, addressing, algorithms for calculating cyclic redundancy check (CRC) value, and error-recovery mechanisms. The PHY specification defines data encoding/decoding procedures, clocking requirements, and framing, among other functions. The PMD specification defines the characteristics of the transmission medium, including fiber-optic links, power levels, bit-error rates, optical components, and connectors. The SMT specification defines FDDI station configuration, ring configuration, and ring control features, including station insertion and removal, initialization, fault isolation and recovery, scheduling, and statistics collection.

FDDI is similar to IEEE 802.3 Ethernet and IEEE 802.5 Token Ring in its relationship with the OSI model. Its primary purpose is to provide connectivity between upper OSI layers of common protocols and the media used to connect network devices. Figure 5.35 illustrates the four FDDI specifications and their relationship to each other and to the IEEE-defined Logical Link Control (LLC) sublayer. The LLC sublayer is a component of Layer 2, the MAC layer, of the OSI reference model.

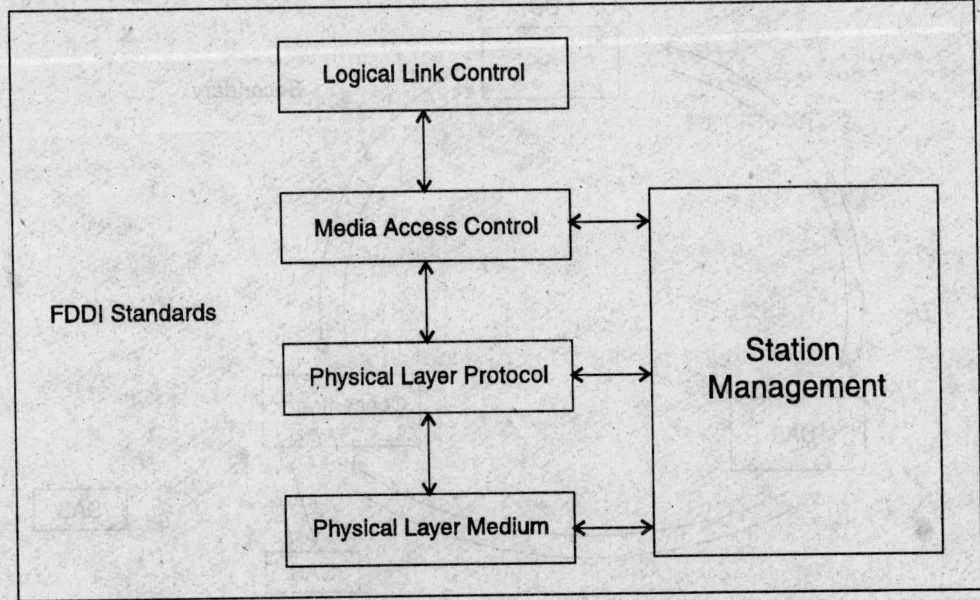

Fig. 5.35 FDDI Specifications Map to the OSI Hierarchical Model

FDDI Station-Attachment Types

One of the unique characteristics of FDDI is that multiple ways actually exist by which to connect FDDI devices. FDDI defines four types of devices: single-attachment station (SAS), dual-attachment station (DAS), single-attached concentrator (SAC), and dual-attached concentrator (DAC).

An SAS attaches to only one ring (the primary) through a concentrator. One of the primary advantages of connecting devices with SAS attachments is that the devices will not have any effect on the FDDI ring if they are disconnected or powered off. Concentrators will be covered in more detail in the following discussion.

Each FDDI DAS has two ports, designated A and B. These ports connect the DAS to the dual FDDI ring. Therefore, each port provides a connection for both the primary and the secondary rings. As you will see in the next section, devices using DAS connections will affect the rings if they are disconnected or powered off. Figure 5.36 shows FDDI DAS A and B ports with attachments to the primary and secondary rings.

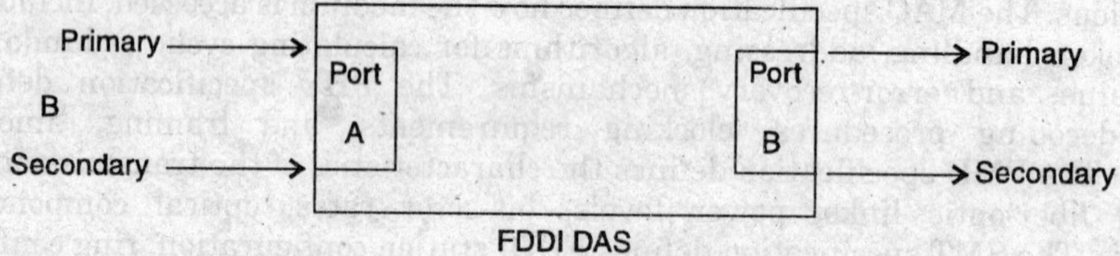

Fig. 5.36 FDDI DAS Ports Attach to the Primary and Secondary Rings

An FDDI concentrator (also called a dual-attachment concentrator [DAC]) is the building block of an FDDI network. It attaches directly to both the primary and secondary rings and ensures that the failure or power-down of any SAS does not bring down the ring. This is particularly useful when PCs, or similar devices that are frequently powered on and off, connect to the ring. Figure 5.37 shows the ring attachments of an FDDI SAS, DAS, and concentrator.

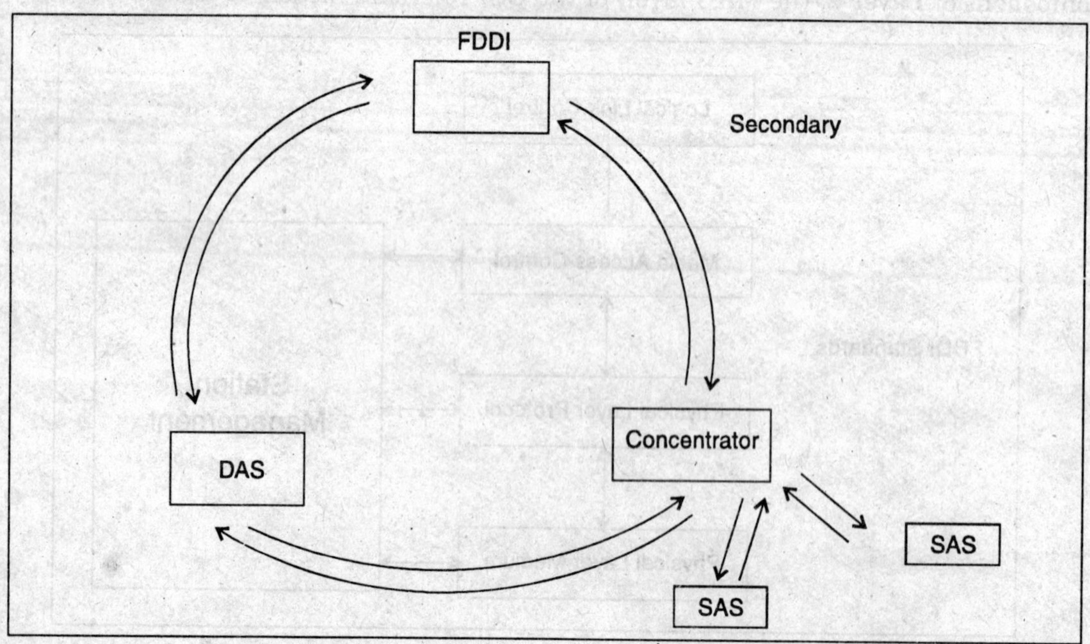

FDDI Fault Tolerance

FDDI provides a number of fault-tolerant features. In particular, FDDI's dual-ring environment, the implementation of the optical bypass switch, and dual-homing support make FDDI a resilient media technology.

Dual Ring

FDDI's primary fault-tolerant feature is the dual ring. If a station on the dual ring fails or is powered down, or if the cable is damaged, the dual ring is automatically wrapped (doubled back onto itself) into a single ring. When the ring is wrapped, the dual-ring topology becomes a single-ring topology. Data continues to be transmitted on the FDDI ring without performance impact during the wrap condition. Figure 5.38 and Figure 5.39 illustrate the effect of a ring wrapping in FDDI.

When a single station fails, as shown in Figure 5.38, devices on either side of the failed (or powered-down) station wrap, forming a single ring. Network operation continues for the remaining stations on the ring.

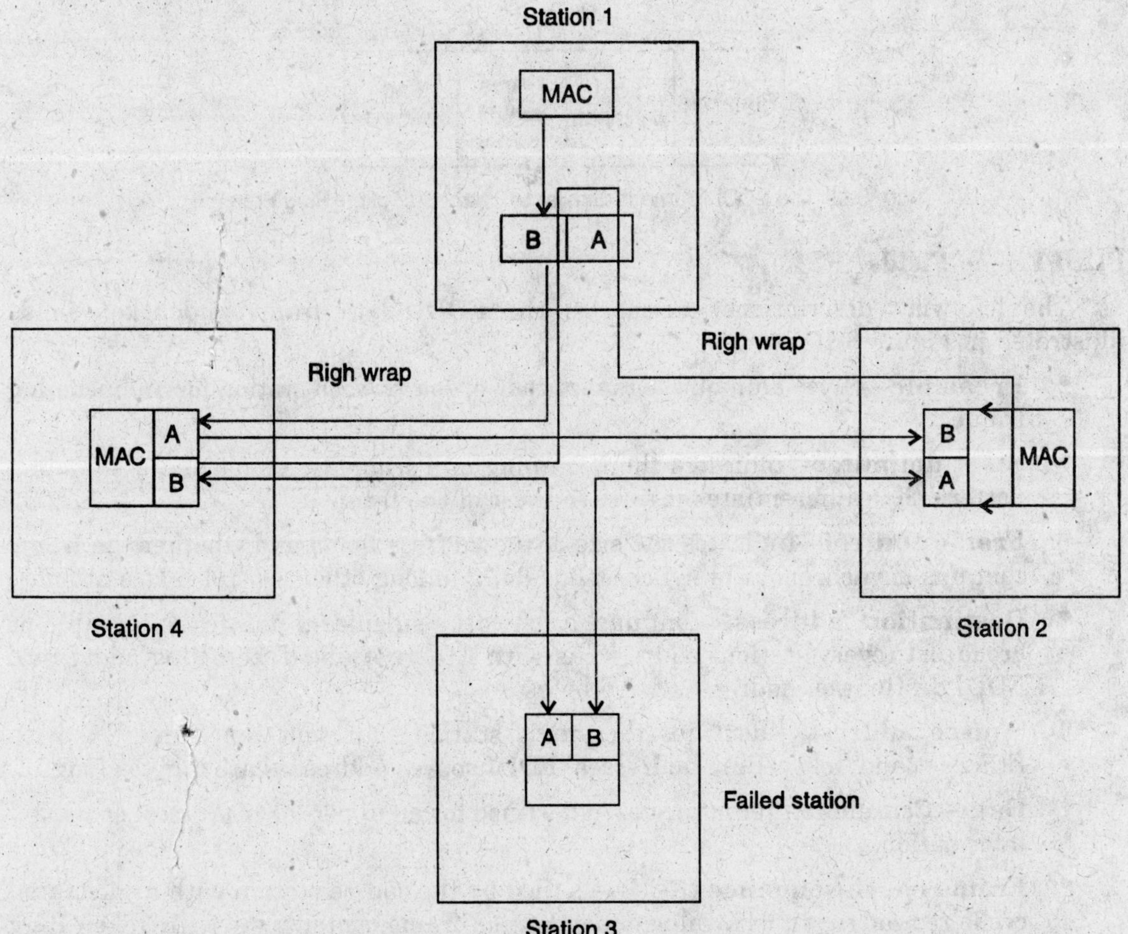

Fig. 5.38 A Ring Recovers from a Station Failure by Wrapping

It should be noted that FDDI truly provides fault tolerance against a single failure only. When two or more failures occur, the FDDI ring segments into two or more independent rings that are incapable of communicating with each other.

FDDI Frame Format

The FDDI frame format is similar to the format of a Token Ring frame. This is one of the areas in which FDDI borrows heavily from earlier LAN technologies, such as Token Ring. FDDI frames can be as large as 4,500 bytes. Figure 5.39 shows the frame format of an FDDI data frame and token.

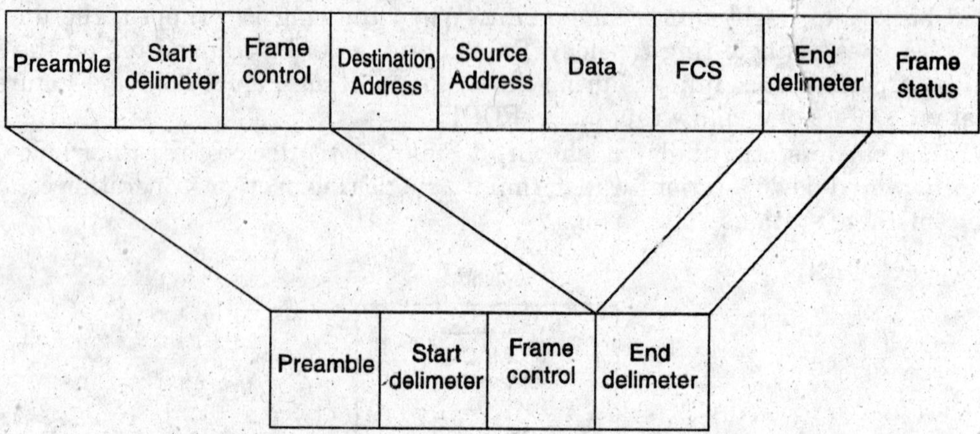

Fig. 5.39 The FDDI Frame Is Similar to That of a Token Ring Frame

FDDI Frame Fields

The following descriptions summarize the FDDI data frame and token fields illustrated in Figure 8.10.

- **Preamble**—Gives a unique sequence that prepares each station for an upcoming frame.
- **Start delimiter**—Indicates the beginning of a frame by employing a signaling pattern that differentiates it from the rest of the frame.
- **Frame control**—Indicates the size of the address fields and whether the frame contains asynchronous or synchronous data, among other control information.
- **Destination address**—Contains a unicast (singular), multicast (group), or broadcast (every station) address. As with Ethernet and Token Ring addresses, FDDI destination addresses are 6 bytes long.
- **Source address**—Identifies the single station that sent the frame. As with Ethernet and Token Ring addresses, FDDI source addresses are 6 bytes long.
- **Data**—Contains either information destined for an upper-layer protocol or control information.
- **Frame check sequence (FCS)**—Is filed by the source station with a calculated cyclic redundancy check value dependent on frame contents (as with Token Ring and Ethernet). The destination address recalculates the value to determine whether the frame was damaged in transit. If so, the frame is discarded.

- **End delimiter**—Contains unique symbols; cannot be data symbols that indicate the end of the frame.
- **Frame status**—Allows the source station to determine whether an error occurred; identifies whether the frame was recognized and copied by a receiving station.

5.5 CDDI : Copper Distributed Data Interchange

Copper Distributed Data Interface (CDDI) is the implementation of FDDI protocols over twisted-pair copper wire. Like FDDI, CDDI provides data rates of 100 Mbps and uses dual-ring architecture to provide redundancy. CDDI supports distances of about 100 meters from desktop to concentrator.

CDDI is defined by the ANSI X3T9.5 Committee. The CDDI standard is officially named the Twisted-Pair Physical Medium-Dependent (TP-PMD) standard. It is also referred to as the Twisted-Pair Distributed Data Interface (TP-DDI), consistent with the term Fiber Distributed Data Interface (FDDI). CDDI is consistent with the physical and media-access control layers defined by the ANSI standard.

The ANSI standard recognizes only two types of cables for CDDI: shielded twisted pair (STP) and unshielded twisted pair (UTP). STP cabling has 150-ohm impedance and adheres to EIA/TIA 568 (IBM Type 1) specifications. UTP is data-grade cabling (Category 5) consisting of four unshielded pairs using tight-pair twists and specially developed insulating polymers in plastic jackets adhering to EIA/TIA 568B specifications.

Figure 5.40 illustrates the CDDI TP-PMD specification in relation to the remaining FDDI specifications.

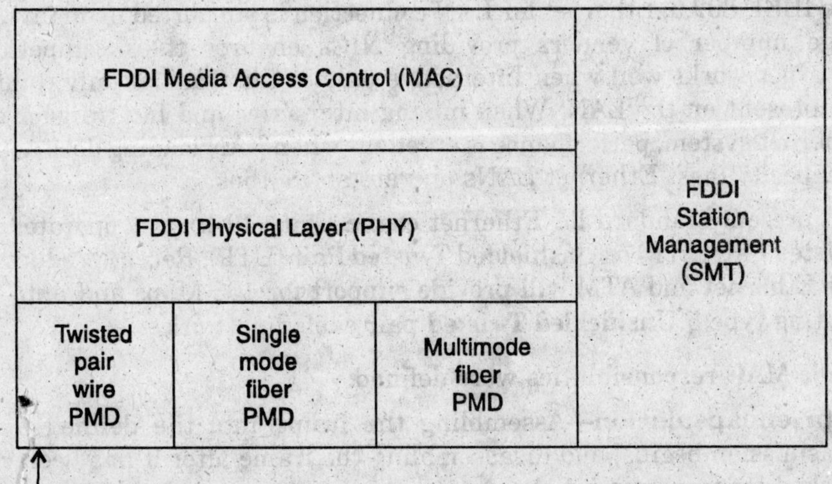

Fig. 5.40 CDDI TP-PMD and FDDI Specifications Adhere to Different Standards

5.6 Summary

- Token Ring NICs were originally IBM products but are now provided and supported by many PC and UNIX vendors. The IEEE 802.5 defines the standards for the interface. Token Ring NICs are particularly desirable for LANs that are collocated with and IBM mainframe.
- They are also useful when Intervallic use is combined on the same LAN with high volume file transfer or print image communications. Token Ring LANs operate at 4 or 16 Mbps. Shielded twisted pair is required by some vendors for 16 Mbps processing but unshielded twisted pair (UTP) cable is supported by many at 16 Mbps and all at 4 Mbps.
- The rapid decline in price for 10 bases T Ethernet and the increasing availability of fast Ethernet means that despite some technical advantages the future of town ring is limited.
- Token Ring technology was developed in the 1970s by IBM. Token-passing networks move a small frame, called a token, around the network. Possession of the token grants the right to transmit. If a node receiving the token has no information to send, it passes the token to the next end station. Each station can hold the token for a maximum period of time. If a station possessing the token does have information to transmit, it seizes the token, alters 1 bit of the token (which turns the token into a start-of-frame sequence), appends the information that it wants to transmit, and sends this information to the next station on the ring.
- The IEEE 802.3, Ethernet for LAN connection is supported by many vendors. The large number of vendors providing NICs ensures their competitive pricing. Ethernet works well when Interactive only or file transfer only communications are present on the LAN. When mixing interactive and file transfer on the same Ethernet system, performance is excellent when LAN loading does not exceed 30% of capacity most Ethernet LANs operate at 10Mbps.
- The present standard for Ethernet connectivity 10 Base T operates on Shielded Twisted Pair (STP) or Unshielded Twisted Pair (UTP). Recent products supporting fast Ethernet and ATM will provide support for 100 Mbps and upto 2.4 Gbps on existing type 5 Unshielded Twisted pair cabled network,

The basic MAC responsibilities were defined:

- **Data encapsulation**—Assembling the frame into the defined format before transmission begins, and disassembling the frame after it has been received and checked for transmission errors.
- **Media access control**—In the required CSMA/CD half-duplex mode, and in the optional full-duplex mode.

Two optional MAC capability extensions and their associated frame formats were discussed. The VLAN tagging option allows network nodes to be defined with logical as well as physical addresses, and provides a means to assign transmission priorities on a frame-by-frame basis. A specific format for the pause frame, which is used for short-term link flow control, is defined in the standard but was not covered here because it is automatic MAC capability that is invoked as needed to prevent input buffer overrun.

The PHY layer discussions included descriptions of the signaling procedures and media requirements/limitations for the following:

- 10Base-T.
- 100Base-TX, 100Base-T4, and 100Base-T2.
- 1000Base-T, 1000Base-CX, 1000Base-LX, and 1000Base-SX.

Although 100Base-FX was not specifically discussed, it uses the same signaling procedure as 100Base-TX, but over optical fiber media rather than UTP copper.

The remaining sections of the chapter were devoted to systems considerations for both twisted-pair and optical fiber LAN implementations:

- Link crossover requirements in UTP networks
- Matching of PMDs and network media to ensure desired data rates
- Use of link aggregation to create higher-speed logical trunks
- Implementation of multispeed networks After essentially finishing the chapter, you should have a reasonable working knowledge of the Ethernet protocol and network technology. The next section should help determine whether you need to go back and reread the chapter.
- Fiber distributed data Interchange is a Protocol originally defined for high speed communications over glass fiber. FDDI provides 100 Mbps through put today. NICs for FDDI are becoming available for more processing environments.This through put is necessary when applications. Deals with large images, large file transfers or multimedia using full motion video. The rapid advances in fast Ethernet and ATM means that FDDI will see limited rollout except for building internet working and WANs.
- The Fiber Distributed Data Interface (FDDI) specifies a 100-Mbps token-passing, dual-ring LAN architecture using fiber-optic cable. FDDI is frequently implemented as a high-speed backbone technology because of its support for high bandwidth and greater distances than copper
- Copper distributed data interchange provide supports for FDDI communications over copper wires. The same 100 Mbps through put is supported over type 1 cobbling shielded twisted pair and standards are emerging to provide support over type 3 cabling unshielded twisted pair that is carefully selected and installed.This Technology is now called Fast Ethernet. CDDI be the protocol of choice for LAN/ WAN Internetworking.

REVIEW QUESTIONS

1. Token Ring networks differ from Ethernet networks in what w]—ays?

   [**Ans.** They are deterministic, meaning that the time before the next token will be passed can be calculated. Extra credit: There are fewer collisions on a Token Ring network than on Ethernet.

2. For what types of applications is this beneficial?

   [**Ans.** Applications in which delay must be predictable, and applications that require a robust network operation.

3. What are the benefits of using FDDI instead of CDDI?

   [**Ans.** Longer distance, no RFI, no EFI.

4. What role does the DAC play in the FDDI network?

   [**Ans.** The concentrator is a dual-attachment station device and ensures that when single-attachment station devicessuch as PCsare turned off, they do not interrupt the network ring.

Chapter 6

Client/Server Systems Development

6.1 Client/Server Systems Development—Service and Support

The services and support regarding to client/server measurely deals with the following activities as:

1) System Administration.
2) Reliability.
3) Survivability.
4) Software Distribution.
5) Performance.
6) Network Management.
7) Help Disk.
8) Remote System Managemen.t
9) Security.
10) LAN / Network Management Issues.
11) Availability.

For a long life of Client/Server system the measure and dense intensity based activity is system Administration.

6.1.1 System Administration

For a right track of system administration, which is responsible for an error free, hanger free and no noise transmission of data is the measure job of the system administrator. The basic principle while system administration is to do it right very first time, that means whenever a network is initially established, its coordination should be devoted at the most in terms of time, cost and available human resources with in the organization.

To host a effective network, which is very much required for the reliable client/server services, the first step is to analyze the whole network system *i.e.*, Analysis of remote workstation of clients, the requirements of the clients, the assisting application to fulfil the requirement of the clients at their own workstation and the remote centralized workstation *i.e.*, on server as well. By identifying the application requirements, the corresponding hardware, network topologies, network media as cabling, hubs etc are identified.

Afterwards, the network (as physical) is established, the next applications are installed at the client and server workstation and afterwards the security system is observed, security system is hosted, network security is analyze, network security chokes are established, and Finally the whole secure network system is tested on the basis of initial analyzed blue prints or pictorial representation.

NOTE : What are Data Centers?

—Data centers are used by highly skilled professionals in the central location, which are prominently deals with the recovery of the data and along with the security of the centralized node data. Example the mirrored disk work as data center.

6.1.2 Reliabilitiy

Reliability in the Client/Server Network application is also one of the important factor but inferred to the system administration. As it has mentioned above the approach of system administration is to do it right at very first time *i.e.*, if the system administration is reliable and efficient it directs whole Client/Server development as Reliable.

The Reliability, Measurely requires application to be protected from overwriting each other and required shared memory to be accessed by the authorized task only i.e. again the secure system is require, which is the responsibility of system administration. Security must be implemented to allow access to resources only by authorized users.

6.1.3 Serviceability

As Reliability, serviceability is also an inferior factor to the system administration. It deal with the access of data at the back and at a front, it deals with the interfaces that has been generated at the server, for the purpose of remote workstation, *i.e.*, the measure impact of GUI provided by the server to the clients. That should be easy to understand, and use to the users.

As an interface importantly, which is not a part of client knowledge or remote users knowledge. A system works that provides the network services with the help of different net protocols and LAN managers along with numerous network applications. Example SMTP (Simple Mail Transfer Protocol).

6.1.4 Software Distribution

Software distribution is an activity which is necessary as per the client requirement *i.e.*, to make the software available which are required for the clients at their workstation to get the facilities or services being provided by the server. For Example, Internet Explorer, Netscape, Navigator, MOSIAC are the browsers by which a user can use the services provided by the application Yahoo, Rediffmail, Hotmail etc.

The application likes yahoo messenger, MSN messengers are used for the purpose of commercial chatting and business dealing visual graphical adaptors software which away clients the facility of webcam, video conferencing etc. It is an important art for an effective client/server system that the server application should built in such a manner, as for them the software distribution is comfortable *i.e.*, Security of the availability of the software should not be there in the market and which is suppose to use at client workstation to get the facility of the server.

6.1.5 Performance

As Reliability, serviceability and the software distribution, the performance is also an inferer factor to the system administration. Performance tells us about the expected output for the certain given input.

In the centralized minicomputer and mainframe environment, trained technical support personnel and operations staff monitor performance on an ongoing basis. If trends show performance degrading, systems managers can add hardware or make adjustments to improve performance before it affects the user community.

The organization learns in advance the resource requirements of new applications changes can be made to the operating environment to ensure that performance will be acceptable.

6.1.6 Network Management

The use of effective LAN manager, LAN server and client/server environments which has already been identified at the time of analysis of networking system (client/server Networking system) while system administration being performed.

Network management tools such as those from open vision, IBM's and Digital Equipment corporation's EMA Products, to name a few all provide a level of remote monitoring that can track response and network loading.

It is impossible to provide adequate support for distributed client/server applications without the capability to support the desktop and the server remotely.

6.1.7 Help Disk

The Help Documentation which should be available at the server side and client side as well, so that if any misunderstanding occurs at the server, professional can use the help contents likewise any problem occurs at the remote workstation i.e. Clients to use effectively the application. The client can use help contents.

For example— In the software installation there is an read me file in which all help contents how we install particular software is given, clients can use this help and works efficiently.

The most efficient and effective way to provide support to client/server users is through the use of the help disk. A help disk is a set of systems and procedures used by technical and applications staff to provide support to end users in areas ranging from basic how to do and problem determination to advanced trouble shooting and diagnosis.

A professional help disk is one of the keys to successful implementation of the client/server model. Remote users require immediate access to assistance. Effective implementation of a Client/Server application depends on the availability of immediate supports when problem occurs.

6.1.8 Remote Systems Management

LAN administrators' would be able to connect remotely to and then manage the workstation of any user who has a problem. LAN from microcosm provides support for the window 3-x desktop.

6.1.9 Security

In any application environment, managers must assess the security requirements. It is necessary to walk a thin line between enough security and over bearing security measures users should find security to be invisible when they are authorized for a function and impenetrable when they are unauthorized. Security of the sever should start by placing physical barriers around unauthorized access. Every user of a client/server application should be assigned a personal ID and password. The ID can be used to assign authority and track access.

6.1.10 LAN and Network Management Issues

LAN management has changed from managing an isolated LAN to managing a LAN that is part of an enterprise network. The challenges of managing local networks, remote networks and interconnections among them are complicated by the lack of global network administration software.

LAN administrators are working more closely with the existing host systems support group the management inform system department. Although the N/W administrator's job is becoming more difficult, it is also is becoming increasingly important as the network plays a more strategic role in business critical application.

6.1.11 Availability

Availability means system uptime or the capability of the system to be available for processing information and doing its expected work whenever called on. Mini-computer and mainframe data centers should provide at least 99.8% availability with today's technology to achieve this level of availability, a combination of technological and procedural steps is followed. Most availability failure today is caused by human error.

6.2 Summary

- To host a effective network, which is very much required for the reliable client/server services, the first step is to analyze the whole network system, *i.e.*, Analysis of remote workstation of clients, the requirements of the clients, the assisting application to fulfil the requirement of the clients at their own workstation and the remote centralized workstation ie. on server as well.
- Data centers are used by highly skilled professionals in the central location, which

are prominently deals with the recovery of the data and along with the security of the centralized node data. Example—the mirrored disk work as data center.

- Reliability in the C/S Network application is also one of the important factor but inferred to the system administration. As it has mentioned above the approach of system administration is to do it right at very first time, *i.e.*, if the system administration is reliable and efficient it directs whole C/S development as Reliable.
- Serviceability is also an inferior factor to the system administration. It deal with the access of data at the back and at a front, it deals with the interfaces that has been generated at the server, for the purpose of remote workstation, *i.e.*, the measure impact of GUI provided by the server to the clients. That should be easy to understand, and use to the users.
- The performance is also an inferer factor to the system administration. Performance tells us about the expected output for the certain given input.
- Network management tools such as those from open vision, IBM's and Digital Equipment corporation's EMA Products, to name a few all provide a level of remote monitoring that can track response and network loading.

REVIEW QUESTIONS

1. Explain the Network Management issues
2. Explain the Help Disk.
3. Explain the Remote Systems Management.
4. Explain the security features.
5. Explain the centalised workstation concepts.
6. Explain the term performance.
7. Explain the serviceability.
8. Explain the Reliability.

Chapter 7

Client / Server Training Concepts

The term training refers to the acquisition of knowledge, skills, and competencies as a result of the teaching of vocational or practical skills and knowledge that relate to specific useful competencies. The need to continue training beyond initial qualifications to maintain, upgrade and update skills throughout working life. People within many professions and occupations may refer to this sort of training as professional development.

Some commentators use a similar term for workplace learning to improve performance: training and development. One can generally categorize such training as on-the-job or off-the-job:

- On-the-job training takes place in a normal working situation, using the actual tools, equipment, documents or materials that trainees will use when fully trained. On-the-job training has a general reputation as most effective for vocational work.
- Off-the-job training takes place away from normal work situations - implying that the employee does not count as a directly productive worker while such training takes place. Off-the-job training has the advantage that it allows people to get away from work and concentrate more thoroughly on the training itself. This type of training has proven more effective[citation needed] in inculcating concepts and ideas.

Training differs from exercise in that people may dabble in exercise as an occasional activity for fun. Training has specific goals of improving one's capability, capacity, and performance.

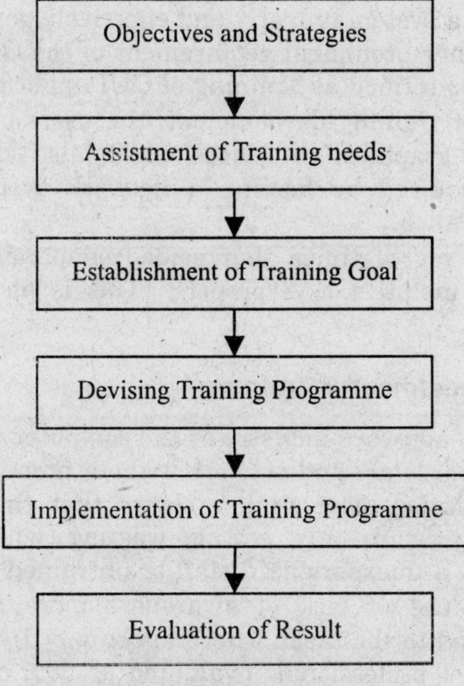

Fig. 7.1 Training process

7.1 Training

Training is basically of two types :

- Graphical Training
- Non-graphical Training

"Training is an investment in human resource with a promise of better returns in the future". Successful candidates placed on jobs, needs training to perform their duties effectively. Workers must be trained to operate the machines, reduce scrap and avoid the accidents.

It is not only the workers who need training, supervisors, managers executives and system administrator also need to be develop in order to help them to grow and acquire maturity of thought and actions.

7.2 Training Advantages

- Reduce the cost of Investment and training
- Effective Technical Staff : Towards cost schedule and quality.

The major activity for the Client/Server services is the system administration. If the system administration is effective, rest activities like reliability, usability, serviceability etc are of inferred nature. For a best ever hosting of Client/Server network system, the effective training of the staff is required.

The first step of effective training to the system administrative staff is to understand by a first look i.e. the training towards the understandability of GUI which measurably gives the directives to host a system properly and effectively generate a best coordinated network system and the other prominent requirement of the Client/Server applications. The above sometimes is also termed as Training of GUI application.

Usually in this kind of training development, the users or the administrators are trained by showing some graphical interfaces which also keeps the information of applications which are required by hosting a network system and the way these applications, should be installed.

It has been observed no. of times that some commercial package provides the graphical tutorial how to install a S/W properly. This is also termed as training of applications with GUI.

7.2.1 Reduce cost of Investment & Training

Previous observation of software industry or the computer industry makes as aware collapsing of the assisting hardware and network without proper guidance installation or without trend staff installation. The studies shows that the around 40%–45% cost (Schedule) towards the hardware only, getting wasting, when client/server network systems are setup either by a unexperienced staff or untrained staff.

Apart from this, because of lack of awareness more number of professionals (administrators) are engaged to the tasks where infect only 1/4 of present professionals are required. So this cost of professionals evaluated as 58% of the total Client/Server Network system cost on an average the extra investment towards the computer Hardware, the network Hardware, the assisting network Software and finally towards the professionals is evaluated as 65% of the total investment of the organization.

The other aspects of the training i.e. if an organization is having efficient trend staff then the training cost of the lower level staff in the other organization can be reduced and apart from this the training cost of lower level staff with the help of GUI application can also be reduced within the same organization. As things can be repeatedly shown not required separate Hardware and stably analysis at any point of time.

7.2.2 Effective Technical Staff

With the help of effective technical staff as we have discussed the cost of extra investment towards the Hardware and professionals can be reduced. Apart from this the measure orientations of the organization is maintain i.e. Schedule, things or the projects must be delivered within the prespecified time. As with the effective technical staff, the integration of Hardware has done in the best ever manner and the integrated Hardware resources are the best-coordinated resources, with the existing Client/Server application. So the input as request and output as provider is done in a speed with in the time and with the expected quality level. The quality level is analyzed on the basis of following parameters like :

- Efficiency (Seek time, Run time, Through put and Response time).
- Correctness (the expected output with the given input)
- Reliability (the correct output with the pre-specified efficiency)
- Interactive usability (easy to understand and use)

- Maintainability (directives to update the Client/Server network system, i.e. Data dictionary and flexi records) etc.

7.3 Training for System Administration

The cost of training experts administrators and technicians in such that most organization will need to provide remote LAN and WAN management support specially. Other than this they also take care of the protocol, which deals with the request of remote clients or human. The operating system is also one of the parts of consideration in system administration training program. Other than this for the best coordinated Software and Hardware resources at the workstation the administrator training is required in following areas :

8 LAN Administration Issues.
9 WAN Administration Issues.
10 Operating system Issues.
11 Workstations S/W and H/W Resource.
12 Assisting C/S S/W Issues.

7.3.1 LAN Administration

The LAN administrator training prominently deals with the issues a Naming (identifying the remote clients), security of the centralized system, and help procedure for the both and so on. Must be understood and implemented uniformly between the applications and protocols.

LAN administration also take of the security of the central system as backing up the database with either mirrored disk or other devices. In a similar way LAN administration also provides the help documentations at the different remote workstations so that the error regarding to the coordination between the workstation and server can be sorted out at their own without the interference of system administrator or system analyst.

Likewise, the security system of the LAN administration provides certain logging or logging group name with unidentified password in text. The disk space management is also the part of system administrator training that is why hosting a LAN.

7.3.2 WAN Administration

WAN is the network of network. All the same WAN network issues associated with remote terminal access to host systems exists in the client/server to WAN access. Additional complexities arises when data is distributed to the remote LAN. Application programs that are distributed to remote servers present many of the same problems as do distributed databases. Administrators must be trained in software and in procedures to handle network definition network management and remote backup and recovery. It is imperative to train the WAN administrator in the use of remote management tools.

Training developers in WAN issues is also critical because of the WAN's impact on communication issues. Where data is stored and how it is to be retrieved must be considered in the development of applications. Training WAN administrators to understand all of the options available to establish an optimal topology is more expensive.

7.3.3 Operating System Issues

Administrators must be expertly trained in the operating system used by clients and servers in the client/server applications. The bestly coordinated operating system which is identified on the basis of its memory management system, LAZY swapper, virtual memory and other fragmentation & defragmentation concepts of the operating system. It should have certain availability of the application which are able to coordinate the utility of the server with the help of the LAN

7.3.4 Workstation Software and Hardware Resources Issue

Administrators must be trained in the basis Hardware components of the workstation. Many problems that occur in the field can be fixed remotely by a user with direction from the remote administrator common problems such as unplugged devices, loose cards or lost configuration can often be repaired by a user with some willingness to follow directions.

Administrators and support personnel should be trained in the software to support remote PC workstations losing. He gives directives to remote users about some basic problems related to software. Example, Software installation etc.

7.3.5 Assisting Client / Server Software Issues, i.e., Application Issues

Administrators must be well versed (trained) in the applications to enable rapid and effective communications with remote users. They should be trained in both the Functionality and technology of the applications. It is common to designate a user as the support administrator for an application, because most problems related to applications, the applications support administrator should be an expert in how business users utilize the application.

7.4 Database Administrator Training

Database administrator faces additional challenges in a client/server implementation when data is distributed. Even in single site, shared database applications, the client/server model typically leads to adhoc end user access. Most current host implementations operate in an environment where trained operations and technical support staff are operating and supporting the applications.

This ensures that standard operating procedures will be followed and that problems can be solved quickly by experienced technical support personnel. In the client/server environment, distributed data implies that data may be stored where no skilled staff are available to provide support. In addition the additional complexity of the new environment requires new training for existing database administration staff.

Design issues are particularly critical here because performance can be dramatically affected by location of data. Remote control of utility functions is mandatory and training existing staff to handle these procedures presents real challenges, especially when they continue to operate existing system. The use of SDE developed standard procedures that are reused between applications will allow this training to be provided once and applied to all new Client / Server applications.

7.5 End User Training

End user should be trained once in the user interface standards defined by the organization as part of the SDE (Software Development Environment). The best time to provide this training is in conjunction with the first application. It is likely that user will already know how to use a workstation for personal productivity. The new standards will not be dramatically different from those currently used unless a very different technology is being employed.

i) Workstation Operations.
ii) Applications and New Technologies

7.5.1 Workstation Operations

It is important to train in the shared use of the workstation for personal productivity and client/server application functionality. Users will be very unhappy if their existing valued capabilities are lost as a result of the new system. This training should include such standard features as security, help, navigation, (How to gel groom one function to the next), table management and scrolling, as well as standard business processes such as viewing, adding changing and deleting information.

7.5.2 Applications and New Technologies

When the standard environment is understood, the particular application processes can be trained within this environment. In the future, new applications, should require only training in the new business processes, training can not take place on software is faculty user confidence and concentration will be lost if errors are regularly encountered. Version releases of the software should enable training to be provided on portions of the applications as it is ready, without the need to wait for products to be completed.

7.6 Future of Client / Server Computing

The single-system image is a reality. In the future, cheap and powerful workstation technology will be available to everyone-with truly distributed applications using processing power wherever it is available and providing information wherever it is needed. In the future, information will be available for use by owners and authorized users, without the constant need for professional systems developers and their complex programming languages. The future will bring information captured at its source and available immediately to authorized users.

The future will provide information from data in its original form: image, video, audio, graphics, document, spreadsheet, or structured data, without the need to be aware of specific software for each form. Successful organizations of the future-those that are market-driven and competitive-will be ones using client/server as an enabling technology to add recognized value to their product or service. The future is now for early adopters of technology. By the turn of the century, the enterprise on the desk will be the norm for all successful organizations.

Client/Server architecture is really a fundamental enabling approach that provides the most flexible framework for using new technologies like the World Wide Web, as they come along. The old paradigm of host centric, time shared computing has given way to a new client/server approach, which is message based and modular. The examples below show how most new technologies can be viewed as simply different implementation strategies built on a client/server foundation.

File Server

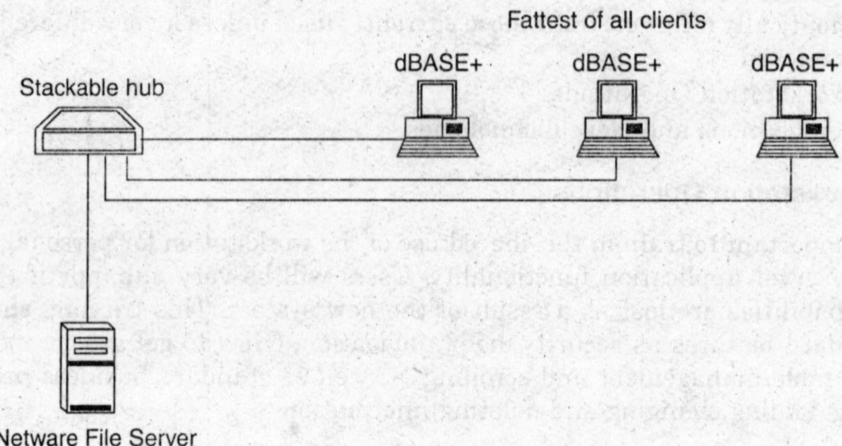

Fig. 7.2 File Server

Even though most people use the term "client/server" when talking about group computing with PC's on networks, PC network computing evolved before the client/server model started gaining acceptance in the late 1980's. These first PC networks were based on the file sharing metaphor illustrated in the figure entitled FILE SERVER. In file sharing, the server simply downloads or transfers files from the shared location to your desktop where the logic and data for the job run in their entirety. This approach was popularized mostly by X-base style products (d-BASE, FoxPro and Clipper). File sharing is simple and works as long as shared usage is low, update contention is very low, and the volume of data to be transferred is low compared with LAN capacity.

As PC LAN computing moved into the 90's two mega trends provided the impetus for client/server computing. The first was that as first generation PC LAN applications and their users both grew, the capacity of file sharing was strained. Multi-user X-base technology can provide satisfactory performance for a few up to maybe a dozen simultaneous users of a shared file, but it's very rare to find a successful implementation of this approach beyond that point. The second change was the emergence and then dominance of the GUI metaphor on the desktop. Very soon GUI presentation formats, led by Windows and Mac, became mandatory for presenting information. The requirement for GUI displays meant that traditional mini or mainframe applications with their terminal displays soon looked hopelessly out of date.

2 Tier Architecture

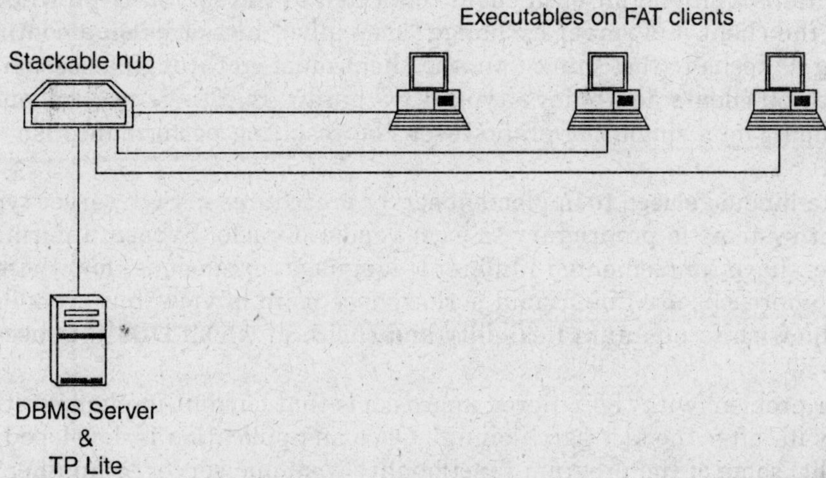

Fig. 7.3 2 Tier Architecture

The architecture and technology that evolved to answer this demand was client/server, in the guise of a two-tiered approach. By replacing the file server with a true database server, the network could respond to client requests with just the answer to a query against a relational DBMS (rather than the entire file). One benefit to this approach, then, is to significantly reduce network traffic. Also, with a real DBMS, true multi-user updating is now easily available to users on the PC LAN. By now, the idea of using Windows or Mac style PC's to front end a shared database server is familiar and widely implemented.

In a 2-tier client/server architecture, as shown in the figure entitled 2-TIER ARCHITECTURE, RPC's or SQL are typically used to communicate between the client and server. The server is likely to have support for stored procedures and triggers. These mean that the server can be programmed to implement business rules that are better suited to run on the server than the client, resulting in a much more efficient overall system.

Since 1992 software vendors have developed and brought to market many toolsets to simplify development of applications for the 2-tier client/server architecture. The best known of these tools are Microsoft's Visual Basic, Borland's Delphi, and Sybase's PowerBuilder. These modern, powerful tools combined with literally millions of developers who know how to use them, means that the 2-tiered client/server approach is a good and economical solution for certain classes of problems.

The 2-tiered client/server architecture has proven to be very effective in solving workgroup problems. "Workgroup", as used here, is loosely defined as a dozen to 100 people interacting on a LAN. For bigger, enterprise-class problems and/or applications that are distributed over a WAN, use of this 2-tier approach has generated some problems.

Client/Server in Large Enterprise Environments

What typically happens with client/server in large enterprise environments is that the performance of a 2-tier architecture deteriorates as the number of on-line users increases. The reason for this is due to the connection process of the DBMS server. The DBMS maintains a thread for each client connected to the server. Even when no work is being done, the client and server exchange "keep alive" messages on a continuous basis. If something happens to the connection, the client must go through a session reinitiating process. With 50 clients and today's typical PC hardware, this is no problem. When one has 2,000 clients on a single server, however, the resulting performance isn't likely to be satisfactory.

The data language used to implement server procedures in SQL server type data base management systems is proprietary to each vendor. Oracle, Sybase, Informix and IBM, for example, have implemented different language extensions for these functions. Proprietary approachs are fine from a performance point of view, but are a disadvantage for users who wish to maintain flexibility and choice in which DBMS is used with their applications.

Another problem with the 2-tiered approach is that current implementations provide no flexibility in "after the fact partitioning". Once an application is developed it isn't easy to move (split) some of the program functionality from one server to another. This would require manually regenerating procedural code. In some of the newer 3-tiered approaches to be discussed below, tools offer the capability to "drag and drop" application code modules onto different computers.

The industry's response to limitations in the 2-tier architecture has been to add a third, middle tier, between the input/output device (PC on your desktop) and the DBMS server. This middle layer can perform a number of different functions - queuing, application execution, database staging and so forth. The use of client/server technology with such a middle layer has been shown to offer considerably more performance and flexibility than a 2-tier approach.

Just to illustrate one advantage of a middle layer, if that middle tier can provide queuing, the synchronous process of the 2-tier approach becomes asynchronous. In other words, the client can deliver its request to the middle layer, disengage and be assured that a proper response will be forthcoming at a later time. In addition, the middle layer adds scheduling and prioritization for the work in process. The use of architecture with such a middle layer is called "3-tier" or "multi-tier". These two terms are largely synonymous in this context.

There's no free lunch, however, and the price for this added flexibility and performance has been a development environment that is considerably more difficult to use than the very visually oriented development of 2-tiered applications.

3-Tier with a TP Monitor

The most basic type of middle layer (and the oldest, the concept on mainframes dating from the early 1970's) is the transaction processing monitor or TP monitor. You can think of a TP monitor as a kind of message queuing service. The client connects to the TP monitor instead of the database server. The transaction is accepted by the monitor, which queues it and then takes responsibility for managing it to correct completion.

TP monitors first became popular in the 1970's on mainframes. On-line access to mainframes was available through one of two metaphors - time sharing or transaction processing (OLTP). Time sharing was used for program development and the computer's

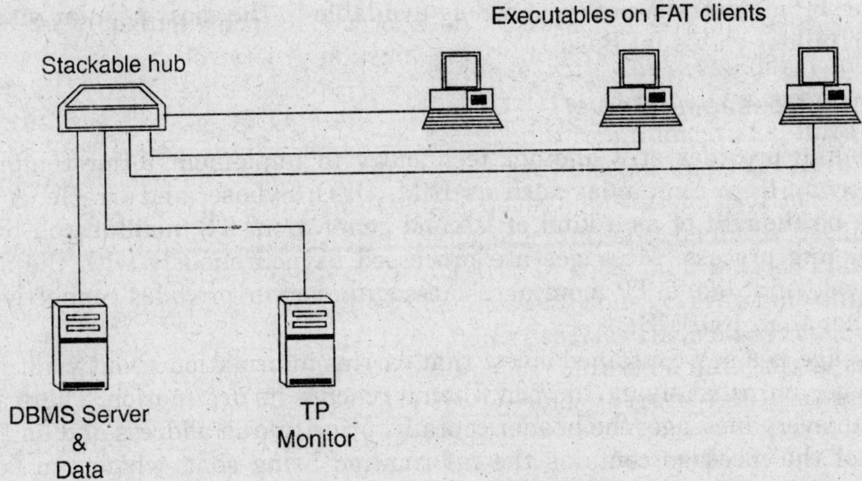

Fig. 7.4 3-Tier TP monitor

resources were allocated with a simple scheduling algorithm like round robin. OLTP scheduling was more sophisticated and priority driven. TP monitors were almost always used in this environment, and the most popular of these was IBM's CICS (pronounced "kicks").

As client/server applications gained popularity over the early 1990's, the use of TP monitors dropped by the wayside. That happened principally because many of the services provided by a TP monitor were available as part of the DBMS or middleware software provided by vendors like Sybase, Gupta, and Oracle. Those embedded (in the DBMS) TP services have acquired the nickname "TP Lite". The "Lite" term comes from experience that DBMS-based transaction processing works OK as long as a relatively small number (d) of clients are connected.

TP monitors (TP Heavy) have staged a comeback because their queuing engines provide a funneling effect, reducing the number of threads a DBMS server needs to maintain. The client connects with the monitor, which accepts the message and queues it for processing against the database. Once the monitor has accepted the message, the client can be released for further processing. The synchronous session based computing of a 2-tier architecture, then, becomes asynchronous through the insertion of the TP monitor into the equation. The monitor smoothes out and lowers the overhead of accessing the database server.

Some other key services a monitor provides are: the ability to update multiple different DBMS in a single transaction; connectivity to a variety of data sources including flat files, non relational DBMS, and the mainframe; the ability to attach priorities to transactions; and robust security, including Kerberos. The net result of using a 3-tier client/server architecture with a TP monitor is that the resulting environment is FAR more scaleable than a 2-tier approach with direct client to server connection. For really large (e.g., 1,000 user) applications, a TP monitor is one of the most effective solutions.

As you might expect, however, there is a downside to network-based TP monitors. At this point in time, the major problem with using this approach is that the code to implement TP monitors is usually written in a lower level language (like COBOL), and support for TP monitors is not (yet) widely available in the most popular visual toolsets like PowerBuilder or Visual Basic.

3-Tier with a Messaging Server

Messaging provides still another technology to implement 3-tier computing. It is available today from companies such as IBM, DEC, Sybase, and Oracle. A messaging server can be thought of as a kind of "second generation" TP monitor and provides the same funneling process. Messages are processed asynchronously with the appropriate priority level. And, like a TP monitor, a messaging server provides connectivity to data sources other than RDBMS.

A message is a self contained object that carries information about what it is, where it needs to go, and what should happen when it reaches its destination. There are at least two parts to every message; the header contains priority, and address and an ID number. The body of the message contains the information being sent, which can be anything including text, images or transactions.

A primary difference from TP Monitors is that message server architecture is designed around intelligence in the message itself as opposed to a TP monitor environment which places the system intelligence in the monitor or the process logic of the application server.

In a TP monitor environment the transactions are simply dumb packets of data. They travel over a pre-existing and pre-defined connection to the TP Monitor. The TP Monitor interrogates and processes the transaction, usually submitting the request to a server tier application. If the TP Monitor doesn't understand the data, it doesn't get processed. Ultimately, the TP Monitor needs to know as much about the transaction as the server tier does.

Contrasting with this, in a message-based architecture there's intelligence in the message itself. The message server just becomes a container of messages and their stored procedures. The operations performed by the message server on the message are communications related (e.g. encrypt message over one service and decrypt message ser. over another service). For the most part, messages are treated as discrete objects. The message contains all the information needed to transverse network services (i.e. network addresses, both logical and physical). Because the message contains the intelligence, the middle tier of a message-based system is more flexible than a TP monitor. For one kind

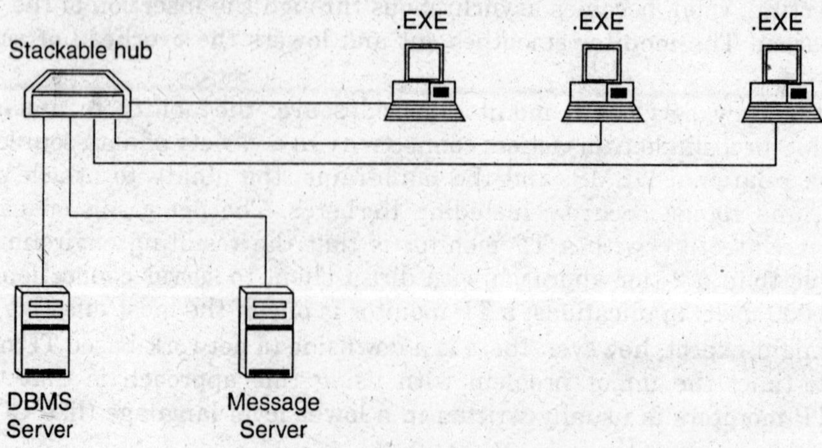

Fig. 7.5 Message based client/sever

of message, the middle tier may simply serve as a routing point between two kinds of network services. For another kind of message, the middle tier may execute a stored procedure or business rule as directed by the message. This abstraction of the middle-tier away from the contents and behavior of the information flowing through it makes the system more portable to different environments and networks. The specifics of communicating the information are hidden underneath the messaging service.

Messaging systems are designed for robustness. By using store and forward logic, they provide message delivery after and around failures. They also provide independence from the enabling technologies such as wired or wireless or protocols. They don't require a persistent connection between the client and server. They are robust because message delivery can be programmed to occur after or around failures. Because messaging systems support an emerging wireless infrastructure, they should become popular for supporting mobile and occasionally connected workers.

A typical message server architecture would look like the figure entitled MESSAGE BASED CLIENT/SERVER, which of course, looks just like any of the other 3-tier approaches we're going to discuss. The architecture of an application that uses messaging services will turn out to look similar to an approach that depends on distributed objects and object request brokers (ORB's) for communication. If you're unwilling or unable to wait for the arrival of distributed object technologies to build your application (widespread popularity probably won't happen with ORB's until the end of the 1990's), you can construct a reasonable clone using the messaging approaches that are now available. When distributed objects are a reality, you can migrate your application if that seems like the best move.

3-Tier with an Application Server

When most people talk of 3-tier architectures, they mean the approach of an application server (illustrated below). With this approach most of the application's business logic is moved from the PC and into a common, shared host server. The PC is basically used for presentation services - not unlike the role that a terminal plays on a mainframe. Of course, because we are talking about a real PC here, it still has the advantages of being used for client side application integration (via OLE or other approach) if desired.

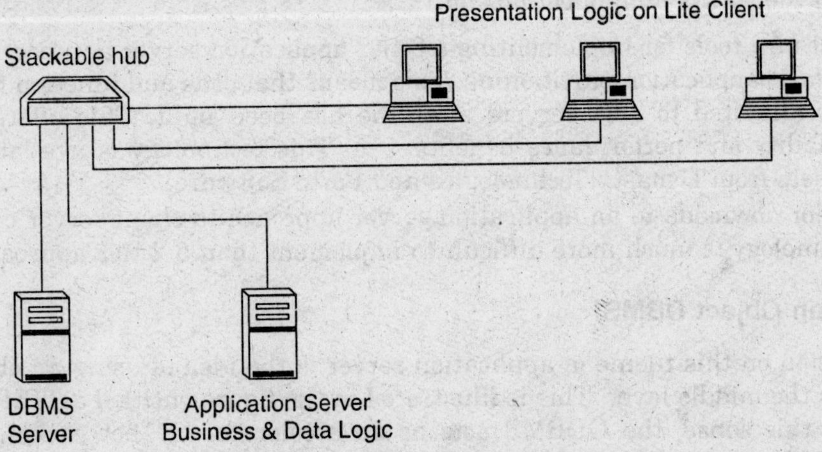

Fig. 7.6 3-Tier Applications

The application server approach is similar in overall concept to the X architecture that was developed at MIT in the 1980's. In X the goal is to allow host-based computing with graphical interfaces on the desktop (I'm using the term "desktop" here because in the X architecture, the term "server" refers to the graphical server which sits on the desktop and the term "client" refers to where the application runs - on the shared host). The similarity between X and a 3-tiered client/server architecture with an application server is that both architectures have the goal of pulling the main body of application logic off the desktop and running it on a shared host.

The application server is also similar to a mainframe in that it doesn't need to worry about driving a GUI, and therefore it's a shared business logic, computation, and data retrieval engine. This server normally operates under a 32 bit multitasking OS like NT, OS/2, NetWare or UNIX. As an option, these OS' all run on symmetric multiprocessing (SMP) configurations. In addition, some are available on massively parallel hardware. Therefore, the server is very scaleable in terms of performance. As new versions of the application software are developed and released, the installation of that software occurs on the one server rather than hundreds or thousands of PC's.

The approach of putting business logic on a server offer a number of important advantages to the application designer:

- When less software is on the client, there is less worry about security since the important software is on a server in a more controlled environment.
- The resulting application is more scalable with an application server approach. For one thing servers are far more scalable than PC's: While a server could be a single Pentium based Compaq or Dell, it could also be a symmetric multiprocessing Sequent, with 32 or more processors. Or, it could be a massively parallel UNIX processor like IBM's SP2.
- The support and installation costs of maintaining software on a single server is much less than trying to maintain the same software on hundreds or thousands of PC's.
- With a middle application server tier it's much easier to design the application to be DBMS- agnostic. If you want to switch to another DBMS vendor, it's more achievable with reasonable effort with a single multithreaded application than with thousands of applications on PC's.
- Most new tools for implementing a 3-tier application server approach offer "after the fact" application partitioning. This means that code and function modules can be reallocated to new servers after the has been built. This offers important flexibility and performance benefits. (e.g. This technology is available today in toolsets from Dynasty Technologies and Forte Software).

The major downside to an application server approach to client/server computing is that the technology is much more difficult to implement than a 2-tier approach.

3-Tier with an Object DBMS

A variation on this theme of application server is the idea of using an object DBMS (ODBMS) as the middle layer. This is illustrated in the figure entitled 3-TIER WITH AN ODBMS. In this sense, the ODBMS acts as an accelerator or "hot cache". Data in a relational DBMS is usually stored in normalized fashion across many tables and for access

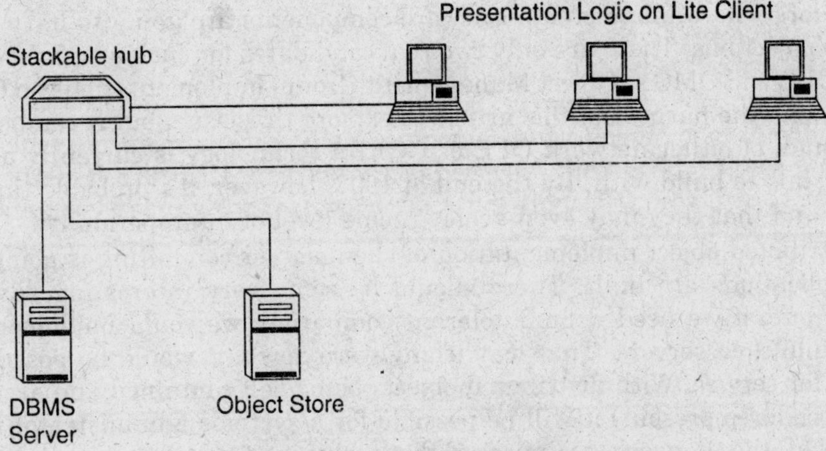

Fig. 7.7 3-Tier with an ODBMS

by different applications and users. This generalized form of storage may prove inadequate (performance wise) for the needs of any one particular application. An ODBMS can be used to retrieve the data from the common store, assemble it for efficient usage by your application, and provide a persistent store for that data as long as your application might need it. Since extended data types like video or voice are not typically supported in today's RDBMS, those data types might also be stored in the ODBMS, which could then associate the appropriate multimedia data with the data retrieved from the RDBMS.

Distributed Components and the 3-Tier Architecture

This brings us to distributed object computing and components. Many software pundits are predicting a software future with the creation of application systems through assembly of software components as is illustrated in the ORB BASED ARCHITECTURE figure. That kind of software approach is available today in a few proprietary object environments like NeXT's NeXTStep and ParcPlace's VisualWorks. The emergence of a broad based industry for component based software will require the prior emergence of industry standards for interchangeable parts. For components to be assembled like tinker toys, they are going to have to match up in terms of connectors. Translated, that means

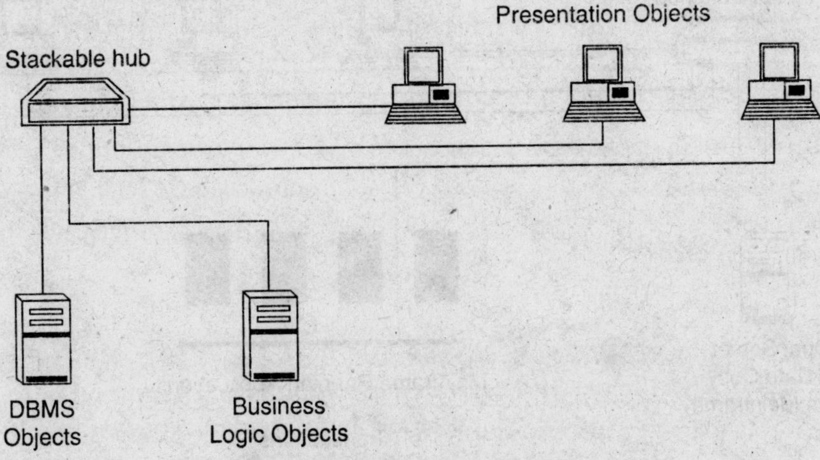

Fig. 7.8 ORB based architecture

that all vendors who want to create software components are going to have to agree on the software object bus. There are only two real candidates for such a standard backbone: Microsoft's OLE and OMG's (Object Management Group) implementations on CORBA and OpenDoc. It isn't the purpose of this article to explore this issue, but it can be mentioned that not enough of either network OLE or CORBA technology is currently available for ordinary mortals to build with. By the end of 1997, however, it's probable that both will be available and that they may even achieve some level of interoperability.

The distributed object implementation of client/server computing is going to change the way applications are built. There should be some very interesting advantages to observe. For one, if we needed fault tolerant computing, we could implement copies of objects onto multiple servers. That way if any were down, it would be possible to go to another site for service. With distributed objects being self contained and executable (all data and procedures present) it will be possible for a systems administrator to tune the performance of the network by moving those objects from overloaded hardware to underutilized computers. This approach is called tuning through "drag and drop", referring to the metaphor the administrator uses on a workstation to move the components.

A distributed object architecture should also offer other benefits for application developers. For example, consider the following:

- The same interface will be used for building a desktop, single location application or a fully distributed application.
- The application can be developed and tested locally and you'll know that it will work fine when it's distributed - you depend on the known services of an object request broker for distribution.
- Since the application developer is dealing with an object request broker for transmission services, technical issues like queuing, timing and protocols aren't an issue for the application developer.

Data Warehouse and 3-Tier

A 3-tier architecture is also useful for data mining or warehouse types of applications.

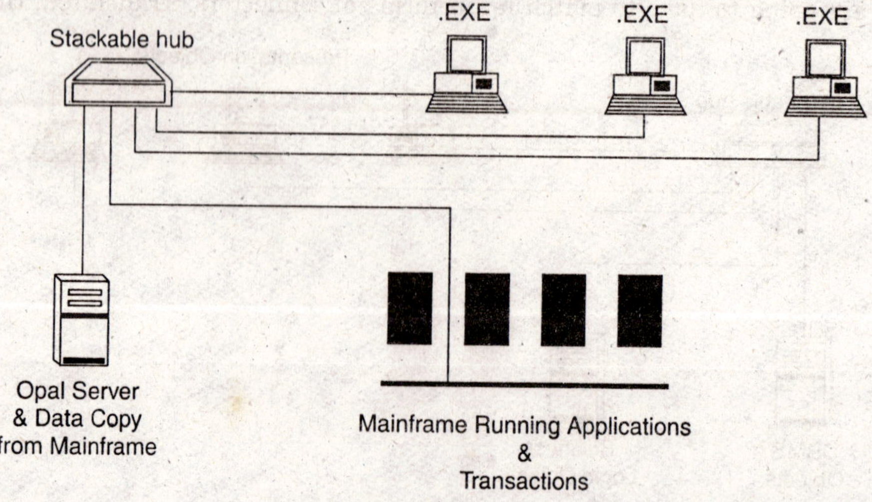

Fig. 7.9 3-Tier warehosue

These applications are characterized by unanticipated browsing of historical data. The databases supporting this type of application can sometimes be huge (up to a few terabytes -10(12) bytes) and have to be structured properly for adequate performance (a few second turnaround).

Data mining and decision support applications typically need response times of a few seconds. If the system can't provide that kind of performance, the thought process of the human analyst is disrupted and the overall purpose of the system is foiled. A production database established for multiple users isn't typically in a form that can support ad-hoc inquiries. The approach to support this browsing is then to make data copies available for that browsing and to organize the data in those copies in the best supporting fashion. This typically means that the data is denormalized, summarized, and stored in a multidimensional table - all of which is very non-relational. IT systems and operations managers usually don't want access to those tables to be on the mainframe. Unpredictable performance from ad hoc browsing can have a nasty impact on production OLTP systems that require predictable response times.

For cost, management, security, and other reasons, it makes sense to load this data copy on its own server rather that leaving it on the mainframe. Often this server is called OLAP - on-line analytical processor. In other circumstances this server can be a symmetric or massively parallel processor running an RDBMS. Since the OLAP server is typically a UNIX or PC-based technology, the MIPS costs are much lower than the same cycles executed on a mainframe. The figure entitled 3-TIER WAREHOUSE illustrates this approach. (The graphic for mainframe is a little different, of course, but the reader has probably noticed that nothing has really changed architecturally here from any of the other multi-tier approaches.)

3-Tier and the Future

By now the point is made. Client/server architectures are flexible and modular. They can be changed, added to, and evolved in numbers of ways. All of the above described 3-tier approaches could be mixed and matched in various combinatorial sequences to satisfy almost any computing need. As the Internet becomes a significant factor in computing environments client/server applications operating over the Internet will become an important new type of distributed computing. (This is probably an understatement, since the use of Internet and intranet based applications will very shortly dwarf all of the distributed computing initiatives of the past)

The Internet will extend the reach and power of client/server computing. Through its promise of widely accepted standards, it will ease and extend client/server computing both intra and inter-company. The movement in programming languages to the technology of distributed objects is going to happen at light speed - because of the Internet.

Client/server still remains the only and best architecture for taking advantage of the Internet and other new technologies that come along. We'll have to add "changes in client/server computing" to death and taxes in our inevitable list. But, regardless of what comes, client/server computing is likely to remain the underpinning for most computing developments we'll see over the next decade.

7.7 Enabling Technologies

Client/server computing describes a model for building application systems, along with the core hardware and software technology that helps in building these systems. The material in the following paragraphs describes aggregations of these core technologies that have created enabling technologies. Enabling technologies are combinations of hardware and software that can be used to assist in creating a particular kind of application system.

7.8 Expert Systems

The main business advantage of using expert systems technology is the opportunity to protect business know-how. Many organizations are severely short of experts. With the aging of the work force, and as a large number of experienced workers retire together, this shortage will become worse. Encapsulating the rules that describe an expert's response to a business situation into a stored electronic rules base, provides the substantive opportunity for higher productivity and reduced costs as these stored rules are consistently applied.

In applications using expert systems products, such as those from Trinzic Corp., Nexpert, and others, objects are created that include this expert knowledge. These objects can be reused in applications to support decision-making throughout the entire organization. Figure 7.10 illustrates the benefits organizations can obtain by using expert systems technology.

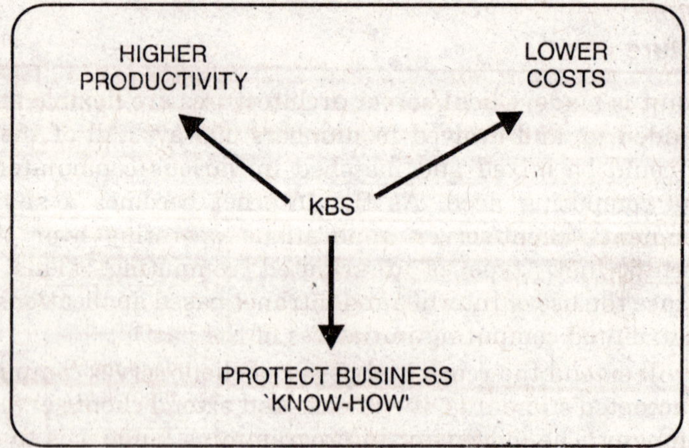

Fig. 7.10. Expert system

Many expert systems products are merely glitz. They are simplified to enable trivial applications to be developed but are not useful because they do not have the capacity to handle the complexity of real-life business processes. A major flaw in many products is their inability to integrate with a company's information systems and databases. If a product cannot be integrated into the organizational SDE or cannot use the organization's databases directly, it is not useful. It isn't practical to create multiple development environments and copies of data to support real-time decision-making. Some expert systems products are used for after-the-fact analysis, but the best products are integrated into the business. Figure 7.11 illustrates a typical integrated architecture.

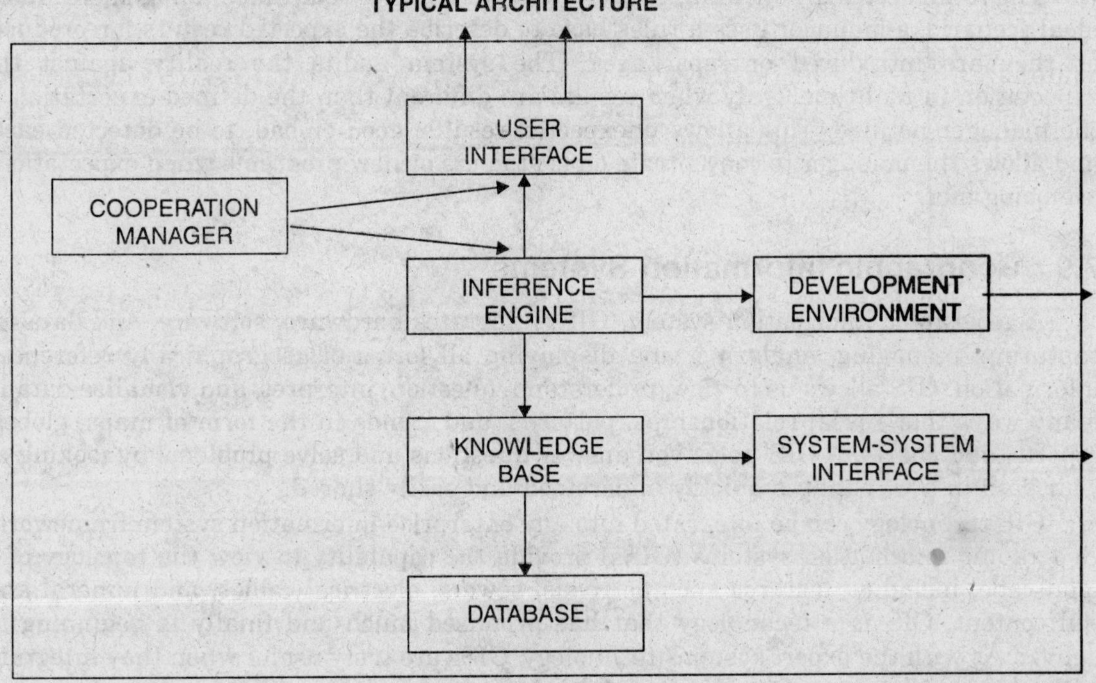

Fig. 7.11 Typical architecure of expert system

Expert systems applications are well suited to the client/server model. In addition to the advantages offered by the user interface component, the rules base benefits from the processing power and ease of use at the workstation. In most implementations, rules should be managed by a knowledgeable user and not by a professional programmer, because the user is the only one intimately familiar with how his or her job works-a job the expert system must emulate.

The rules are enforced by the inference engine, a CPU-intensive process that takes advantage of the low-cost processing and RAM available with client/server technology. Most applications will be implemented using existing databases on host-based DBMSs. The client/server model provides the necessary connectivity and services to support access to this information.

Expert systems currently are used mainly in government and financial organizations. In the government sphere, knowledgeable personnel create rule bases to determine people's eligibility for programs such as welfare aid. Welfare programs, in particular, change these rules rapidly, and an expert system that manages and applies these rules can improve the fairness and decrease the cost of adjudication for the program.

The financial community has built loan determination rules that can significantly reduce the time required to analyze loan application and determine the loan's risk of default. A new application of expert systems is network management. In particular, remote LAN management is an ideal application for expert systems technology. The network alerts are processed by a rules-based analyzer to help diagnose problems. Historical data is captured and maintained for subsequent comparison. The rules base also can invoke regular preventive maintenance.

The retail sector is beginning to use expert systems for real-time management. In an ideal scenario, a manager uses a rules base to describe the expected results for products as they are introduced or repackaged. The system audits the reality against the expectation in real time. Only when results are different than the defined expectation is the manager notified. This allows unexpected results, good or bad, to be detected early and allows the manager to concentrate on customers or new programs when expectations are being met.

7.9 Geographic Information Systems

A geographic information system (GIS) integrates hardware, software, and data for capturing, managing, analyzing, and displaying all forms of geographically referenced information. GIS allows us to view, understand, question, interpret, and visualize data in many ways that reveal relationships, patterns, and trends in the form of maps, globes, reports, and charts. A GIS helps you answer questions and solve problems by looking at your data in a way that is quickly understood and easily shared.

GIS technology can be integrated into any enterprise information system framework. Geographic information systems (GISs) provide the capability to view the topology of a landscape, including features such as roads, sewers, electrical cables, and mineral and soil content. GIS is a technology that has promised much and finally is beginning to deliver. As with the expert systems technology, GISs are truly useful when they integrate with the business process. From a technological perspective, GISs must operate on standard technologies, integrate with the organization SDE, and directly access the organizational databases.

Conceptually, GISs enable users to store virtually unlimited geographic information as a series of layers. Some layers, such as street layouts, compose the base map. Other layers, such as wetlands and subterranean water sources, are thematic layers that serve a specific, sometimes narrow purpose. A GIS user can custom design a printed map to fill a particular need by simply selecting the relevant layers. Selecting the street layer and the wetlands layer would produce a map of wetlands and their relationship to the streets. Selecting the subterranean water sources layer and the wetlands layer would show the wetlands superimposed on the features of the underlying aquifer.

Each line, curve, and symbol in a map is fixed in space by a series of numbers, called the spatial data. Spatial data describes the precise positioning of map objects in three-dimensional space. Besides storing map objects such as street segments and wetland boundaries, GISs enable designers to specify attributes the users want to associate with any map object. Such attributes may be descriptive data, detailed measurements of any kind, dates, legal verbiage, or other comments. When viewing a map on-screen, the user can click any map object, and a data-entry window will open to display the attributes associated with that object. Attribute information is usually stored in RDBMS tables, and each map layer can draw attributes from multiple tables.

GIS applications are naturals for client/server technology. Powerful workstations manage the mapping. Connectivity enables shared access to the layers maintained by various departments. The GIS database is related to attributes stored in other databases that provide considerably more value in combination. For example, combining the voters list with the street maps allows polling booths to be located with easy access for all and ensures that no natural or artificial barriers are blocking the way.

Three Views of a GIS

A GIS is most often associated with a map. A map, however, is only one way you can work with geographic data in a GIS, and only one type of product generated by a GIS. A GIS can provide a great deal more problem-solving capabilities than using a simple mapping program or adding data to an online mapping tool (creating a "mash-up").

A GIS can be viewed in three ways :

1. **The Database View:** A GIS is a unique kind of database of the world-a geographic database (geo database). It is an "Information System for Geography." Fundamentally, a GIS is based on a structured database that describes the world in geographic terms.

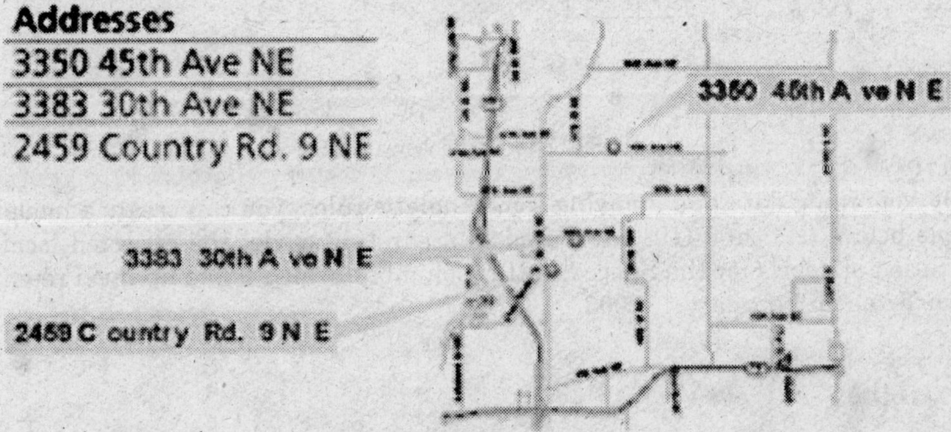

Fig. 7.12 Database view of GIS

2. **The Map View:** A GIS is a set of intelligent maps and other views that show features and feature relationships on the earth's surface. Maps of the underlying geographic information can be constructed and used as "windows into the database" to support queries, analysis, and editing of the information.

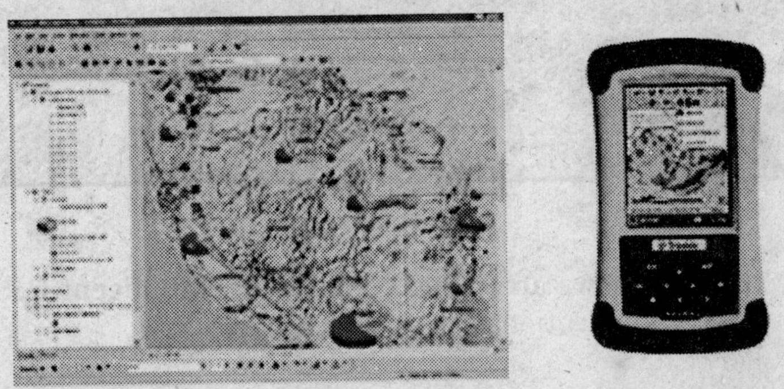

Fig. 7.13 Map view of GIS

3. **The Model View:** A GIS is a set of information transformation tools that derive new geographic datasets from existing datasets. These geo-processing functions take information from existing datasets, apply analytic functions, and write results into new derived datasets.

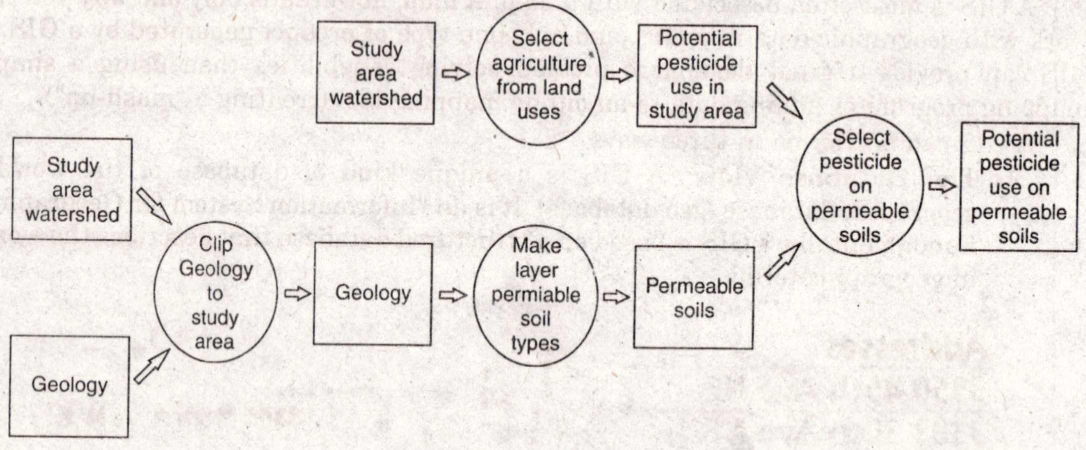

Fig. 7.14 Model view of GIS

By combining data and applying some analytic rules, you can create a model. In the example below, GPS and GIS were used to accurately model the expected location and distribution of debris for the Space Shuttle Columbia, which broke up upon re-entry over eastern Texas on February 1, 2003.

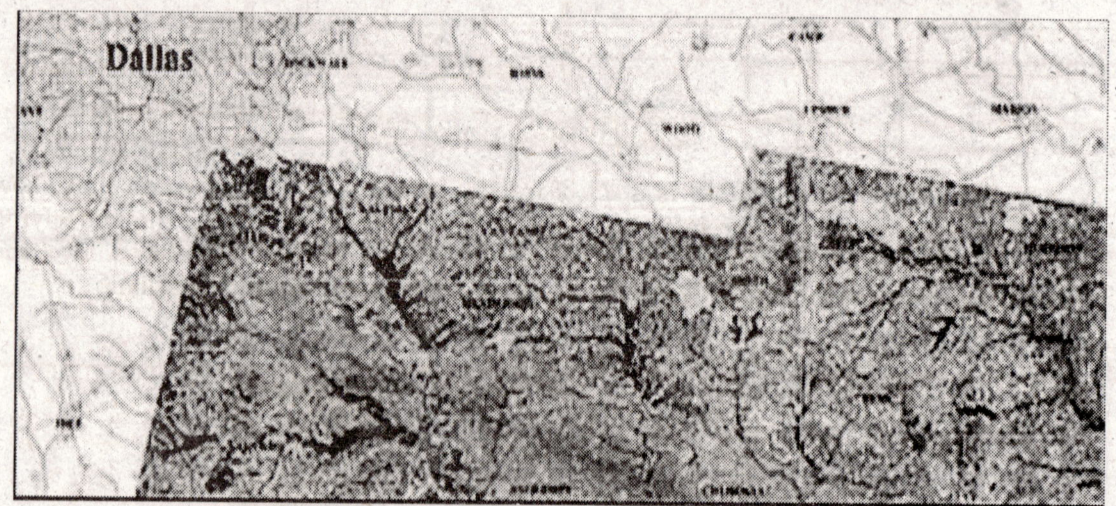

Fig. 7.15

Together, these three views are critical parts of an intelligent GIS and are used at varying levels in all GIS applications.

7.10 Point-of-Service (POS)

Point-of-service (POS) technologies-traditionally known as point-of-sale technologies-are ubiquitous. Every restaurant, supermarket, most department stores, and even auto service stations use POS technology at the site for pricing, staff management, accounting, product distribution, and inventory control. POS is one of the most widely installed examples of client/server technology. Implementations use an intelligent cash register, bar code scanner, scale, or gas pump as the client working with a UNIX or OS/2 server.

The integration of technology, business process, and management information in POSs is a model for the implementation of client/server applications. Some older implementations continue to use dumb client devices, but lower technology costs and the growing use of object-oriented development techniques are moving more processing to the client. These applications have a specific set of characteristics; namely, they run in a large number of distributed sites and are frequently used by users with little training in a business environment demanding rapid change. Appendix A describes a large POS application built and implemented for the United States Post Office.

There is a growing demand for POSs, such as applications, to improve service and reduce costs. Self-service customs and excise processing, postal counters, help services, libraries, and even vending machines are demanding the processing power and ease of use that can be provided by this technology.

7.11 Imaging

Imaging is the conversion of documents from a physical medium (for example, paper) to a digital form where they can be manipulated by computers. Imaging should be viewed as an enabling technology. Information that is available in machine-readable form never should be converted to paper and scanned back into machine-readable form. The business process should strive to maintain and use information in machine-readable form from the earliest moment.

There is an unfortunate tendency to automate existing processes by converting recycled paper to digital form without considering whether the information printed on the form can be captured elsewhere and used without rekeying. Optical character recognition (OCR) is an existing technology that offers powerful capabilities to convert the image of typed information on a form to text. Intelligent character recognition (ICR) enables handwritten input to be recognized. Our experience in text form processing shows this technology to be capable of a high degree of reliability. Even more efficiency can be gained, whether through EDI or capture-at-source techniques, so the information on the form can be maintained in machine-readable form at all times and communicated electronically where needed.

Figure 7.16 shows a typical document imaging system. Information is entered into the system from a scanner. The scanner, similar to a fax machine, converts the paper image into digital form. This image is stored on a permanent medium, such as a magnetic or optical disk. Information must be indexed on entry so it can be located after it is stored. The index usually is stored in a relational database on a high-speed magnetic disk. Access to stored images is always initiated by an index search. High-resolution screens enable

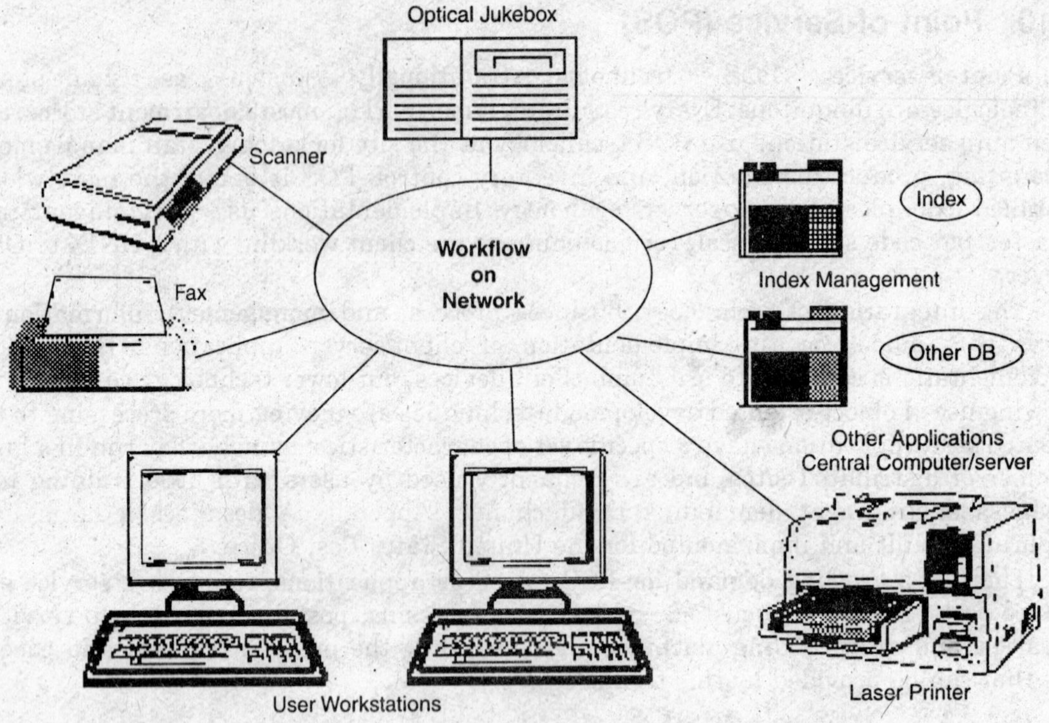

Fig. 7.16 Imaging

users to view the images after storage. Laser printers are used to recreate the image on paper as required.

Document images are stored and accessed through standard data access requests. The only difference between the image of an application form and the textual information keyed from the form is the amount of space required to store the image. Typically, a black-and-white image occupies 35K of storage space. The keyed data from a form typically occupies less than 2K of storage space.

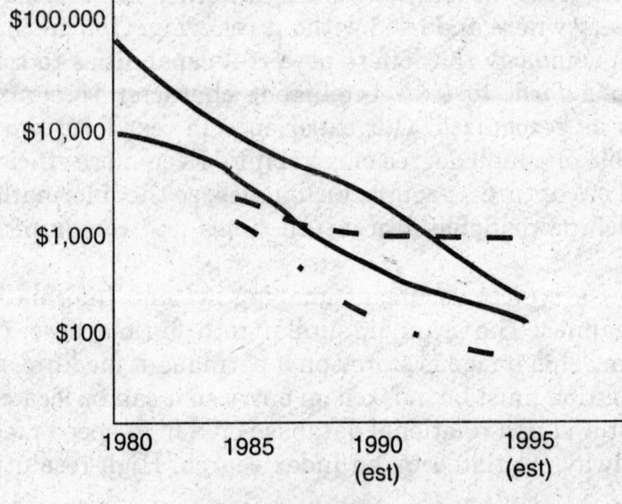

Fig. 7.17

As Figure 7.16 illustrates, images can be accessed by any workstation with access to the image server. Note that the image server replaces the filing cabinet but provides the additional advantage of allowing multiple access to the same documents or folders. The movement toward standards for the creation, distribution, indexing, printing, display, and revision of images has enabled a large number of vendors to enter the market with products. This has led to a dramatic reduction in the price of these components. Figure 7.17 plots this price change.

7.12 Electronic Document Management-Multimedia

The concepts of electronic image management relate to the manipulation of information contained in forms, blueprints, x-rays, microfilm, fingerprints, photographs, and typewritten or handwritten notes. Electronic document management adds the capability to manipulate information from other media, such as audio and video. In addition, the "folder" device gives the user an intuitive interface to information equivalent to, but more flexible than, a filing cabinet. The information is always available on the desktop. Several users can use the folder simultaneously. Folders are always refilled in the correct location. Billions of these documents exist and are used daily in the process of providing government services. Consider that the Los Angeles County municipal hospitals alone have 5 billion pieces of paper, x-rays, scans, photographs, audio reports, and videos (and so on) filed to maintain patient records. Currently, the cost of this technology is prohibitively high for most organizations, but these systems will come down in price as all computer components do.

Figure 7.18 illustrates the range of information sources that can be manipulated

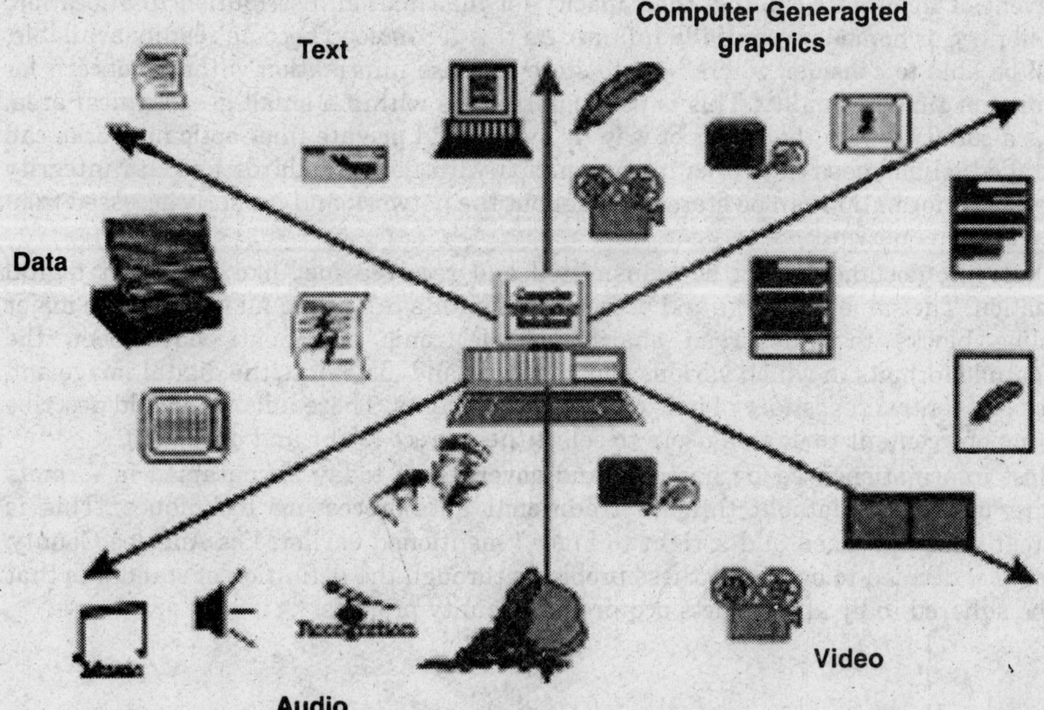

Fig. 7.18 Electronic Document Management

digitally. To make efficient and effective use of this information, the means must exist for rapid filing, retrieval, and sharing of this information among all persons. This is the principle of making information available only to those with a "need and a right to know."

Electronic mail can be delivered routinely in seconds anywhere in the United States. Consumers can have direct access to suppliers. Goods can be ordered and paid for electronically. A retired engineer in Northern California can teach algebra to disadvantaged children in Compton, located in the southern part of the state. A parent can deliver office work to an employer in downtown Los Angeles while he cares for children at home. Library and museum materials can be explored at the users' own pace, with their personal interests in mind, to tap into a rich assortment of interactive, graphical how-to lessons. The community library can provide the conduit to government services: taking drivers' photographs and producing drivers' licenses on-site, producing birth certificates, or searching the titles on properties. Lawyers can file case data, review their calendars, or locate their clients' criminal records all from the law office and under the safeguards provided by electronic passwords, user auditing, and caller ID validation.

Each of these functions can be conveniently provided to citizens and consumers without them having to travel to an office location. The cost savings and environmental impact of this convenience are important considerations in today's society. Businesses no longer need to rent or buy expensive office space close to clients and suppliers. Individuals can live where they want and commute electronically to work. It is easy to imagine how the provision of these services in such a convenient manner can generate significant revenues that more than offset the cost of providing the service.

High-speed communications networks can provide the capability to distribute information other than voice conversations throughout a county, state, or country. With the advent of fiber-optic cabling, the capacity for information distribution to a location, office, library, or home is essentially infinite. As this technology become readily available, we will be able to consider where best to store and use information without concern for transmission time or quality. This is particularly true within a small geographical area, such as a county where the "right of way" is owned and private fiber-optic networks can be installed. High-speed networks in conjunction with new standards for data integrity ensure that information can be stored throughout the network and properly accessed from any point in the network.

Electronic documents can be transmitted and received just like any other digital information. The same networks and personal computers can send and receive. The major stumbling blocks to widespread sharing of electronic documents have been the incompatible formats in which various vendors store and distribute the digital image and the lack of a central repository of indexes to the documents. These indexes should describe the document content to enable users to select the correct folder and document.

Most information used by business and government today is contained in formats that are not manipulatable through traditional data-processing techniques. This is consistent with the "need and a right to know," mentioned earlier. Los Angeles County, for example, decided to overcome these problems through the definition of standards that must be adhered to by all products acquired for county projects.

7.12.1 Full-Text Retrieval

An area of explosive growth, coincident with the availability of high-powered workstations and RISC servers, is full-text retrieval. Originally a technology used by the military to scan covert transmissions and media communications, full-text retrieval is now a mainstream technology. Vendors such as Fulcrum and PLS have packaged their technology to be used in more traditional business applications. Northern Telecom bundles a product, Helmsman, with all its switch documentation to facilitate document access. All major news services provide an electronic feed of their information. This information is continuously scanned by reporters, businesses, and government offices to identify significant events or locate trends. Dow Jones provides their news retrieval system with access to 10**12bytes (that's three billion pages) of textual data. Many criteria searches can be run against all this text in a few seconds. Figure 7.19 illustrates the flow of information in a full-text retrieval application.

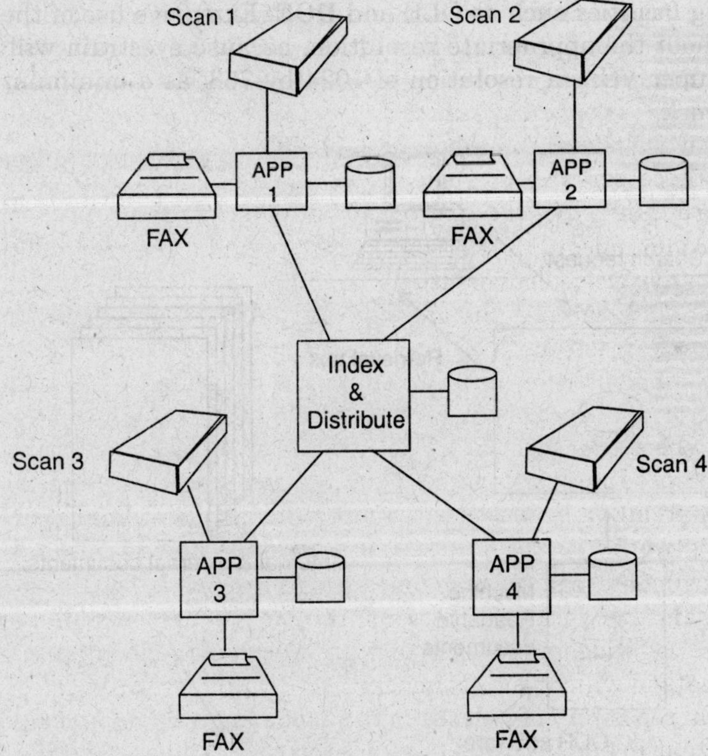

Fig. 7.19 Full-text retrieval

The major hardware and software technologies that have made this technology production viable are Optical Character Recognition (OCR), ICR, optical storage, powerful workstations, large D-RAM, software algorithms, and high-resolution monitors. OCR and ICR technologies convert the paper documents to text files. Companies such as Colera provide software to convert typewritten documents directly into WordPerfect format. Recent improvements in these algorithms provide support for most major fonts.

Improvements in handwriting recognition promise to enable users to enter data from handwritten documents as well. Colera provides a fax link that enables documents to be entered by way of OCR as they are received from a fax. Mitek provides high-speed ICR engines to be used with document workflow applications. Embedded diagrams are maintained in image format.

Full-text indexing of documents is a CPU-intensive function, and the availability of low-cost, high-powered workstations has made the technology viable. (See Figure 7.20.) PC products such as Lotus Magellan enable the casual user to create full-text indexes of all their files. Viewers and launchers within the products enable users to access these files in their native format and manipulate them using a data editor of choice. With the advent of Object Linking and Embedding (OLE 2.x) and CORBA-based object solutions such as DOE, full-text access will become much more common to support capture and inclusion of source material. For high-performance retrievals, the indexes must support Boolean search requests. The availability of large and low-cost D-RAM provides the necessary environment. High-resolution monitors are necessary as we move to a multi windowed environment using facilities such as OLE and DOE. Extensive use of these facilities will not be viable without the appropriate resolution, because eyestrain will discourage use. We recommend Super VGA, a resolution of 1024 by 768, as a minimum for this type of multiwindowed work.

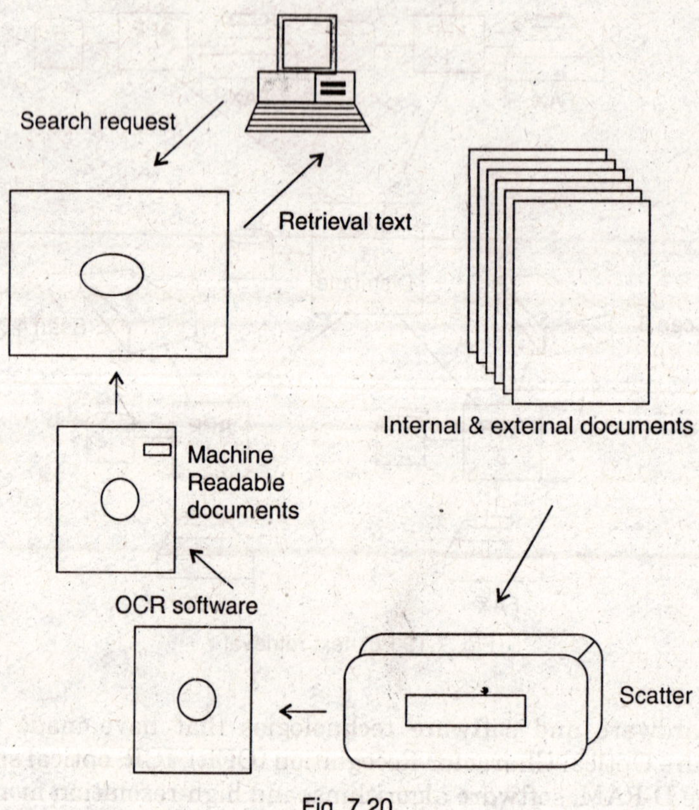

Fig. 7.20

7.13 Transformational Systems

In the more than 40 years since the introduction of the stored program computer in 1951, we have seen tremendous advances in the capabilities of this technology. Computers have proven over and over that they can add numbers at mind-numbing rates. We have extrapolated from this capability the functionality to maintain accounts, calculate bills, print checks, and create memos. All this functionality has enabled organizations to grow and do more work with fewer clerical and administrative staff.

As the world economy becomes more integrated, goods and services are provided by companies and individuals from all parts of the world. Consumers can and will buy the most cost-effective quality product and service available. This substantially increases the necessity for organizations to demonstrate their value. Western economies, with their higher salaries and cost of plant, are particularly threatened by this trend. However, Western economies have the advantage of a highly educated population. Educated staffs are willing to accept decision-making responsibility and are better able to adapt to change. The challenge is to find ways in which technology can enable the West to capitalize on these advantages.

Many organizations and industries are finding solutions that use client/server technology to truly transform the working environment. The following are brief examples of business solutions and technology partnerships that apply this technology to fundamentally change the business process.

7.14 Emergency Public Safety

Emergency dispatch operators are responsible for sending the right emergency response vehicles to an incident as quickly as possible and at the same time dealing with the crisis being reported over the telephone. This functionality must be provided 24-hours-per-day, 365-days-per-year, with the maximum possible performance.

As you can imagine, most 911 callers are in a state of anxiety. The telephone switch provides the caller's telephone number and address to the dispatcher workstation. Traditional technical design of a 911 system involves the use of redundant minicomputers connected to character-based terminals. This design solution provides the benefits of fault tolerance and high performance with the costs of complex user interfaces, considerable redundancy, and excess capacity.

Through the use of client/server computing, it is now possible to duplicate all of the functionality of such an existing traditional design with the additional advantages of better performance, a graphical user interface (GUI), a single point of contact, higher reliability, and lower costs. With a client/server-based system, the dispatch operator is empowered to oversee how staff and equipment are allocated to each incident. The operator uses a GUI to dynamically alter vehicle selection and routing. Maps may be displayed that show the location of all incidents, emergency response centers, and vehicles. Vehicles are tracked using automatic vehicle locator (AVL) technology. Obstacles, such as traffic congestion, construction, and environmental damage (such as earthquakes) are shown on the map so the dispatcher can see potential problems at a glance.

The implementation of such an E911 service can dramatically improve the rate at which emergency calls can be answered and reduce the incidence of unnecessary dispatches. Workstation technology provides the dispatcher with a less stressful and more functional user interface. The dispatcher can respond quickly to changes in the environment and communicate this information immediately to the vehicle operator. The system is remarkably fault-tolerant. If a single workstation is operating, the dispatcher can continue to send emergency vehicles to the incident. This architecture is general enough to apply to any application that has reasonable quantities of transient data.

7.15 Electronic Data Interchange

Electronic data interchange (EDI) technology enables unrelated organizations to conduct their business computer to computer without the need to use the same computer applications or technology in all locations. Combining just in time (JIT) manufacturing with EDI truly transforms the process:

1. A salesperson accepts an order through a laptop computer system.
2. Using the electronic mail facilities of the organization, the order is shipped to the order entry system.
3. The component parts are determined, and electronic purchase orders are generated to each supplier.
4. The EDI link routes the order, which is processed by the supplier's order system.
5. An EDI link is used to validate the purchaser's credit worthiness.
6. The paperless invoice is sent by way of EDI back to the purchaser.
7. When it is time for payment, an EDI link is used to generate the electronic funds transfer (EFT) to pay.

With EDI, a single entry by the person closest to the customer causes the facilities of the manufacturer and its suppliers to schedule appropriate production, shipping, and billing. The maximum possible time is allowed for all parties to process the order, thus reducing their need to carry inventory. A further advantage comes when production is driven by orders, because only those products that will actually be sold are manufactured. Manufacturers are able to offer more flexibility in product configuration, because they are manufacturing to order. The use of EDI standards allows organizations to participate in this electronic dialog regardless of differences among their individual technologies or application systems.

7.15.1 Overview of EDI Benefits and Drawbacks

The EDI process provides many benefits. Computer-to-computer exchange of information is much less expensive than handling paper documents. Studies have shown that manually processing a paper-based order can cost Rs. 70 or more while processing an EDI order costs a rupees or less. Much less labor time is required. Fewer errors occur because computer systems process the documents rather than processing by hand.

EDI transactions between companies flow faster and more reliably than paper documents. Faster transactions support reduction in inventory levels, better use of warehouse space, fewer out-of-stock occurrences and lower freight costs through fewer emergency expedites.

Paper purchase orders can take up to 10 days from the time the buyer prepares the order to when the supplier ships it. EDI orders can take as little as one day.

Drawbacks are few, but there are some. For example, companies choosing to implement both paper and EDI processes must manage both of these processes. However, as stated before, using EDI is much more efficient than using paper, lending strength to the argument against paper documents. Also, companies must ensure that they have the resources in place to make an EDI program work; however, the need for these resources (or their hiring) may be offset by the increased efficiency that EDI provides.

7.15.2 EDI example

Here is an example of how the electronic data interchange process works. A buyer prepares an order in his purchasing system and has it approved. Next, the EDI order is translated into an EDI document format called an 850 purchase order.

The EDI 850 purchase order is then securely transmitted to the supplier either via the internet or through a VAN (Value Added Network). The buyer's VAN is a like an electronic post office that interconnects with the supplier's VAN. The VANs make sure that EDI transactions are sent and received. The supplier's VAN ensures that the supplier receives the order. The supplier's computer system then processes the order. In the case of Covalent Works' clients, we provide VAN transportation and our servers provide all of the software and hardware required to process EDI documents. Only internet access and email are needed.

Data security and control are maintained through out the transmission process using passwords, user identification and encryption. Both the buyer's and the supplier's EDI applications edit and check the documents for accuracy.

7.15.3 EDI Requirements

Each trading partner has unique EDI requirements. These will include the specific kinds of EDI documents to be processed, such as the 850 purchase order used in the example above, 856 advance ship notices and 810 invoices. The fact is that most any business document that one company would exchange with another company can be sent via EDI. However each EDI document must be exchanged with the partner in exactly the format they specify.

Many partners will have an EDI implementation guide or kit that explains their specific requirements. Maps are required to translate the EDI documents from the trading partner's format into the format that is useable by the receiving party. Covalent Works handles all of the mapping and translation requirements for our clients.

EDI capability involves either buying or outsourcing the following components:

- Software for communications
- VAN service for EDI transmission
- Mail boxing of EDI transactions
- Mapping
- Translation

VAN, ASYNC, BISYNC, FTP and AS/2 Internet communications will be required by various partners. A server or PC, communication devices and peripherals will be needed as well as secured office space, monitored security, backups and redundant power. Additional software will be needed if integration of the EDI transactions with back office systems is desired. A VAN will need to be contracted for transmissions. Personnel must be trained in how to use the software and communication devices. Maps will then need to be developed.

7.15.4 Advantages vs. Disadvantages of using EDI

Advantages

There are several advantages of using EDI all of which provide distinct benefits to the user. One of the most notable benefits to using EDI is the time-saving capability it provides. By eliminating the process of distributing hard copies of information throughout the company, easy access to electronic data simplifies inter-department communication. Also, another time-savings advantage is the ability to track the origin of all information therefore significantly reducing time spent on corresponding with the source of the information.

Another benefit for the user of this information system is the ultimate savings in costs for the company. Although the initial set-up costs may seem high, the overall savings received in the long run ensures its value. For any business, regardless of its size, hard-copy print outs and document shipping costs add up. EDI allows for a paper-less exchange of information reducing handling costs and worker productivity that is involved with the organization of paper documents.

Electronic data interchange has another strong advantage over paper-based information exchange which has to do with accuracy of information. When the information is already stored electronically, it speeds up an organization's ability to check for accuracy and make any necessary corrections as the data is already inputted in the system. Also, unlike paper-based methods, EDI allows for the ability to send and receive information at any time thereby tremendously improving an organization's ability to communicate quickly and efficiently.

Disadvantages

There are a few barriers to using electronic data interchange. One of the most significant barriers is the accompanying process change. Existing processes built around slow paper handling may not be suited for EDI. For example, a business may receive the bulk of their goods by 1 or 2 day shipping and all of their invoices by mail. The existing process may therefore assume that goods are typically received before the invoice. With EDI, the invoice will typically be sent when the goods ship and will therefore require a process that handles large numbers of invoices whose corresponding goods have not yet been received.

Another significant barrier is the initial set-up. The preliminary expenses and time that arise from the implementation, customization and training can be costly and therefore may discourage some users.

Note: EDI is defined as the inter-process communication (computer application to computer application) of business information in standardized electronic forms. The primary benefits of EDI to business is a considerable reduction is transaction costs by improving the speed and efficiency of filling orders. EDI is not widely used.

Electronic commerce is often equated with EDI, so it is important to clarify that electronic commerce embraces EDI and much more. EDI is one well known example of structured document inter change, which enables data in the form of document content to be exchanged between software applications that are working together to process a business transaction.

- EDI is the paperless exchange electronic transfer from one computer to another of computer from one computer to another of computer process able data using an agreed standard to structure the data.

7.15.5 EDI Layered Architecture

EDI Semantic Layer	Application level Services	
EDI Standard Layer	EDI Business from Standard	
	ANSI × 12 Business from Standard	
EDI Transport Layer	Electronic mail	X.435, NIME
	Point to Point	FTP, TELNET
	World Wide Web	HTTP
Physical Layer	Dial up lines, Internet, I-way	

Fig 7.20 Layered Architecture of EDI

EDI architecture specifies four layers, the semantic layer (application layer), the standard translation layer, the packing (or transport) layer and the physical network infrastructure layer.

Semantic Layer

The EDI semantic layer describes the business application that is driving EDI. This layer specific to a company and the software it uses. In other words, the user interface and content visible on the screen are tailored or customized to local environments.

When a company receives the document, their EDI translation software automatically changes the standard format into the proprietary format of their document processing software so that the company can manipulate the information in what ever way it chooses to.

EDI Standard Layer

EDI standards specify business form structure and to some extent influence content seen at the application layer. For instance, a purchase order name field in an X12 standard might be specified to hold a maximum of 50 characters. An application using 75 character field lengths will produce name truncation during the translation from the application layer to standard layer.

In short, the EDI standards and application level, although separate are closely intertwined.

Transport Layer

The EDI transport layer corresponds closely with the non-electronic activity of sending a business form from one company A to company B. The business form could be sent via regular postal service, registered mail, certified mail or private carrier such as united parcel service (UPS) or simply faxed between the companies.

In other words, the content and structure of the form are separated from the transport carrier. EDI document are exchanged rapidly over electronic networks using the existing email programs and infrastructure.EDI document transport is far more complex than simply sending email messages or sharing files through a network. These EDI documents are more structured than email.

EDI Vs E-mail

- EDI is a structured document where email is an unstructured document there is no fixed structure in email.
- In EDI, the interchange is composed by one software for interpretation by another software. If a reply is involved it is composed by a software to be interpreted by another software i.e. EDI is a software to software interface.
- In E-mail, the message is composed by a human and or interpreted by a human and/or a reply is composed by a human and interpreted by a human. ie. S/W can not understand E mail document.
- In EDI, there is typically no human involvement in the processing of the information. Whereas in E-mail, the human involvement is necessary. A Human-to-Software interface is involved at minimum of one end of the interchange.

Note : EDI—Structured doc, S/W to S/W interface.
E-mail—Unstructured doc, human to S/W interface

EDI in Action

The idea behind EDI is very simple. EDI seeks to take what has been a manually prepared form or a form from a business application, translates that data into a standard electronic format and transmit it. At the receiving end, the standard format is

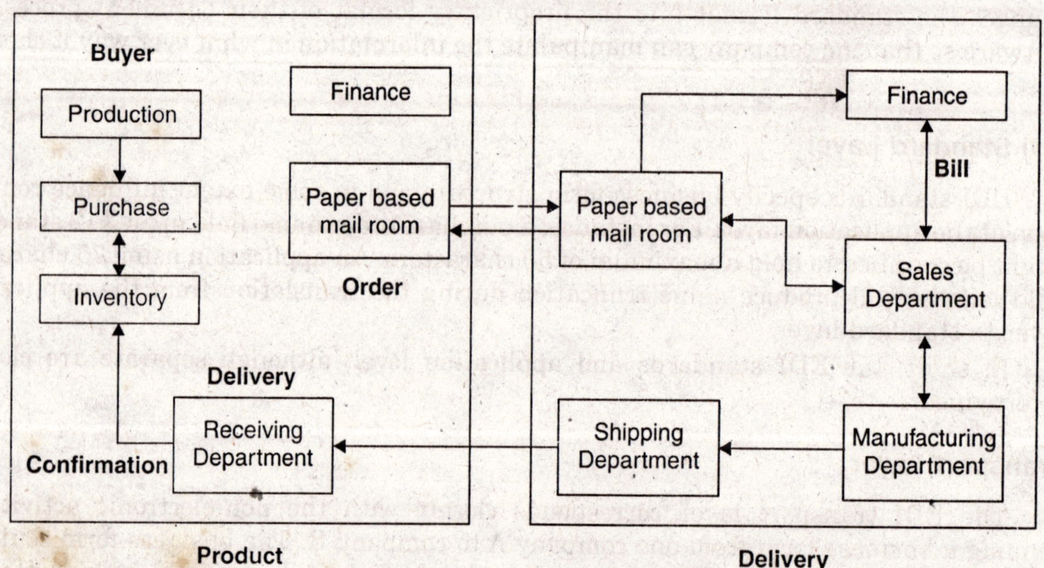

Fig. 7.21 Information Flow without EDI.

"un-translated" into a format that can be read by the recipient applications. Hence output from one application becomes input to another through the computer to computer exchange of information.

When the buyer sends a purchase order to a seller, the relevant data must be extracted from the internal database and recorded on hard copy. This hard copy is then forwarded to the seller after passing through several intermediate steps. Sellers receive information in the form of letters and in some cases a vast number of facsimiles. This information is manually entered into the internal information systems of the recipient by data entry operators. This process generates a considerable amount of overhead in labour costs and time delays.

Disadvantage

- Overhead in labor costs
- Time delays
- Increase the risk of error

7.15.6 Benefits of EDI

- Paperless Exchange
- Improved problem resolution and services.
- Less time in comparison of manual.
- Reduce costs
- Decrease the risk of error
  o Transmission error: 1299 - 1929
  o Transcription error: 1299 - 12992
- Expanded customer base/supplier

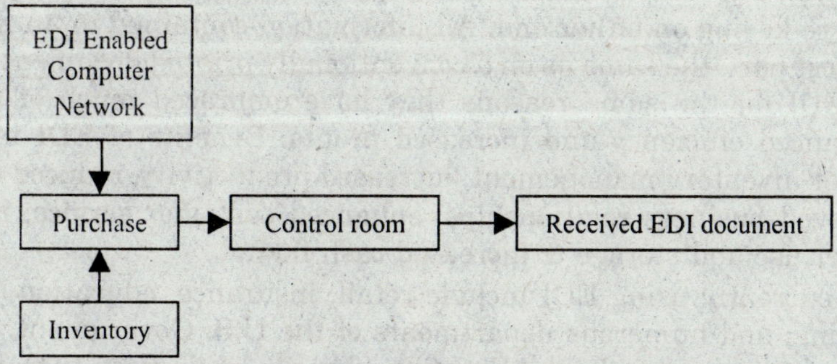

Fig. 7.22 Information Flow with EDI

7.15.7 EDI Application in Business

Although EDI was developed to improve transportation and trade, it has spread everywhere. EDI has grown from its original and somewhat limited use as expediter of the transfer of trade goods to Facilitator of standard format data between any two-computer systems.

The four different scenarios in industries that use EDI extensively -

i) International or cross border trade.

ii) Electronic funds transfer (EFT).

iii) Health care EDI for insurance claim processing.

iv) Manufacturing and retail procurement.

Companies have applied a number of EDI - based solutions to improve business processes for both strategic and competitive advantages. EDI has shaped a company's marketing and distribution efforts by helping to create new distribution channels, introduce new market research method and introduce better customer services.

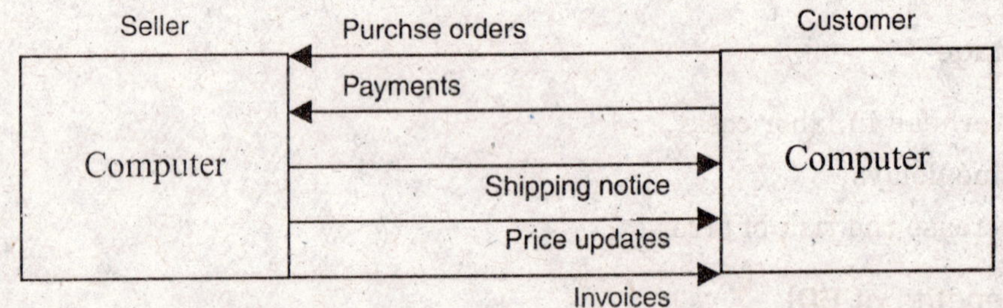

Fig. 7.23 Electronic Data Interchange

Companies can use EDI to automate electronic commerce applications. Purchase orders and payments can be transmitted directly from the customer's computers to the seller computer. The seller can transmit shipping notices, price changes and invoices electronically back to the customer.

7.15.8 EDI and VAN (Value Added Network)

Electronic Data Interchange (EDI) is the computer-to-computer exchange of business data in standard formats. In EDI, information is organized according to a specified format set by both parties, allowing a "hands-off" computer transaction that requires no human intervention or re-keying on either end. All information contained in an EDI transaction set is, for the most part, the same as on a conventionally printed document. Organizations have adopted EDI for the same reasons they have embraced much of today's modern technology-enhanced efficiency and increased profits. Benefits of EDI include: reduced cycle time, better inventory management, increased productivity, reduced costs, improved accuracy, improved business relationships, enhanced customer service, increased sales, minimized paper use and storage & increased cash flow.

Industries currently using EDI include retail, insurance, education, entertainment, mortgage banking, and numerous departments of the U.S. Government. Note, however, that this list is far from complete! As more and more businesses turn to EDI, several standards committees - including the Accredited Standards Committee X12 (ASC X12) and EDIFACT - are working to include appropriate transactions in its body of standards.

A **Value-Added Network (VAN)** is a private network provider (sometimes called a turnkey communications line) that is hired by a company to facilitate electronic data interchanges (EDI) or provides other network services. Before the arrival of the World Wide Web, some companies hired value-added networks to move data from their company to other companies. With the arrival of the World Wide Web, many companies found it more cost-efficient to move their data over the Internet instead of paying the minimum monthly fees and per-character charges found in typical VAN contracts. In response, contemporary value-added network providers now focus on offering EDI translation, encryption, secure e-mail, management reporting, and other extra services for their customers.

Value added networks are essential part of B2B e-commerce as they provide a common EDI platform connecting various participating organizations of trade partners and take care of various technical network management and communication issues involved in EDI so that the trading partners can concentrate on their core business rather than bothering about conforming to the EDI standards :

VAN's in EDI play a vital role in :

- EDI program management
- Alternative delivery methods for messages and EDI documents.
- Edi consulting.
- EDI software management.

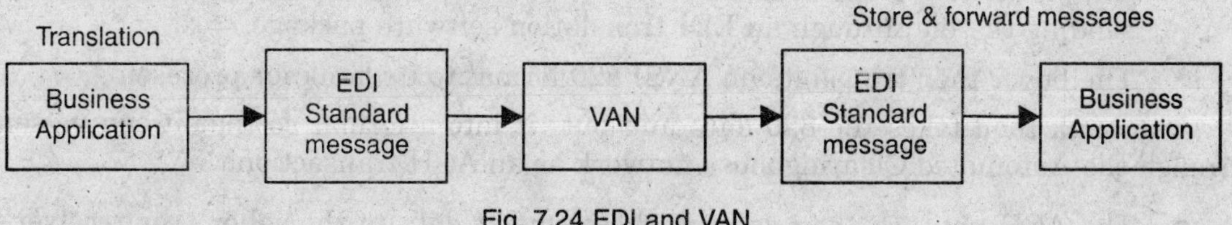

Fig. 7.24 EDI and VAN

VAN's are mostly provided by third party service providers like ISP's. the advantages by VAN's to EDI are :

- Flexibility and Scalability.
- Adherence to local rules and regulations governing communication and transactions.
- Infra-structure allocation, development and sharing.

There are three basic components of VAN's :

Technical -Message formatting / communication protocols.

Mail - Maintaining email boxes and buffering to support EDI transactions.

Links - Between various VAN Networks

VAN's in EDI business offer additional peripheral services other than just direct connections. For example

- Direct communication links between trading partners.
- Maintenance of the EDI standards and technologies by the VAN service provider.
- VAN support to multiple data format standards.
- Store and forward systems.
- Varied protocol / access support.
- Availability round the clock.

- VAN's dial up services to connect to companies which do not participate in VAN.

7.15.9 Financial EDI

Financial EDI (FEDI) is the computer-to-computer exchange of payment and payment-related information between companies using a standard format. Financial EDI works much like non-Financial EDI - which involves the electronic exchange of business data such as price quotes, purchase orders, and shipping information - but is also significantly different in that, to move a payment, a bank must be involved. Because of this difference, the buyer and seller must work closely with their respective banks to effect a Financial EDI transaction. Today, it is estimated that 60,000 companies are doing EDI in the U.S. and a growing percentage is starting to adopt FEDI.

This is the sequence of events:

- The buyer, or originator, electronically extracts payment information from the company's accounts payable system.
- The buyer formats the data into an EDI ANSI standard, the ANSI 820 transaction set, or the ANSI 835 transaction set for health care. (This is usually done by sending the file through an EDI translation software package.)
- The buyer then transmits an ANSI 820 format to its bank for processing.

The bank then takes the 820 data and puts it into a format so that it can be sent through the Automated Clearinghouse network as an ACH transaction.

- The ACH network then delivers the payment data to the seller's, or receiver's, bank.
- The receiving bank credits the seller's account with the proceeds and delivers the remittance information to the seller for automatic accounts receivable posting. The remittance data can be delivered electronically in a variety of formats: ANSI 820, 835 or 823 format (true EDI formats), and in a BAI format. (Information can also be sent in other ways that cannot generally result in automatic cash application for the seller: through a bank's on-line balance reporting system, or in a paper report via fax or mail.)

The Benefits of Financial EDI

To be successful in any business practice usually means that all the participants affected by the process share in the benefits. In Financial EDI, there are ample advantages for both the buyer and the seller.

The buyer enjoys a number of benefits: increased productivity, the ability to use a less expensive payment method (electronic vs. paper check) that does not require reconciliation, a reduction in the risk of fraud, and the ability to invoice electronically. The seller benefits because it can reduce the average age of its receivables, lower processing costs by automatic A/R posting, improve quality by minimizing errors, and generate predictable cash flows. The result of these benefits is that both buyer and seller become more valued trading partners to one another.

Expanding the Use of Financial EDI

Financial EDI has been actively used by corporations for the last five or six years and has increasingly become the payment method of choice as more and more trading partners have seen the benefits provided to their competitors and have consequently adopted an EDI platform for their own company.

As corporations reengineer their current business practices, many are looking to outsource their payments processing, which results in a single file of all payment instructions being sent to the bank in an EDI format. The bank will then execute all payment orders, including ACH and wire transfers, and will also print and mail the payable checks. In this way, a company can deal electronically with all of its payments even though some are being converted to paper checks by the bank for those trading partners who still want the paper.

On the collection side, companies are also streamlining the receivables process by having remittance information collected by their bank - whether through the ACH, lockbox, or wire transfer payments - and then sent electronically to the companies' accounts receivable system for automatic cash application. Here again, the company is deriving the benefit of streamlined, automated posting for all of its collections, even though some or perhaps most of its payments received are paper based.

Another Kind of Receivables Application

Several financial institutions are going one step beyond this and are beginning to provide true matching of accounts receivable. In this scenario, a company has outsourced a good portion of its A/R processing to its bank.

It works in the following manner:

- The company electronically sends its receivables file to the bank on either a daily or weekly basis.
- The bank stores this data in a data base.
- As lockbox receipts or ACH collections are received, the database is queried to determine if there is a match between an open receivable item and a remittance.
- If there is a match, then the database is appended with the remittance information and a file of the matched items is created.
- Unmatched items are separately batched.
- Optionally, a bank might display the unmatched remittance information on its balance reporting systems.

Also optionally, the company can then view this data and, based on information it has, now match the previously unmatched items.

- Matched items and the remaining unmatched items are electronically sent to the customer in any desired format, EDI or proprietary.
- The customer automatically updates its accounts receivable system.

Financial EDI for Consumer Payments

Although Financial EDI has been confined to business-to-business transactions, it can also be successfully deployed in the handling of consumer payments and associated remittance data. As an example, consumer payments initiated through a bill payment service or a home banking system can be directed through Visa's ePay network by having this data handled by a bank's Financial EDI system. The bank can reformat the remittance data and deliver it electronically to the biller (for example, a utility company) for automated posting. This new way of using Financial EDI benefits large billers by eliminating the expense and operating inefficiency of receiving a check and a list and having the billet manually key in the remittance data for cash application.

Financial EDI comprises the electronic transmission of payments and remittance information between a payer, payee and their respective banks. Financial EDI allows businesses to replace the labour - intensive activities associated with issuing, mailing and collecting cheques through the banking system with automated initiation, transmission and processing of payment systems. Thus it eliminates the delays inherent in processing cheques.

Types of financial EDI

Business to business payment is accomplished using cheques, EFT and automated clearing houses (ACH) for domestic and international funds transfer.

Bank Cheques : Cheques are instruments for debit transfers, where payees collects funds from payers. Businesses use cheques to make payments for two reasons :

- They are a familiar and readily accepted form of payment despite some uncertainly about receiving final payments.
- Businesses benefit from the float created by the delays in the check collection processes.

Businesses find float valuable because they continue to use or invest funds for several days after they have issued a cheque. Float is created when a delay between the initiation of a payment and the availability of the funds to the recipient.

7.15.10 Electronic Funds Transfer

- Electronic funds transfers are credit transfers between banks where funds flow directly from the payer's bank to the payee's bank.
- EFT is one of the earliest examples of payment systems that use on-line transactions although these transactions are carried out on private networks.

For electronic funds transfer :

Two types of Automated clearing house transfers are used:

- Credit transfers.
- Debit transfers.

Credit transfers are similar to large dollar funds transfers in that funds flow directly from the payer's bank to the payee's where as ACH debit transfers are used when the payee's bank initiates the transfer and receives funds immediately from payers.

- An ACH provides the following services -
  - ✦ Preauthorized debits - such as repetitive bill payments and consumer initiated payments.
  - ✦ Preauthorized credits - such as the direct deposit of payrolls.

To provide these and other services, banks not only have set up their own systems but also have shared ACH systems with other banks.

Note : CHIPS = Clearing house inter-bank payments systems.
SWIFT= Society for world wide inter-bank financial telecommunications.

7.16 Financial Analysis

Financial analysts are overloaded with data. It is impossible for them to process all the data received. They must read it, looking for gems of information. Powerful workstation technology enables these analysts to specify personal filters to be applied against the data in order to present only information of likely interest and to present it in order of most likely interest. These filters provide search criteria specific to each analyst and provide only information satisfying the filter criteria to the analyst.

Improvements in technology enable the data to be scanned in real time. Alerts can be generated to the analyst whenever a significant event is detected. In this way, the analyst's job is transformed. He or she is now concerned with developing the rules to drive the filters and with understanding how to react to the significant events that are detected. Meaningful and useful data is available to support the analyst's decision making. He or she has more time to make informed decisions.

7.17 Summary

- "Training is an investment in human resource with a promise of better returns in the future". Successful candidates placed on jobs, needs training to perform their duties effectively. Workers must be trained to operate the machines, reduce scrap and avoid the accidents.
- The first step of effective training to the system administrative staff is to understand by a first look i.e. the training towards the understandability of GUI which measurely gives the directives to host a system properly and effectively generate a best coordinated N/W system and the other prominent requirement of the C/S applications. The above sometimes is also termed as Training of GUI application.
- With the help of effective technical staff as we have discussed the cost of extra investment towards the H/W and professionals can be reduced. The cost of training experts administrators and technicians in such that most organization will need to provide remote LAN and WAN management support specially. Other than this they also take care of the protocol which deals with the request of remote clients or human.
- LAN administration also take of the security of the central system as backing up the database with either mirrored disk or other devices. In a similar way LAN administration also provides the help documentations at the different remote

workstations so that the error regarding to the coordination between the workstation and server can be sorted out at their own without the interference of system administrator or system analyst.

- Database administrator faces additional challenges in a client/server implementation when data is distributed. Even in single site, shared database applications, the client/server model typically leads to ad-hoc end user access.
- End user should be trained once in the user interface standards defined by the organization as part of the SDE (Software Development Environment). The best time to provide this training is in conjunction with the first application.

REVIEW QUESTIONS

1. Explain the concepts of Training.
2. Explain the advantages of Trainging.
3. Explain the procedure for Trainging of a Database Administrator.
4. Discuss the procedure for Trainging of a Network Administrator
5. Discuss the procedure for Trainging of a END USER.
6. Differentiate trainging of a Database Administrator with development of Managers.
7. What do you understand by the term EDI? What role EDI plays in business?
8. What is client server technology? How to handle the threats imposed in client server network?

Short Answer Type Questions

Q. 1. What is Client-server Computing?

Ans : *The short answer* : Client/server is a computational architecture that involves client processes requesting service from server processes.

The long answer : Client/server computing is the logical extension of modular programming. Modular programming has as its fundamental assumption that separation of a large piece of software into its constituent parts ("modules") creates the possibility for easier development and better maintainability. Client/server computing takes this a step farther by recognizing that those modules need not all be executed within the same memory space. With this architecture, the calling module becomes the "client" (that which requests a service), and the called module becomes the "server" (that which provides the service).

The logical extension of this is to have clients and servers running on the appropriate hardware and software platforms for their functions. For example, database management system servers running on platforms specially designed and configured to perform queries, or file servers running on platforms with special elements for managing files.

Q. 2. What is a Client process?

Ans : The client is a process (program) that sends a message to a server process (program), requesting that the server perform a task (service). Client programs usually manage the user-interface portion of the application, validate data entered by the user, dispatch requests to server programs, and sometimes execute business logic. The client-based process is the front- end of the application that the user sees and interacts with. The client process contains solution-specific logic and provides the interface between the user and the rest of the application system. The client process also manages the local resources that the user interacts with such as the monitor, keyboard, workstation CPU and peripherals. One of the key elements of a client workstation is the graphical user interface (GUI). Normally a part of operating system i.e. the window manager detects user actions, manages the windows on the display and displays the data in the windows.

Q. 3. What is a Server process?

Ans : A server process (program) fulfills the client request by performing the task requested. Server programs generally receive requests from client programs, execute database retrieval and updates, manage data integrity and dispatch responses to client requests. Sometimes server programs execute common or complex business logic. The server-based process "may" run on another machine on the network. This server could be the host operating system or network file server; the server is then provided both file system services and application services. Or in some cases, another desktop machine provides the application services. The server

Process acts as a software engine that manages shared resources such as databases, printers, communication links, or high powered-processors. The server process performs the back-end tasks that are common to similar applications.

Q. 4. What is Two-Tier Architecture?

Ans : Two-tier architecture is where a client talks directly to a server, with no intervening server. It is typically used in small environments (less than 50 users).

A common error in client/server development is to prototype an application in a small, two-tier environment, and then scale up by simply adding more users to the server. This approach will usually result in an ineffective system, as the server becomes overwhelmed. To properly scale to hundreds or thousands of users, it is usually necessary to move to three-tier architecture.

Q. 5. What is Three-Tier Architecture?

Ans : Three-tier architecture introduces a server (or an "agent") between the client and the server. The role of the agent is manifold. It can provide translation services (as in adapting a legacy application on a mainframe to a client/server environment), metering services (as in acting as a transaction monitor to limit the number of simultaneous requests to a given server), or intelligent agent services (as in mapping a request to a number of different servers, collating the results, and returning a single response to the client.

Q. 6. What is Middleware?

Ans : Connectivity allows applications to transparently communicate with other programs or processes, regardless of their location. The key element of connectivity is the network operating system (NOS). NOS provides services such as routing, distribution, messaging, file and print, and network management services. NOS rely on communication protocols to provide specific services. The protocols are divided into three groups: media, transport and client-server protocols. Media protocols determine the type of physical connections used on a network (some examples of media protocols are Ethernet, Token Ring, and Fiber Distributed Data Interface (FDDI), coaxial and twisted-pair). A transport protocol provides the mechanism to move packets of data from client to server (some examples of transport protocols are Novell's IPX/SPX, Apple's AppleTalk, Transmission Control Protocol/ Internet Protocol (TCP/IP), Open Systems Interconnection (OSI) and Government Open Systems Interconnection Profile (GOSIP)). Once the physical connection has been established and transport protocols chosen, a client-server protocol is required before the user can access the network services.

A client-server protocol dictates the manner in which clients request information and services from a server and also how the server replies to that request (some examples of client-server protocols are NetBIOS, RPC, Advanced Program-to-Program Communication (APPC), Named Pipes, Sockets, Transport Level Interface

(TLI) and Sequenced Packet Exchange (SPX).

Q. 7. What is Cooperative Processing?

Ans : Cooperative processing is computing which requires two or more distinct processors to complete a single transaction. Cooperative processing is related to both distributed and client/server processing. It is a form of distributed computing where two or more distinct processes are required to complete a single business transaction. Usually, these programs interact and execute concurrently on different processors. Cooperative processing can also be considered to be a style of client/server processing if communication between processors is performed through a message passing architecture.

Q. 8. What is Distributed Processing?

Ans : The distribution of applications and business logic across multiple processing platforms. Distributed processing implies that processing will occur on more than one processor in order for a transaction to be completed. In other words, processing is distributed across two or more machines and the processes are most likely not running at the same time, i.e. each process performs part of an application in a sequence. Often the data used in a distributed processing environment is also distributed across platforms.

Q. 9. What is an "Intranet"?

Ans : The explosion of the World Wide Web is due to the world-wide acceptance of a common transport (TCP/IP), server standard (HTTP), and markup language (HTML). Many corporations have discovered that these same technologies can be used for internal client/server applications with the same ease that they are used on the Internet. Thus was born the concept of the "Intranet" : the use of Internet technologies for implementing internal client/server applications.

One key advantage of Web-based intranets is that the problem of managing code on the client is greatly reduced. Assuming a standard browser on the desktop, all changes to user interface and functionality can be done by changing code on the HTTP server. Compare this with the cost of updating client code on 2,000 desktops.

A second advantage is that if the corporation is already using the Internet, no additional code needs to be licensed or installed on client desktops. To the user, the internal and external information servers appear integrated.

A rapidly-disappearing disadvantage is that there is limited ability to provide custom coding on the client. In the early days of the Web, there were limited ways of interacting with the client. The Web was essentially "read-only". With the release of code tools such as Java and JavaScript, this limitation is no longer a major issue.

Q. 10. What are the characteristics of client/server architecture ?

Ans : The basic characteristics of client/server architectures are :

(1) Combination of a client or front-end portion that interacts with the user, and a server or back-end portion that interacts with the shared resource. The client process contains solution-specific logic and provides the interface between the user and the rest of the application system. The server process acts as a software engine that manages shared resources such as databases, printers, modems, or high powered processors.

(2) The front-end task and back-end task have fundamentally different requirements for computing resources such as processor speeds, memory, disk speeds and capacities, and input/output devices.

(3) The environment is typically heterogeneous and multivendor. The hardware platform and operating system of client and server are not usually the same. Client and server processes communicate through a well-defined set of standard application program interfaces (API's) and RPC's.

(4) An important characteristic of client-server systems is scalability. They can be scaled horizontally or vertically. Horizontal scaling means adding or removing client workstations with only a slight performance impact. Vertical scaling means migrating to a larger and faster server machine or multi servers.

Q. 11. What are the different types of servers?

Ans : The simplest forms of servers are disk servers and files servers. With a file server, the client passes requests for files or file records over a network to the file server. This form of data service requires large bandwidth and can slow a network with many users down considerably. Traditional LAN computing allows users to share resources, such as data files and peripheral devices, by moving them from standalone PCUs onto a Networked File Server (NFS).

The more advanced form of servers are database servers, transaction server and application servers (Orfali and Harkey 1992). In database servers, clients passes SQL (Structured Query Language) requests as messages to the server and the results of the query are returned over the network. The code that processes the SQL request and the data resides on the server allowing it to use its own processing power to find the requested data, rather than pass all the records back to a client and let it find its own data as was the case for the file server. In transaction servers, clients invoke remote procedures that reside on servers which also contains an SQL database engine. There are procedural statements on the server to execute a group of SQL statements (transactions) which either all succeed or fail as a unit. The applications based on transaction servers are called On-line Transaction Processing (OLTP) and tend to be mission-critical applications which require 1-3 second response time, 100% of the time and require tight controls over the security and integrity of the database.

The communication overhead in this approach is kept to a minimum as the exchange typically consists of a single request/reply (as opposed to multiple SQL statements in database servers). Application servers are not necessarily database centered but are used to server user needs, such as. Download capabilities from Dow Jones or regulating a electronic mail process. Basing resources on a server allows users to share data, while security and management services, which are also based in the server, ensure data integrity and security.

Q. 12. What are the different client/server processing styles?

Ans : Gartner group came out with the five ways of describing the different client/server styles based on how they split the three components of any application : user interface, business or application logic, data management. The five styles are distributed presentation, remote presentation, distributed function, remote data management and distributed data management.

Q. 13. What is distributed or remote presentation?

Ans : For people whose roots are embedded in the mainframe IBM world, client-server is essentially distributed or remote presentation. This style maps a workstation Graphical User Interface (GUI) front end onto an existing application's text-based screen. This is also called Remote, Mapping, Front-ending or HLLAPI (High-Level Language Application Programming Interface). The mode of operation is typically intelligent workstations intercepting and interrogating text-screen (e.g. 3270) data streams sent from a host for display in a windowed environment. This is "front ware" solution, where a GUI front end is added to an IBM/MVS 3270/5250 application and is placed on a workstation. However, most processing remains on the host or server, with the exception of user interface translation logic and possibly validation logic. For example, data from an application program is sent to a 3270 screen program on the mainframe to be displayed.

The merged data is sent to the workstation as a 3270 data stream. The workstation interprets the data and converts it to graphical form in a window. (Typically every mainframe screen used by the application has a corresponding window on the workstation and vice versa). When the user enters the data in a GUI window, it is transformed by the front ware application into a corresponding 3270 data format and is sent to the host computer.

Q. 14. What is Remote Data Management?

Ans : In remote data management, the entire application resides on the client and the data managment is located on a remote server/host. Remote Data Management is relatively easily to program for because there is just one application program. The client communicates with the server using SQL, the server then responds with data that satisfies the query. RDBMS products that offer remote data management provide a layer of software on the client to handle the communication with the DBMS server. This style represents a more traditional LAN database server or file server approach.

Workstations support the presentation and function logic and interface with the data server through the data manipulation language. Distributed data management is an extension of remote data management and uses the distributed facilities of the DBMS to access distributed data in a manner transparent to users. This is most relevant for architectures having data spread across several servers and when access to a DBMS on another server is required.

Q. 15. What is distributed function processing?

Ans : Distributed function applications are the most complex of the three typologies since two separately compiled application programs must be developed. Developers must analyze where each function should reside and what type of dialog must occur between the two programs. The underlying communications facilities may implement either a message-based or remote procedure call (RPC) mechanism for transfer of dialog and data. However, there are many variants of this typology. One variant of the distributed function style is where data management and application function occur at both the client and server. In this instance, data management at the client would include referential, read-only data. Data frequently updated or accessed by many users would reside on the server.

Q. 16. What is IBM's System Application Architecture?

Ans : SAA is a collection of selected software interfaces, conventions, and protocols that are used as a framework for developing consistent, integrated applications across the major IBM computing environments.

Four major components of this architecture are :

- ☐ Common User Access (CUA) defines conventions for GUI look and feel.
- ☐ Common Programming Interface (CPI) provides languages, tools, and APIs that give applications greater portability and more consistent user interfaces across multiple platforms.
- ☐ Common Communication Support (CCS) supports existing communications standards, such as LU 6.2.
- ☐ Common Applications, written by IBM, will serve as demonstrations of SAA concepts and make it easy for users to migrate between systems.

Q. 17. What is APPLE's VITAL architecture?

Ans : VITAL provides a way of building information systems constructed from generalized modules that can be reused and shared. It specifies how to construct and provide interfaces for these modules. A cornerstone of Apple's client/server architecture is Data Access Language (DAL). DAL consists of software components for the client and the server (Macintosh System 7 includes the client component, DOS and Windows clients are sold separately). DAL sits between the client and server components.

This approach allows varied clients to communicate with many different servers. With DAL, a change in the DBMS does not affect the front-end; it simply requires the appropriate DAL link.

Q. 18. What is Sun's Open Network Computing Architecture?

Ans : Open Network Computing (ONC) is the Sun architecture, with third party alliances providing the missing pieces. Sun's RPC is licensed by more than 300 companies, including DEC, IBM, and Apple Computer. It is a lean, efficient RPC that is particularly effective for installations not requiring WAN support. Transport Independent Remote Procedure Calls (TI-RPC) were co-developed by Sun and AT&T. TI-RPC runs independent of the underlying network transport, allowing applications to run unmodified over multiple transport protocols including NetWare, PCNFS, AIX/6000, Solaris, UNIX/SVR4, AIX/ESA. Net Wise developed the TI-RPC Application Toolkit source code generation technology.

Q. 19. What is Digital's Network Application System (NAS) architecture?

Ans : NAS is a software suite that enables applications to be integrated across a distributed network of multivendor systems: NAS services are divided into four main groups:

- ☐ Application Access Services which support user interface (forms based, graphical or character terminal based)
- ☐ Communication and Central services which support communications using electronic mail and EDI
- ☐ Information and resource sharing, which supports database access and compound documents (collection of images, graphics and conventional text)
- ☐ System Access services which provides a standard operating system interface.

Q. 20. What is OSF-DCE?

Ans : DCE is the Distributed Computing Environment, from the Open Software Foundation. DCE consists of multiple components which have been integrated to work closely together. They are the Remote Procedure Call (RPC), the Cell and Global Directory Services (CDS and GDS), the Security Service, DCE Threads, Distributed Time Service (DTS), and Distributed File Service (DFS). The Threads, RPC, CDS, Security, and DTS components are commonly referred to as the "secure core" and are the required components of any DCE installation. DFS is an optional component.

DCE is called "middleware" or "enabling technology". It is not intended to exist alone, but instead should be integrated or bundled into a vendor's operating system offering. DCE's security and distributed file system, for example, can completely replace their current, non-network, analogs.

Q. 21. What are Distributed Object Management Systems (DOMS)?

Ans : DOMS provide a way of pulling diverse components together and managing their communications. They are aimed at addressing the following:

- ☐ A single interface to manage the complexities of a heterogeneous environment
- ☐ A uniform framework, based on standards and extensibility, to build, integrate, and deploy open distributed-computing applications
- ☐ A method for creating location independence for client applications.

Q. 22. What is CORBA?

Ans : CORBA stands for the Common Object Request Broker Architecture. It is a set of standard mechanisms for naming, locating, and defining objects in a distributed computing environment.

Q. 23. What is DAE?

Ans : Distributed Application Environment is designed to allow businesses to use IBM's RISC System/6000 and PS/2 computers in a client/server network (or standalone) for their business applications.

Distributed Application Environment consists :

(1) MESSAGING services;

(2) DATABASE services;

(3) PRESENTATION Services;

(4) DEVICE services to capture data and to control a broad category of controllers, devices, equipment and sensors.

Q. 24. Define business-focused client/server architecture.

Ans : When analysing a business there are three views of the organisation:

- ☐ A functional model, which reflects organisational responsibilities and the way in which the people who use the system view their work.
- ☐ A process model, which details the business functions of the organisation (eg accepts orders, make goods, deliver goods, bill customers, receive money). The functional structure and process model rarely, if ever, agree..
- ☐ An information model, which details the information that the organisation needs to function.

Q. 25. Define client/server business application architectures.

Ans : Traditional applications architectures have been based on function. Today, to meet the needs of the business application architecture should reflect the complete range of business requirements. Therefore, client/server computing demands a three layer view of the organisation.

(1) The user interface layer, which implements the functional model.

(2) The business function layer, which implements the process model.

(3) The data layer, which implements the information model.

It should be noted that this application architecture does not demand multiple hardware platforms, although such technology can be utilized, if the environment is robust and reliable enough and the business is prepared to pay the additional costs associated with workstation and LAN technology.

Q. 26. Define Business Drivers.

Ans : Client/server computing has arisen because of a change in business needs. Businesses today need integrated, flexible, responsive and comprehensive applications to support the complete range of business processes.

Problems with existing systems include:

- ☐ Applications were developed to model vertical applications.
- ☐ Applications were built in isolation.
- ☐ Applications were implemented as monolithic systems.
- ☐ Applications were complex.
- ☐ The supporting technology was based on a centralized control model.

Information technology, which is an enabling factor in systems building, has almost reached the stage where these systems can be designed and created. Unfortunately, most businesses have existing systems based on older technology, which must be incorporated into the new, integrated environment.

The development and implementation of client/server computing is more complex, more difficult and more expensive than traditional, single process applications. The only answer to the question "why build client/server applications?" is because the business demands the increased benefits.

Q. 27. Business Benefits

Ans : There is a perceived need for vendor independence. This includes application development methodologies, programming paradigms, products and architectures.

- ☐ Organisation have changed from steep hierarchies to flattened hierarchies
- ☐ Network management is replacing vertical management
- ☐ There is a change to team based management
- ☐ The customer should have a single point of contact for all business with the organisation
- ☐ The customer should deal with the same person over multiple contacts.
- ☐ The user will perform as much processing as possible during customer contact time
- ☐ The time required to complete the work will be minimized
- ☐ There is a need for empowerment of staff and audit trail of actions
- ☐ Multi-skilled and multi-function teams need access to multiple applications

28. What does business expect from IT?

Ans : New applications should be aligned with both the user's view and the business process view. Existing functionally aligned systems are not appropriate

- ☐ Applications need to provide a consistent user interface
- ☐ Application complexity needs to be hidden
- ☐ The user interaction must be flexible
- ☐ Consistent information across all applications
- ☐ A variety of user interface styles to reflect the needs of the work
- ☐ Users should be able to modify business rules without reference to IT staff
- ☐ IT systems will support all activity performed by the user, not just a part
- ☐ An ability to evolve IT systems to reflect changing business requirements
- ☐ It is essential that there be integrity of transactional processes

29. What is Business Process Reengineering?

Ans : Reengineering is the organizational process required to align people, processes and technology with strategies to achieve business integration. It can also be thought of as taking a business in its current state and forming an organizational and operational blueprint to redirect skills, policies, information (data), cultural values, organizational structures, processing and incentives towards targeted improvements.

Multiple Choice Questions

Q. 1. What is Client-server Computing?

(a) Client/server is a computational architecture that involves client processes requesting service from server processes.

(b) Client/server is a computational architecture that involves Server processes requesting service from Client processes.

(c) Hardware and software systems containing more than one processing element or storage element

Q. 2. What is a Client process?

(a) The client is a process (program) that sends a message to a server process (program)

(b) A client process (program) fulfills the client request by performing the task requested

Q. 3. What is a Server process?

(a) A server process (program) fulfills the client request by performing the task requested

(b) The server process (program) that sends a message to a server process (program)

Q. 4. What is a Two-Tier Architecture?

(a) A two-tier architecture is where a client talks directly to a server, with no intervening server

(b) A two-tier architecture is where a client can not talks directly to a server.

(c) A two-tier architecture introduces a server (or an "agent") between the client and the server

Q. 5. What is a Three-Tier Architecture?

(a) A three-tier architecture introduces a server (or an "agent") between the client and the server

(b) A three-tier architecture is where a client talks directly to a server, with no intervening server

(c) A two-tier architecture is where a client can not talks directly to a server.

Q. 6. What is Cooperative Processing?

(a) Cooperative processing is computing which requires two or more distinct processors to complete a single transaction

(b) Cooperative processing is computing which requires single processors to complete a single transaction.
(c) Is an architecture introduces a server (or an "agent") between the client and the server

Q. 7. What is Distributed Processing?
(a) The distribution of applications and business logic across multiple processing platforms.
(b) The distribution of applications and business logic inside single processing platforms.
(c) Computing which requires single processors to complete a single transaction.

Q. 8. What is Remote Data Management?
(a) In remote data management, the entire application resides on the client and the data management is located on a remote server/host.
(b) In remote data management, the entire application resides on the Server and the data management is located on a remote Client
(c) Is computing which requires two or more distinct processors to complete a single transaction

Q. 9. What is OSF-DCE?
(a) DCE is the Distributed Computing Environment, from the Open Software Foundation.
(b) DCE is the Distributed Computing Environment, from the Open Hardware Foundation.

Q. 10. What is CORBA?
(a) CORBA stands for the Common Object Request Broker Architecture.
(b) Confederation of Regions Broker Architecture.
(c) Certificate of Registration Broker Architecture.

Q. 11. Which of the following protocols is used in the internet
(a) X.25 (b) IBM
(c) TCP/IP (d) UUCP

Q. 12. A port no. 2000 is used on both PCs of a network for an application. Then the following layer in a Network is needed for handling such a connection.
(a) Network layer (b) Transport layer
(c) Physical layer (d) Data link layer

Q. 13. One needs to send the data to hosts on the network at once. The data must be received only by the hosts for whom it is intended. The following topology should be used.
(a) Broadcast (b) Point to point
(c) Multicast (d) None of the above

CLIENT/SERVER COMPUTING QUESTION BANK

1. What are the advantages of Client Server Computing?
2. Differentiate between single system image and client server computing.
3. Discuss the OLE and CORBA.
4. What are the various networking operating system and server operating system, what is the difference between NOS and SOS?
5. What are the ways to improve the performance of client/server developed application?
6. Discuss various internet working devices.
7. Define
   (i) Telnet
   (ii) FTP
   (iii) SNMP
   (iv) Porting.
8. What do you mean by RAID disk array? discuss RAID1, RAID2, RAID3.
9. Explain the following
   (i) EDI
   (ii) WORM
   (iii) Mirrored Disk
   (iv) X Terminals.
10. (a) What are the various types of client hardware available in the market? Explain the remote procedure calls.
11. (a) Define single system image with example?
    (b) What is the mainframe centric c/s computing?
12. (a) What do you mean by RPC? How do you benefit from it?
    (b) Define OLE, DDE and CORBA with differences among them?
    (c) Discuss the architecture of Novell-Netware NOS.
13. (a) Describe OSI model? Where does 802.3 fit
    (b) Define IPC? What are the various implementation of IPC?
    (c) Define system development environment. Describe various components for a system development environment.
14. (a) What are the different kinds of storage devices. Discuss RAID-DISK array in detail?
    (b) Discuss network management issues? Which protocol is used in management of networks? Discuss the protocol in brief.
15. (a) What are the various issues related to system administration? Discuss in detail.
    (b) Discuss the fut.
    (c) Cure of client/server in the light of networking and s/w development.

MODEL QUESTION PAPER-1
CLIENT/SERVER COMPUTING
[MCA-244(4)]

Time : Three hours Maximum Marks : 100

Note : Attempt all questions. Marks are allotted against each question.

1. (a) What do you understand by single system image? Explain the salient features of single system image. **(10)**
   (b) What do you understand by transparency illusion? Explain the different types of transparencies in brief. **(10)**
2. (a) What is client server technology? Discuss the advantages of client server computing. **(10)**
   (b) "The mainframe-centric model uses the presentation capabilities of the workstation to front-end existing applications"-Justify the comment. **(10)**
3. (a) What is remote procedure call? How are the servers functions located and started during the RPC? **(15)**
   (b) Explain fax/print services in brief. **(5)**
4. (a) Explain the following: **(10)**
   (i) OLE; (ii) Common object request broker architecture (CORBA)
   (b) What is NOS? Explain the important features of NOS with relevant examples. **(5)**
   (c) Explain windows services and remote boot services in brief. **(5)**
5. (a) What are the different layers in OSI reference model? Describe how each layer is insulated from the other by a well-defined interface? **(10)**
   (b) Discuss NFS and SMTP briefly. **(10)**
6. (a) What do you mean by inter-process communication? What are the services being provided by IPC? **(10)**
   (b) Explain network management in brief. What are the 5 key OSI management areas? **(10)**
7. (a) What do you understand by RAID? Briefly discuss. **(5)**
   (b) Define the following:
   (i) Token ring.
   (ii) Ethernet.
   (c) Define availability, reliability and serviceability in terms of systems administration. **(5)**
8. (a) "LAN and network management issues are very important in client/server computing". Explain the above fact indicating the sundry issues involved in this connection.
   (b) Define FDDI and CDDI.
9. (a) What are the training advantages of GVI applications? Explain briefly. **(10)**
   (b) Explain Database Administrator Training and End user training with a real life example. **(10)**
10. (a) What do you understand by Expert Systems? Draw the architecture of a typical expert systems system applications areas.
    (b) What do you know about EDI and EDIFACT? Discuss the relation between EDI and Financial analysis with an example.

MODEL QUESTION PAPER-2
CLIENT/SERVER COMPUTING
[MCA-244(4)]

Time : Three hours Maximum Marks : 100

NOTE : Attempt all questions. Marks are allotted against each question.

1. (a) Define client server architecture with data base management concept? **(4)**
   (b) Write advantages of client server computing? **(4)**
   (c) Define single system image? **(2)**
2. (a) Explain mainframe centric client server computing model? **(4)**
   (b) What are the various ways to improve performance of client server architecture? **(3)**
   (c) How to reduce network traffic? **(3)**
3. (a) What is the role of the client and explain its services in detail? **(5)**
   (b) What is the role of the server and explain its functionality in detail? **(5)**
4. (a) What are the basic requirements to design a network operating system? **(4)**
   (b) Give a brief idea about Netware architecture? **(3)**
   (c) Give a comparative study of server operating system (SOS) and network operating system (NOS)? **(3)**
5. (a) Define open system? **(2)**
   (b) Why open systems interconnect came into existence and explains its functionality of seven layers? **(5)**
   (c) Why protocols are required in a communication and uses? **(3)**
6. (a) Define simple network management protocol and network file system? **(4)**
   (b) What are the various services provided by inter process communications (IPCs) and where it is used? **(6)**
7. (a) What is the purpose of system integration life cycle (SILC), define its all phases? **(5)**
   (b) Explain components of the application and technical architecture? **(5)**
8. (a) What do you understand by system development environment (SDE) define IBM's application development cycle model? **(6)**

FOURTH SEMESTER EXAMINATION
2001-2002
CLIENT / SERVER COMPUTING

Time : Three Hours Total Marks : 100

NOTE : (1) Attempt ALL questions.
(2) All questions carry equal marks.

1. Attempt any TWO of the following : **(10 × 2 = 20)**

(i) (a) Explain the DBMS concept in Client / Server architecture in brief.

(b) Is the structure of the data important to consider for processing environments? Discuss.

(c) If two servers process the same database, can it be called a client server system? Explain with example.

(d) "One disadvantage of Client-server system concerns control in a database management environment". Explain the disadvantage with an example.

(e) "Resource sharing architecture is not suitable for transaction processing in client-server environment." Discuss.

(ii) In a typical Client / Server computing under Network environment, explain the following in detail:

(b) What are the server requirements?

(c) What are the hardware requirements?

(d) What are the client requirements?

(e) What are the Network requirements?

(f) What do you mean by a thin client networking?

(g) List some advantages of Thin Client Networking system.

(iii) Client / Server architecture is a modular infrastructure that is intended to improve Usability, Flexibility, Interoperability and Scalability. Explain each of above with an example, in each case how it helps to improve the functionality of a client-server architecture.

2. In client-server computing, explain any FOUR of the following with examples in detail :-- **(5 × 4 = 20)**

(a) RPC

(b) Dynamic Data Exchange

(c) Object Linking and Embedding

(d) Remote Boot Service

(e) Diskless Computer

(f) Object Request Broker (ORB) Architecture

3. (i) Microsoft Windows NT Server provides various network services to support specific requirements of users on the network. All network services impact the capacity of a network. Some of the services are :
   (a) Net Logon
   (b) Computer Browser
   (c) DHCP
   (d) Internet Explorer
   (e) Workstation
   (f) Server

   Explain any FOUR of the above parts in brief in a client-server environment. **(2 × 4 = 10)**

   (ii) Answer any FOUR of the following **(2.5 × 4 = 10)**
   (a) Computing in client-server architecture over Mainframe architecture has certain advantages and disadvantages. Describe atleast two advantages and disadvantages for each architecture.
   (b) Client-server architecture could be explained as a two tier architecture, explain.
   (c) Explain the working of three-tier architecture with an application server.
   (d) How does the client-server interaction work? Explain with a sketch.
   (e) Describe the server function and client responsibility in this architecture.

4. In a client server architecture in a network environment, explain any THREE of the following phenomena with examples : **(20)**
   (a) RAID
   (b) UPS
   (c) Surge Protector
   (d) Optical Disk
   (e) Mirrored Disk

5. (i) In a client-server architecture, you are appointed as a System Administrator. You have about 500 users and it is a mix of WinNT machine, Macintosh machines and a very few DOS machines. Describe any FOUR parts with example wherever necessary : **(2.5 × 4 = 10)**
   (b) What all will you do so that network runs smoothly?
   (c) What will you do to make sure that data is secured?
   (d) What will be your Network Operating Systems for this particular configuration?
   (e) What all you look for to optimize the network function?
   (f) In a network arrangement, when you have several different machines, such as the system in question, you need to watch for certain factors to keep network trouble-free. What are these factors?
   (g) Resource sharing architecture is not suitable for transaction processing in a client-server environment. Discuss.

6. Attempt any one of the following:
   (a) Explain an object web model based on java client and CORBA ORB's on the basis of following points
      (i) Web client
      (ii) Protocol used
      (iii) Web server
   (b) Explain end-to-end working of client-server web model.
      (**Hint** : Use CGI, GET, POST, Web browser and Web server).

MCA
FOURTH SEMESTER EXAMINATION
2005-2006
CLIENT / SERVER COMPUTING

Time : Three Hours Total Marks : 100

1. Attempt any ***FOUR*** of the following :

(a) Why is the client program finite and the server program infinite ? 5

(b) In the client server model, what is the role of the client program ? What is the role of the server program ? 5

(c) What is the relationship between CGI and dynamic documents ? 5

(d) How the client/server model provides opportunity to achieve true open system computing ? 5

(e) Are standard application protocols like TELNET, FTP, SMTP and NFS connectionless or connection oriented ? 5

(f) Give a brief description of the advantages of client/server model. 5

2. Attempt any ***FOUR*** parts of the following :

(a) What is redirection in NOS ? How does it work ? 5

(b) What is object linking and embedding (OLE)? Discuss its advantages in client-server model. 5

(c) Explain the architecture of distributed computing enviromnent. 5

(d) List the features that must be included in the database engine to make it suitable for client server applications. 5

(e) Give a brief description of the functions provided by server in a Network Operating System Environment. 5

(f) What is CORBA ? 5

3. Attempt any ***TWO*** out of the following :

(a) Explain the services provided by interprocers communication. 10

(b) What is Network Basic input output system ? Describe the various services provided by Net BIOS commands. 10

(c) What is Token ring ? In a 16-Mbps Token ring network, the length of the token in three bytes. How long does it take for a station to produce a token ? 10

4. Attempt any ***TWO*** parts out of the following :

(a) Write short comments on the following : 10

(i) WORM

(ii) Erasable optical

(iii) Network interface cards

(iv) CDDI

(b) How the security can be implemented in client server applications explain. **10**

(c) Explain the various LAN and network management issues in the context of client server applications. **10**

5. Attempt ***TWO*** parts of the following :

(a) Explain the benefits that can be obtained by organizations using expert systems technology. **10**

(b) What is EDI ? Discuss its advantages. **10**

(c) Discuss the key issues in the training of systems administration personnel. **10**

M C A
FOURTH SEMESTER EXAMINATION
2006-2007
CLIENT / SERVER COMPUTING

Time : Three Hours Total Marks : 100

NOTE : Attempt **all** questions. All questions carry **equal** marks.

1. Attempt any ***FOUR*** parts : **(5 × 4 = 20)**

(a) Differentiate between centralized and distributed comuting.

(b) What is the difference between database schema and database state ?

(c) Discuss the advantages of a three-tier client server architecture over two-tier client server architecture.

(d) Discuss the role of object technology in client/server development.

(e) Is it always beneficial to go for client/server computing ? Yes or No ? Explain. Give certain applications where it is not recommended to use client server computing.

(f) Discuss some of ways to improve performance in client/server computing.

2. Attempt any ***FOUR*** parts : **(5 × 4 = 20)**

(a) What is meant by object linking and embedding (OLE) ? Explain

(b) Discuss the role of server in detail.

(c) Compare object oriented and relational database management system features.

(d) Discuss the distributed computing environment (DCE) architecture in detail.

(e) Discuss the OSI reference model in detail.

(f) Explain Asynchronous Transfer Mode (ATM).

3. Attempt any ***TWO*** parts : **10 × 2 = 20**

(a) Discuss the client/server systems development methodology in detail.

(b) Write short notes on the following :

(i) X-terminals.

(ii) UNIX work station.

(c) What is meant by WAN ? Discuss the various WAN technologies in detail.

4. Attempt any ***TWO*** parts : **10 × 2 = 20**

(a) Discuss the various LAN and Management issues in detail.

(b) Describe the following

(i) RAID-DISK

(ii) Optical disk

(iii) NICs.

(c) Write short notes on the following :
 (i) Software Distribution in client/server environment.
 (ii) MTTR and MTBF.

5. Attemp any ***TWO*** parts :

(a) Discuss the various training advantages of QUI applications in detail.

(b) Write short notes on the following :
 (i) Expert systems
 (ii) POS.

(c) Describe the following :
 (i) Text-management process.
 (ii) Emergency Public safety.